DATE DUE

DEMCO 38-296

ALLEN SAPP

Allen Sapp

ALLEN SAPP

A Bio-Bibliography

Alan Green

Bio-Bibliographies in Music, Number 62
Donald L. Hixon, Series Adviser

GREENWOOD PRESS
Westport, Connecticut • London

Library of Congress Cataloging-in-Publication Data

Green, Alan, 1962–
    Allen Sapp : a bio-bibliography / Alan Green.
        p.   cm.—(Bio-bibliographies in music, ISSN 0742–6968 ; no.
    62)
    Includes bibliographical references and index.
    ISBN 0–313–28983–2 (pbk. : alk. paper)
    1. Sapp, Allen, 1922–   —Bibliography.   2. Sapp, Allen, 1922–   —
Discography.   I. Title.   II. Series.
ML134.S17G74   1996
016.78′092—dc20   96–21945

British Library Cataloguing in Publication Data is available.

Library of Congress Catalog Card Number: 96–21945
ISBN: 0–313–28983–2
ISSN: 0742–6968

First published in 1996

Greenwood Press, 88 Post Road West, Westport, CT 06881
An imprint of Greenwood Publishing Group, Inc.

Printed in the United States of America

The paper used in this book complies with the
Permanent Paper Standard issued by the National
Information Standards Organization (Z39.48–1984).

10 9 8 7 6 5 4 3 2 1

Every reasonable effort has been made to trace the owners of copyright
materials in this book, but in some instances this has proven impossible.
The author and publisher will be glad to receive information leading to more
complete acknowledgments in subsequent printings of the book and in the
meantime extend their apologies for any omissions.

Affectionately dedicated
to my parents,
DENT EDMUND GREEN
and
RUTH MARIE GREEN

CONTENTS

MUSICAL EXAMPLES cited in the BIOGRAPHY follow page 49.

FOREWORD

WHEN I FIRST MET ALLEN SAPP, I had long known about him. My friend Charles Kletzsch, who has for years been composer-in-residence of Harvard's Dunster House, was once telling me about the composers he had known while he was a Harvard student during the early 1950s. He singled out Allen as one whose music I would one day come to know and love. I also learned from such former Sapp students as Ann Besser Scott and Margaret Fairbank Jory what a magnificent teacher Allen was. So, when Allen came to Yale in the early 1970s, as a member of a visiting committee charged with evaluating the music program in which I taught as an assistant professor, I felt that I already knew him. Allen was the only member of the committee who seemed really interested in helping Yale. He was also the only one willing to listen to the ideas, suggestions, and complaints of the junior faculty. He and I subsequently entered into a fascinating correspondence.

Allen and I became friends in 1978, when we both joined the faculty of the College-Conservatory of Music of the University of Cincinnati, he as dean and I as associate professor. It was at this time that I finally got to know some of Allen's music. Always one to put the music of his colleagues ahead of his own, he agreed only with some coaxing to allow us to include his pieces on our faculty composers' concert series. I was particularly struck by his more individualistic and intimate works, such as the *Nocturne* [W65] for cello that Jack Kirstein played [P65b] and *Taylor's Nine* [W67], premiered by The Percussion Group with five other musicians. Allen and I developed a mutual respect as well as a friendship, and—despite our working in the same building—our correspondence continued! As most people who know Allen realize, he is a generous, prolific, engaging, and perceptive letter writer. Rarely was a composition of either of us performed without a subsequent note explaining our perceptions, reactions, enthusiasm, or even criticism. How the man was able to maintain correspondence with a multitude of people while acting as dean, teacher, and composer, I cannot imagine!

Alan Green's study is extremely interesting and important. In setting forth the details of Allen Sapp's work, Alan helps to show the development of a major creative life. In telling the story of Allen's professional life, Alan does not simply show us a composer's development. He chronicles the life of an important figure in American musical culture. The interrelationship between composing, teaching, and administering (on both local and national levels) is a complex aspect of musical life in the United States in the late twentieth century. Historians who seek to understand how our music came to be what it is, and how it has related to its cultural milieu, will do well to study Alan's book. This is because Allen Sapp's career, though in many ways unique, typifies that of the American academic composer who must deal with the often conflicting demands of artistic expression, educational responsibility, and institutional growth.

Composer and scholar Alan Green is the perfect person to have written this book. A student of Sapp and of his music, Alan offers wonderful insights along with valuable factual accounts. We should all be grateful that Allen Sapp's retirement from administration allowed him to resume his compositional career after a long nearly inactive period, and we should be equally grateful to Alan Green for having made us all aware of the musical richness of Allen's recent burst of creativity and of how it connects to his exciting early career. I hope that this book will lead performers as well as scholars to Allen's compositions, so that his music will finally gain the wide hearing it deserves.

Jonathan D. Kramer
Professor of Music
Columbia University
30 January 1995

ACKNOWLEDGMENTS

I AM INDEBTED TO A GREAT MANY PEOPLE who have assisted me over the past five years in gathering information and advising me in the preparation of this book. At the head of this long list is the subject of this book, Allen Sapp, and his late wife, Norma Bertolami Sapp, who allowed me unlimited access to their personal papers, gave freely of their time, and promptly answered each of my queries in abundant detail. I am particularly grateful to Professor Sapp for the more than 30 hours he devoted to taped interviews with me. I would also like to thank other members of Allen Sapp's family for their communications with me: his sister Nancy O'Reilly, and his sons Christopher Dawson and Anthony Sapp.

It is impossible for me to enumerate the many ways in which I have been assisted by Professors Carol June Bradley and James Coover at the State University of New York at Buffalo. Their assistance ran the gamut from thoughtful advising and careful editing through the mundane task of helping me arrange for financial support. I hope that the research embodied in this book will be a tribute to their teaching.

Many of the composer's past and present colleagues provided interviews that were imperative to my research, among them Robert Commanday, Robert Creeley, Lukas Foss, David Fuller, Harold Laster, Renee Levine, Robert Middleton, Myles Slatin, and Jan Williams. Others who provided me valuable information and advice through correspondence or conversation were Bonnie Blackburn, Bathea Churgin, Frank D'Accone, Jack Dahlquist, Noam Flinker, Elliot Forbes, Martin and Cecilia Gelland, Ralph Hartsock, Thomas F. Heck, James A. Hirt, Catherine M. Kleszczewski, Edward Komara, Jonathan Kramer, David Lesniaski, Roberta Lindsay, Anthony S. Lis, Stephen Long, A. Tillman Merritt, Kevin Michki, Robert and Polly Middleton, Jeremy Noble, Darragh Park, Vivian Perlis, Reginald Phelps, Howard Pollack, Marilyn Shrude, Robert L. Taylor, William Thornhill, and Eleanor Trawick.

I am deeply grateful to the many archivists and librarians who offered assistance in locating materials and information at their respective institutions: Gilles Devincre, Elizabeth Giuliani, and Gérald Grunberg, Bibliothèque nationale de France; Bridget P. Carr, Boston Symphony Orchestra Archives; Bonna Boettcher, Bowling Green State University; Joan Redding, British Broadcasting Corporation; Helen I. Khan and Norma Jean Lamb, Buffalo and Erie County Public Library; Stephen Toombs, Case Western Reserve University; Paul Cauthen, Kevin Grace, Robert Johnson, and Mark Palkovic, University of Cincinnati; Burt Altman and Dale

Hudson, Florida State University; Harley Holden and his staff at the Harvard University Archives; Maic Chomel and Jean-Michel Villaret, Institut national de l'audiovisuel (INA-Paris/Bry-sur-Marne); Samuel Brylawski, Win Matthias, Geraldine Ostrove, and David Sommerfield, Library of Congress; Jeanne E. McConnell, Library of the National Endowment for the Arts; John Shepard and Mark Tolleson, New York Public Library; Robert J. Vidal, Radio France; R. Wayne Shoaf, Archivist, Arnold Schoenberg Institute; Carol June Bradley, Nancy Bren-Nuzzo, James B. Coover, Shonnie Finnegan, Gudrun Kilburn and Richard McRae, State University of New York at Buffalo; Diane Parr Walker, University of Virginia; Steven L. Sundell, University of Wisconsin-Madison, and Ross Wood at Wellesley College. Several administrators also provided me with access to non-public files which were very helpful in my research, including Joseph McCarthy at Harvard University, and Robert J. Werner and Robert Zierolf at the University of Cincinnati College-Conservatory of Music.

Kent and Joy Green, Tim and Ann Marie Johnson, Kevin and Renee Michki, Markie Oliver, and Eleanor Trawick were gracious hosts during my research travels. James B. Davis, Eric Schnell, and Matthew Trawick gave me valuable computer consultation when I needed it most. The musical examples in this book were encoded and printed by Craig Sylvern.

The Music Library Association provided significant financial assistance to this project through their Walter Gerboth Award in 1991. The State University of New York at Buffalo also provided early support through the Mark Diamond Research Fund of the Graduate Student Association. Additional funding and release time was granted by my colleagues at the Ohio State University Libraries, for which I am especially grateful to William J. Studer, Jay Ladd, and Thomas F. Heck.

Donald L. Hixon (University of California at Irvine, and adviser for this series) and Alicia S. Merritt (Acquisitions Editor, Greenwood Press) provided valuable advice in shaping the final format of this book. They were also very understanding and patient with me in granting a much needed deadline extension.

A final note of thanks is due to the primary editors and critics of this book. My dear wife, Joyce Sympson Green, in addition to serving as my second set of eyes, showed incredible patience with me during this project. My dear mother, Ruth Green, also assisted me with editing the final text. Final proofreading was performed by my good friends Jack Dahlquist and Anthony S. Lis. Thanks to their repairs, the readers of this book will not have to endure many of my rambling run-on sentences and late-night typographical errors (my apologies for those that still remain). Lastly, I would like to thank my dear little daughter Laura, whose frequent refrain of 1995, "Dada done with book!" was a great inspiration!

To all listed above, I offer my deepest and most sincere thanks for your time, services, and support.

PREFACE

THIS BOOK HAD ITS HUMBLE BEGINNINGS IN 1990 as a project for a course in music librarianship taught by Dr. Carol June Bradley at the State University of New York (SUNY) at Buffalo (see B138). The assignment was to compile a biographical sketch and descriptive catalog of the complete works of a composer. I chose Allen Sapp as a subject for several reasons. First, I knew that working on his biography would be very interesting since he was a student of Walter Piston, Aaron Copland, and Nadia Boulanger, served as Chief Cryptanalyst for the U.S. Army in Europe at the close of World War II, and had close associations with many other significant artistic figures during his teaching career at Harvard, SUNY at Buffalo, and elsewhere. Secondly, it seemed appropriate to document the career of one of the most significant persons in Buffalo's cultural history; Sapp's leadership in various administrative roles helped SUNY at Buffalo to emerge as an important center of avant garde artistic culture in the 1960s. Most importantly, I was already familiar with Allen Sapp and his music from my composition studies with him in the mid-1980s at the University of Cincinnati College-Conservatory of Music. I knew him as a brilliant and very inspiring teacher, one who not only taught the fine points of compositional technique but also transmitted his broad knowledge of many artistic and humanistic fields. I had come to admire several of his compositions, particularly the *Violin Sonata IV* (W68), *Piano Sonata III* (W19), and *Imaginary Creatures* for harpsichord and chamber orchestra (W118); these works were unpublished and unavailable on commercial recordings, so I felt particularly fortunate to know these powerful, lyrical works. This assignment seemed like an excellent opportunity to survey his entire output and look for additional hidden musical treasures.

I was not disappointed. The composer allowed me into his home in Cincinnati to work directly with his manuscripts and performance programs, and supplied me with photocopies and tapes of dozens of compositions to take back to Buffalo. As the project developed, I was struck by how much of this fine music was virtually hidden from the world; except for eleven scores published by American Composers Alliance and two commercial recordings no longer in print, his music was only readily available to those who knew him personally. Furthermore, dozens of works had not even seen their première performances. Having come to the conclusion that Sapp's music clearly deserved to be given a wider audience, I decided to develop this project into my M. A. thesis in music history at SUNY at Buffalo (see B148), and to seek publication of his bio-bibliography in this Greenwood Press series.

The present volume consists of five major sections:

I. A concise **BIOGRAPHY** of Allen Sapp's professional career;

II. A catalog of **WORKS AND PERFORMANCES** complete to November 1995 (excluding juvenilia). The arrangement of the catalog is classified by genre, with works listed in chronological order within each class. In order to facilitate cross-indexing, each work is assigned a catalog number preceded by the mnemonic "W" (W1, W2, etc.). Following the descriptive entry for each work is a listing of première and other known performances, each identified by the catalog number of the composition preceded by the mnemonic "P" and followed by a lowercase letter. For example, successive performances of composition W68 are labeled P68a, P68b, and so on. If a work has not been performed, the "Notes" field will contain the phrase "No performances." Following the model employed in Karen Perone's *Lukas Foss: A Bio-Bibliography* (Greenwood Press, 1991), I have listed bibliographical entries pertaining to a specific composition (mainly performance reviews) directly following the list of performances in chronological order; each entry is assigned a "WB" ("Works Bibliography") number corresponding to the "W" number for the work, followed by a lowercase letter (WB68a, WB68b, etc.). Each of these entries contains an annotation, often taking the form of a direct quotation from the review, in keeping with the pattern established in previous volumes in this series;

III. A **DISCOGRAPHY/WEBOGRAPHY**, i.e., an alphabetical listing of works which have been made available on commercially produced sound recordings (both in-print and deleted), as well as all known non-commercial recordings located in libraries and archives, or available as sound files on the world-wide web. Each entry is preceded by the mnemonic "D" (D1, D2, D3, etc.). When a non-commercial recording exists in multiple formats, e.g., a master tape recording of a private recital and a world-wide web sound file copy of the same recording, these entries share the same "D" number differentiated by a lowercase letter (D1a, D1b, etc., with the master or "best copy" assigned "a"). Recordings are cross-referenced to the performances ("P" numbers) and record reviews ("WB" numbers) in the "Works and Performances" section;

IV. A chronological annotated bibliography of **WRITINGS BY SAPP**, including all of his known published writings and the extant major unpublished writings. Each citation is preceded by the mnemonic "B" (B1, B2, etc.); and,

V. A chronological annotated bibliography of **WRITINGS ABOUT SAPP**, including all known published items containing biographical information about his professional career. Access to articles by author and subject is provided through the general index. Each citation is preceded by the mnemonic "B," continuing the series begun in the previous section.

Appendices at the end of this volume provide a listing of academic and non-academic positions held by Sapp, and chronological and alphabetical listings of his compositions. A general index concludes the volume.

I hope that readers of this volume will feel the same sense of joy I have experienced in discovering the music of Allen Sapp and in contemplating his many contributions as an educational leader and practitioner.

ALLEN SAPP

I. BIOGRAPHY

1. YOUTH AND EDUCATION, 1922-43

ALLEN DWIGHT SAPP JR. was born in Philadelphia on 10 December 1922, the son of Allen Dwight Sapp Sr. and Edythe (Dawson) Sapp. His father was an investment banker who specialized in municipal bonds. During the composer's early childhood, the Sapp family lived in Lansdowne, a suburb west of Philadelphia.

Sapp's interest in the piano began at an early age, nurtured at first by his maternal grandmother, an amateur pianist. At about age nine, he began playing four hand piano works with his father, and started formal piano lessons. His first piano teacher, Margaret MacDowell Coddington (who claimed relationship with the composer Edward MacDowell), encouraged the young composer's early efforts at writing. At his second public recital at the age of ten, Sapp played his own *Prelude in C-Sharp Minor*,[1] which he believes to be his earliest notated piece. This work was apparently composed in the style of Rachmaninoff's famous *Prelude in C-Sharp Minor*, which Sapp had heard on several occasions when Rachmaninoff visited Philadelphia on concert tours.[2]

After three years' study with Coddington, Sapp was referred to another piano teacher, Robert Elmore, who was also known as a composer and organist. He also studied with a composition and theory teacher, William Happich. Happich drilled him in species counterpoint and critiqued his early compositional works, while Elmore developed Sapp's musicality by coaching him through a great quantity of piano literature.

Sapp attended the Haverford School, where his scholastic work was so extraordinary that he was advanced two grades and completed high school at the age of 16. He was especially fond of reading, everything from biographies of composers and other famous personages, to the literature of American, English, and French poets and novelists. He was fluent in French by his later high school years and also acquired a reading knowledge of Latin and Greek.

The young composer reached a major turning point early in his career while listening to the radio one Sunday afternoon, 20 June 1937: on the weekly broadcast of the CBS Symphony Orchestra, Sapp heard the première performance of Walter Piston's *Concertino for Piano and Orchestra*.[3] Upon hearing this performance, Sapp decided that Piston was the composer with whom he wanted to study in college.[4]

Harvard College, where Piston served on the music faculty, was the only college to which Sapp applied for admittance. His parents initially balked at his decision to apply to Harvard; Allen Sr. wanted his son to go to his and his father's *alma mater,* Kenyon College (in Gambier, Ohio). Family tradition notwithstanding, the Sapps were also facing financial difficulties and could not afford Harvard's tuition.[5] But not only was Allen Jr. accepted by Harvard; he was awarded a university scholarship, as well as an additional scholarship from the Harvard Club of Philadelphia. In September 1939, Sapp left Philadelphia for Boston, which would be the center of his musical life for the next two decades.

Sapp studied with Piston during nearly every semester of his undergraduate and graduate university education in courses or composition seminars or private lessons. Sapp "admired him extravagantly as a young person."[6] He was very much drawn to Piston's "crisp, economical, lean, clear, neo-baroque"[7] contrapuntal style. Sapp adopted many of these traits in his own music, as well as the *grand ligne* approach to composing espoused by Nadia Boulanger and practiced by Piston and several of her other former students. Boulanger believed that "Music is made up of two essential elements (line and rhythm) which are completed by decorative elements (harmony and orchestration)—the goal is attained if the coordinated use of these elements corresponds to the emotion from which is born the idea which they seek to develop."[8] Therefore in the *grand ligne* method, the principal melodic thread and propelling rhythmic elements of an entire movement or section are composed in advance of the "decorative elements" which are then supplied in the proper manner and amount in order to clarify the effect of this primary musical line. Sapp began to use this method almost immediately after he began his studies with Piston, beginning with his *Suite for Two Flutes and Piano* (W48).[9]

Sapp described Piston's teaching style in his Seminar in Composition as follows:

> He preferred if you would play your music, but if you didn't or couldn't or wouldn't, he would play it. If it was a chamber piece or orchestra piece, he would still play. And play it, of course, very impressively. His critique was always very direct. Blunt sometimes. Very seldom did he praise a piece extravagantly. He was reserved in his judgments. If you did get any praise, you treasured it.[10]
>
> The kind of thing that he hated most was the music in which there was too much of this rich Debussy or Ravel kind of harmony. . . . He had very contemptuous feelings about that. . . . He would just leer over at somebody, a poor hapless composer who had written a beautiful sensitive phrase with a lot of ninth chords in it, and say "This is just gumdrops!" You can imagine what that does to a fellow who thinks he has written something of exquisite beauty.[11]

In addition to Piston's Seminar in Composition, Sapp also took his courses in Advanced Harmony and Fugue. Other undergraduate music courses included Tonal Counterpoint with Grosvenor Cooper; Technique of Choral Writing with Archibald T. Davison; Orchestration with Edwin Burlingame Hill, with additional private study in orchestration with William Denny;[12] and seminars on the music of Stravinsky and Hindemith with A. Tillman Merritt.

Sapp performed exceedingly well in most of his non-music courses, so much so that he had two invitations to entertain a change of major. His Latin literature professor, Edward Kennard Rand, encouraged Sapp to change his course of study to the Classics. The following year, a similar situation developed with his French literature professor, Andre Maurice. Both offers Sapp graciously declined. Sapp also greatly enjoyed a course in 17th century English poetry with Francis Otto

Matthiessen, and later set to music many of the texts he studied closely in this class.[13] He also took courses in philosophy, international government, and German, the latter proving to be extremely valuable during his later army service in Europe.

Late in his freshman year, Sapp was asked by the Harvard Dramatic Club to write and perform incidental music for its productions. Sapp joined the Dramatic Club, participating as composer, pianist, and coach of the chorus for two productions; he enjoyed the work immensely. The first was Christopher Isherwood and W. H. Auden's *The Ascent of F-6*, performed 2-4 May 1940.[14] With Harold Shapero, he performed incidental music for piano duet composed by Benjamin Britten, as well as his own supplemental music for the production (see W133).[15] The following autumn, Sapp composed and performed incidental music for the piano for the American première of T. S. Eliot's *The Family Reunion* (see W134).[16] The music for this production earned the seventeen-year-old composer his first critical praise by the press.[17] Some eighteen months later, Sapp shared incidental music writing duties with Irving Fine for a Boston area production of *Alice in Wonderland* (see W135).

Another extracurricular activity which Sapp enjoyed during his undergraduate years was his involvement with the "Crimson Network," the campus radio station at Harvard (800 kHz). He gave occasional programs in which he would perform and discuss his own compositions.[18] Sapp's first publicly performed work at Harvard was broadcast over this radio station during his freshman year: his *Suite for Two Flutes and Piano*, performed by his classmates Robert Commanday and Gabriel Jackson accompanied by the composer.[19] He enjoyed this first taste of radio, and this experience would serve him well a decade later when he became the host of two educational radio music programs for the National Association of Educational Broadcasters (see B5 and B7) and served as an on-air program annotator for the Boston Symphony Orchestra broadcasts on WGBH-FM.[20]

In addition to the *Suite for Two Flutes and Piano*, Sapp composed several other significant chamber works during his undergraduate days at Harvard. One of these was his *Cello Sonata* (W51),[21] performed by Peter G. Swing and accompanied by William W. Austin during a session of Piston's seminar in composition in 1942. This work was awarded the 1942 Bohemians Prize at Harvard. The previous year, Sapp composed his *Piano Sonata I* (W1) for his close friend, the composer and pianist Robert Middleton. Irving Fine gave its première performance; this was the first time Sapp was able to enjoy the performance of one of his compositions given by a truly professional musician. In a letter to his parents, Sapp remarked, "This *Sonata* of mine is fiendishly difficult, and although [Fine] is a superb pianist, he has been practicing it for weeks; oft the time he was very worried about it. . . . The performance was magnificent! Mr. Fine played it so brilliantly I could hardly keep from crying."[22] Sapp considers the *Piano Sonata I* a pivotal work in his early career. "That was the piece in which I really began to think in a more personal way. The first movement of that, even today, as I look at it, has a personality and a sort of severity and bleakness."[23]

Irving Fine was to become an even more significant force in Sapp's life when he became his tutor at Eliot House during the academic years 1940-42.

> That tutorial became a very strong influence. It has influenced my teaching, my work, and my attitude about things deeply. . . . I have tried in every place I've been to translate [the tutorial model] as best I could either personally or institutionally. It's a system of education which is far too costly

> now, which for all kinds of reasons cannot survive I suppose, but what a
> glorious concept: the idea of a master-apprentice relationship built into your
> educational system, with all the advantages of a major university library and
> all that goes with it.[24]

Their weekly sessions would consist of studying the works of a particular composer
or a specific musical problem. Their sessions did not proceed in any particular order:

> It was Mahler one week and Monteverdi the next, and then some harmonic
> problem the following week, and then of course a lot of contemporary music.
> . . . It was the kind of mining technique where you go into a mine and just
> extract the ore and you learn the vocabulary and you learn the mannerisms.
> It was immensely valuable.[25]

A further illustration of the very favorable learning environment of a particular
golden era at Harvard is a paragraph from a letter Sapp wrote to his parents in the
autumn of 1941:

> Friday was a delightful day in many respects. . . . At ten . . . I ran into
> Mr. [Andrew] Haigh of the section men in Music 1, also in my Stravinsky
> class. He suggested we go somewhere for a cup of coffee and since I had had
> no breakfast I was glad to go. At St. Clair's [restaurant] we . . . were joined
> by John Ohl and Dr. [Donald] Grout, also teachers in the music department,
> and a Mr. [Lincoln] Spiess who is an authority on the middle ages. We
> talked and talked and finally at about one-fifteen the bull session broke. It
> was very exciting to talk with really intelligent men. After lunch I went up
> again to see if Miss Ayres had mailed my manuscript.[26] This time I met Mr.
> [William] Denny. On the spot he suggested an impromptu orchestration
> lesson. After about an hour of very intensive work we stopped in at the
> Georgian for a Coke and lingered over this, so the day was almost gone.
> Isn't this a wonderful way to get educated when your teachers really make
> friends of you?[27]

Sapp was unanimously voted President of the Harvard Music Club at the
meeting which immediately followed the performance of his *Piano Sonata I* by Irving
Fine. At the same meeting, Norma Bertolami was elected President of the Radcliffe
Music Club. In a letter to his parents, Sapp wrote, "The rest of the evening I
conferred with the President of the Radcliffe Music Club and discovered that we have
very similar ideas about the plans for next year. Before the end of the year I intend
to see her again and arrange some details for the coming year. She is a very
attractive girl."[28] They would become engaged in the spring of 1942 and married in
the summer of 1943.

On 5 February 1942, Sapp received a telegram from Edilh Sawsin, Chairman
of the Young People's Concerts Committee of the New York Philharmonic,
announcing that Sapp's *Andante for Orchestra* (W110) was selected for performance,
and awarded second prize (tied with Luise Vosgerchien) in the Young Composers'
Contest.[29] The telegram directed Sapp to report to Carnegie Hall on 21 February
to accept the prize at a press conference and to make arrangements to send the
music to the Philharmonic office.[30] Piston was very proud of Sapp for this
achievement, and arranged to have his professional copyist make the parts for the
performance at the university's expense.[31] The *Andante for Orchestra* is an extension
and orchestration of the first movement of the composer's *Piano Sonata I* written,

earlier the same year, 1941.[32] The New York Philharmonic performance took place on 18 April 1942, conducted by Rudolph Ganz. It received a favorable review by Robert Lawrence in the *New York Herald Tribune* the following day: "His prize-winning work revealed definite talent, in a somewhat abstract direction. The scoring for orchestra proved sinewy and effective, while the musical content itself varied in interest."[33]

During the 1939-40 academic year, Igor Stravinsky was in residence at Harvard as occupant of the Charles Eliot Norton Chair of Poetry. Sapp attended every one of the Norton Lectures, which Stravinsky delivered in French.[34] He then was able to interact with Stravinsky in Piston's Seminar in Composition[35] and at meetings of the Harvard and Radcliffe Music Clubs. Stravinsky also held a few private sessions with Harvard composition students, including the young freshman Sapp.[36] This encounter with the great composer led Sapp two years later to perform an extensive graphic analysis of Stravinsky's technique of orchestration in seven works of the previous two decades as the basis of his senior honors thesis in 1942.[37]

In early 1942, Sapp was awarded the John Knowles Paine Fellowship by Harvard, which was traditionally used to send promising Harvard composers to Europe for study with a renowned composer or teacher. However, due to the war, Sapp was not able to travel to Europe, so he arranged (with the help of Piston[38]) to study privately with Aaron Copland. He received permission to use part of the money to attend Tanglewood during the summer of 1942. At Tanglewood he not only participated in a weekly group seminar session with Copland, but also began his private lessons with him. Following Tanglewood, he had a series of weekly private lessons at Copland's apartment in New York City.[39] Copland also arranged for Sapp to study music analysis privately with Nadia Boulanger[40] on a weekly basis during this period.

On 11 June 1942, Sapp graduated from Harvard, A. B., *magna cum laude*, one year ahead of schedule.[41] Sapp's musical achievement during his undergraduate years is evident not only in the Department of Music's awarding him the Paine Fellowship, but also in the texts of the letters of recommendation written by the faculty in support of his application for a commission in the U.S. Navy. For example, Archibald T. Davison wrote:

> I knew Allen Sapp for several years as a student at Harvard University. In the work which he did with me he was pains-taking, resourceful, thorough and accurate. He made a fine record in his chosen subject, but beyond that, he stood out because of his traits of character—traits which are so often lacking in gifted students, namely, promptness, fidelity, and an eagerness to learn. I am glad of this opportunity of speaking a word in behalf of a young man whom I admire both personally and professionally.[42]

Sapp's summer at Tanglewood brought him into close social contact with many great personalities of the coming generation of musicians, most notably Leonard Bernstein, Harold Shapero, and Lukas Foss (Sapp and Foss would later have a long and fruitful collaboration in Buffalo in the 1960s). Copland himself helped to intermingle the Tanglewood composers and conductors, as he held a number of parties at his rented home near the festival grounds. Sapp recalled one of these occasions: " I remember [Copland] and Bernstein playing the version of the *El Salón México* for two pianos. It was a great occasion. . . . Then Bernstein played parts of the [Copland] *Piano Sonata* and there was a lot of discussion and lively social feeling."[43]

In addition to Sapp, the Copland class of the summer of 1942 included the following composers: Pablo Moncayo, Blas Galindo, Harold Gramatges, Barbara Pentland, and Romeo Cascarino.[44] The sessions were especially concerned with orchestration problems. Copland gave sections from his own works to be orchestrated by the students; these assignments were then discussed in the group sessions. Among the assigned music was an excerpt from the piano sketches for *Lincoln Portrait* (1942) and the *Piano Sonata* (1939-41).

> After the first preamble [in *Lincoln Portrait*], there's a big explosion
> . . . and he gave us that. My version, you know, was characteristically lean
> and severe, and the crescendo was all built in by adding instruments and
> working it out very carefully. . . . Copland remarked on the differences of
> approach [between the students]. He didn't say one was right and one was
> wrong. His own version was not in our heads.[45] We just had the problem.[46]

In addition to studying Copland's music, there was also much discussion of the works of Shostakovich. Serge Koussevitzky was rehearsing the top student orchestra for most of the summer for the much touted 14 August American première of the Shostakovich *Symphony No. 7*, which because of its heroic wartime significance would attract an international cast of musicians, dignitaries, and the press.[47] In addition to this work, Copland focused on Shostakovich's *Piano Quintet*, which was also performed at Tanglewood that summer.[48] Copland was a great admirer of Shostakovich and spoke at some length about Soviet music during these sessions. Other topics of discussion in the seminar included the problems of text setting, Copland's *Piano Variations*, the importance of establishing an original style,[49] and the practicalities of making a living as a composer.[50]

The major summer project for Sapp was composing his *Concertino for Piano and Chamber Orchestra* (W111), which had been commissioned by the Town Hall Music Forum in June 1942.[51] This work was strongly influenced by Piston's composition of the same name which had made such an impact on Sapp five years earlier. In fact, the second movement of Sapp's *Concertino* started as a project for Piston's Seminar in Fugue at Harvard in the spring of 1942. Piston composed a passacaglia theme and assigned the students to use this as the basis for their final projects. Sapp completed the assignment but was not totally satisfied with his first setting.[52] For the Town Hall Forum commission, he decided to return to Piston's passacaglia theme and use it as the basis of the slow middle movement of the *Concertino*. This movement, "Passacaglia on a Theme of Walter Piston," was performed as an independent work at Tanglewood in the summer of 1942 under the direction of Walter Hendl with Sapp's fiancée, Norma Bertolami, as soloist.[53] Sapp also completed the first movement and made several revisions to the second under Copland's tutelage before leaving Tanglewood. Something of Copland's teaching style and his influence on this work is described by the composer:

> I worked out most quickly the first part of it, which was this
> "Passacaglia." I brought that to him. Again, he was very helpful in matters
> of orchestration. He thought my orchestration was unusual because it was
> not very fancy and it was rather severe. Then I wrote the first movement
> with him, using very much this *grande ligne* approach. He, of course, knew
> what that was all about from his work with Boulanger. He found my
> harmonic language interesting. It was a kind of melange of Harris and Piston

and Copland, I guess you would say. It had a classic character. He never made any comments, for example, to the effect that the piano part was not really a concerto-like part. It was sometimes integrated with the orchestra more than it should, and so on. But he was very kind about that. It was obvious that I wasn't writing a brilliant piano concerto from the beginning. So he just accepted that, you see. That was very characteristic of him, to accept your artistic predilections, whatever they were, and then be diagnostic. [He would] show you where you could do something better or make a point. He often made points about proportions, like "This phrase goes on a little too long," or "Maybe this idea needs a little more working out." . . . It was not "This F-sharp is the wrong note here," or "This chord here is one that you've used too much," or anything like that. It [had] much more to do with phraseology.[54]

Following Tanglewood, Sapp moved to Bryn Mawr to live near his parents. Since it was wartime, it was difficult to travel reliably even in North America. The suburban Philadelphia location allowed Sapp to commute more easily to New York City on a weekly basis for his lessons with Aaron Copland.[55] It was in Bryn Mawr that Sapp would complete the last movement of the *Concertino* in late August.

The private lessons with Copland were relaxed and spontaneous, primarily focusing on Sapp's music. At first they concentrated on the final revisions of the *Concertino*, mainly alterations in orchestration. The main work of the autumn was Sapp's *Violin Sonata I* (W52).[56] One very direct influence Copland had on this work was the choice of the slow-fast-slow movement sequence, a direct result of their discussions of the concept of occasionally needing to invert expected time schemes.[57] In addition to discussing Sapp's music, they would occasionally branch out into discussions of music by other modern composers or specific musical and artistic problems. Sapp recalled one such discussion which focused on the concept of writing music for a greater population, or *Gebrauchsmusik*, something very much in the air at this time.

> This is quite an important point. [Copland] said, "You do not expect a person in church to speak the way that a politician speaks, the way that a university professor speaks, the way that you speak when you have quite intimate things to say to your loved one." And he made a galaxy, so to speak, of different ways in which we normally communicate with each other. We converse, in formal ways, informal ways, intimate ways, public ways. He said that he based his philosophy of communicating in the music on the fact that he felt free to move from one mode of communication, so to speak, to another. That made so much more sense to me than the casual division of, well, "There's a lot of hard music and severe music and intellectual music, and then there's the popular music."[58]

After several weeks of lessons, Copland felt that Sapp would also benefit from lessons in musical analysis with Nadia Boulanger. Sapp enthusiastically agreed and made arrangements with her for a second weekly lesson funded by the Paine Fellowship. Boulanger was then teaching at two institutions, the Longy School of Music in Cambridge and the Peabody Conservatory of Music in Baltimore. From October 1942 through January 1943, the composer met Boulanger on her weekly train ride from Boston to Baltimore by boarding in Philadelphia. Here they began their lessons during the approximately two-hour ride to Baltimore. Upon arriving in Baltimore, they walked to her studio at the Peabody Conservatory and continued for several hours more (her regular teaching duties at Peabody did not occur until the following day). Sapp then caught the last train back to Philadelphia.[59]

Sapp and Boulanger immediately established a warm relationship, no doubt due in part to Sapp's fluency in French and deep interest in French literature and music; in fact, these lessons moved spontaneously back and forth between English and French. At first he was assigned arrangements of Bach chorales and some part-writing exercises from the Vidal *Manuel pratique d'harmonie*.[60]   However, Sapp recalls that "the Boulanger lessons . . . were mostly discussions with her rather than formal lessons. Piston had told her (and Copland confirmed) that I had had plenty of formal instruction and needed some broader perspectives."[61]   Their discussions focused mainly on analyses of French music, from the baroque (e.g., Rameau, Couperin) to the more contemporary (e.g., Ravel, Fauré, D'Indy, and Françaix). They also spent a great deal of time discussing and analyzing several Bach fugues. Sapp also recalls showing her his recent compositions, including the *Piano Sonata I*, the *Concertino for Piano and Orchestra*, and the *Violin Sonata I*:

> I did bring the *Violin Sonata*, and she was very pleased with it, the crispness and incisiveness that she admired. . . . She had very strong . . . positive reactions. I expected her to be very critical. She wasn't. . . . She liked my harmonic style and diatonic style at that time.   She saw the Stravinsky influences and the Piston influences, and the Copland influences of course, but she sensed some originality.[62]

Boulanger later "came to the concert in New York of the *Violin Sonata* and wrote [me] a very sweet note about it."[63]

With his studies at Harvard completed and his twentieth birthday fast approaching, Sapp knew that he would soon be called into war service. He tried to arrange (with his father's assistance) a naval commission for himself, and began to study cryptanalysis in the fall of 1942 through a navy correspondence course. This plan eventually fell through, as the composer was drafted into the army on 23 January 1943, one week before he would receive his officer's commission from the navy. On 4 February 1943 the composer reported to the local draft board in Bryn Mawr, and a few weeks later he was bound for an army boot camp in Missouri.[64] He returned the unused Paine Fellowship funds to Harvard, and his period of private study with two great teachers came to an unfortunate and premature halt.

2. SERVICE IN WORLD WAR II, 1943-47

DURING FEBRUARY AND MARCH OF 1943, Sapp spent a very trying period in army basic training at Camp Crowder near Neosho, Missouri. The following month, however, found him at Vint Hill Farms Station[1] in Warrenton, Virginia receiving specialized training in cryptanalysis.

While boot camp was totally disconnected from the previous heady musical life of studying with Copland and Boulanger, at least Vint Hill provided opportunities for music making. There Sapp befriended a teacher at a local private school for girls who asked him to perform his *Piano Sonata I* at a student assembly. He also frequently played four-hand piano music with a colleague at Vint Hill, Gabriel De Haan. Most importantly, Sapp began sketches for a *Symphony in D Minor*, which would eventually find its final form as his *Four Hand Piano Sonata I* (W42), composed and refined during his various stations in Europe the following year.

Norma Bertolami, Sapp's fiancée, graduated from Radcliffe in June 1943. The couple chose to marry before he was sent to Europe; they were married at St. James Episcopal Church in Warrenton on 22 July 1943. They spent the rest of the summer together, living off-base in a room rented from the church pastor. But at the beginning of September Sapp was ordered to New York to prepare for departure for England. On 12 September Sapp boarded his ship and bade farewell to his wife and parents.

He arrived in London one week later and was stationed there for several weeks. The city was enjoying a respite from the earlier heavy bombing, and some of its artistic life had resumed. While off-duty he attended several concerts, including a performance of Vaughan Williams *D-Major Symphony* at Albert Hall, and a concert by Dame Myra Hess at the British Museum.

In October, Sapp was assigned to an intelligence unit at a large shoreline estate in Eastbourne on the southern coast of England, where he learned to intercept radio messages from German patrol boats and submarines. There was little time for any music until December, when his unit moved to another large estate near the town of Battle, a few miles northeast of Eastbourne.

> I was promoted a couple of times [in Battle]. That meant more income and more freedom. [Voice interception] was routine work, so I continued work at this time on the *Symphony*. I realized that I didn't really have the material for a symphony and decided to keep the basic structure.

> So during the time in Battle was the time that I really completed the *First Four-Hand Sonata*. . . . That was pretty well sketched out and finished by the time we made our last move, which was up to a suburb of London called Bexley.[2]

In Battle Sapp had access to a piano at a local church, and to another one at the USO club which he used occasionally. Fortunately, at Harvard he had learned to compose without the aid of a piano; this allowed him to continually compose small amounts of music during the war. His unit moved to Bexley in March 1944. There they remained for several months, again allowing the composer to occasionally enjoy London's cultural offerings. He remembers making a pilgrimage to Kent, at one point, to visit Ralph Vaughan Williams, who was a good friend of Professor Archibald Davison.

In early August 1944, Sapp's unit was shipped over to France, landing near the Cherbourg Peninsula. By the end of the month his unit arrived fresh on the heels of the liberation forces in Paris and set up operations in a beautiful apartment hotel on Boulevard Maurice Barrès, opposite the Bois de Boulogne, which had been the former headquarters of German naval intelligence for the western front. They remained there for approximately three months, during which time Sapp was assigned to the intelligence headquarters of the 12th Army Group under General Omar Bradley. His task was to synthesize all of the information gathered by the unit and write a daily intelligence report for the senior commander.

Surprisingly, this work did not occupy Sapp for more than a few hours each morning, leaving him most of the day to roam Paris and enjoy the euphoria of the great city in the days following liberation. As in London, he attended many concerts, but he did not make contact with any significant French musicians during this time; many, such as Boulanger, had not yet returned from their sanctuaries in safer lands.[3]

Around the first of November, his unit was committed to assignments in the field, across the French countryside, and eventually into the city of Luxembourg. Here it set up headquarters in a convent, and during this time Sapp was fully occupied with intelligence work near the front.

The Germans beat back the 12th Army Group during the December 1944 "Battle of the Bulge," with Sapp's unit retreating to the Belgian town of Namur. While there Sapp befriended the head of the Conservatoire de Musique de Namur, the composer René Barbier, and his daughter Lucienne, an aspiring pianist.[4] The Barbiers apparently premiered the *Four Hand Piano Sonata I* in a concert at the Conservatoire after his departure. Sapp learned of this by letter at some time during 1945. Apparently the piece "made a big sensation"[5] at the concert.

In late February 1945, his unit advanced to Verviers, Belgium, about 80 kilometers east of Namur.[6] In early March, General Bradley's 12th Army Group crossed the Rhine. Sapp's unit rapidly advanced to the southeast, reaching Nuremberg one month later. From there the unit continued southward to Munich, arriving shortly after V-E Day (8 May 1945). It set up intelligence operations in Pullach, just south of Munich, in a military complex that was the former headquarters of Martin Bormann. With the war over, the charge of the unit shifted to civil censorship work, especially the monitoring of resurgent German terrorist groups.

Shortly after arriving in Pullach, Sapp returned to composing. During the summer he composed his *Piano Sonatina I* (W12).[7] This work is dedicated to "DD" (Dédé), the nickname of Lucienne Barbier. This dedication was in thanks for the Barbiers' having given the première of Sapp's *Four Hand Piano Sonata I* in Namur.

The dedication was also inspired by the very special package Sapp received in July. It not only contained a fair copy of the *Sonata* in Lucienne's hand,[8] but also a "victory present" of a wartime delicacy: a large quantity of hard boiled eggs!

At some point in the early autumn of 1945, the composer flew from Munich to Paris for an official trip lasting a few weeks. While there he discovered

> that the *Concertino* had been performed [by l'Orchestre de la Radiodiffusion Française] and recorded and deposited in a "Filmothèque" library if I remember correctly.[9] . . . What I can recall is a meeting with [the pianist who performed the work] Monique Haas—a most dynamic and attractive person—and her taking me to a studio and my hearing of the tape of the performance. I had the impression that it had been broadcast in the euphoria surrounding the American liberation of Paris. I did not supply the parts, and was quite astonished that some technician of the RDF had prepared the whole thing. Miss Haas got excited about the third movement where she finally had something to do; it was certainly not a conventional concerto-like piece. . . . Perhaps Nadia Boulanger had something to do with causing it all to happen; she was a great supporter of mine at this time."[10]

Sapp returned to Munich to set up a branch office of the U. S. Army Civil Censorship Division, which had its headquarters in Frankfurt. During this time, he wrote an extensive three-volume training manual, *Censorship Cryptanalysis* (see B2). This manual was immediately put to use in the division and was praised by a senior official in a letter of commendation: "You have prepared manuals and operating instructions, based on original thought, which have been of great value, not only to this organization but also to the more general field of cryptanalysis."[11]

Though the war in Europe was over, Sapp could not expect to be discharged for some time,[12] and thus he looked for other means to be reunited with Norma. In autumn 1945, he was approached by one of his superiors and offered a civilian post at a much higher assimilated rank and salary. This appointment would also make it possible to return to the United States briefly in order to bring Norma to Germany. He accepted the offer and received his honorable discharge from the army on 23 November 1945, at the final rank of Technician Fourth Grade. While Sapp was in the United States, a performance by Hans Rosbaud and Martin Piper of the *Four Hand Piano Sonata I* took place at the Prinzregententheater, Bayerische Staatstheater in Munich on 16 December 1945. As with the other two European performances of his music, army duties prevented the attendance of the young composer.

During the next two years, Sapp served in several different positions in the army's Civil Censorship Division, ultimately attaining very high positions at European Theater Headquarters (Frankfurt am Main): Chief of Code Research, and Chief Cryptanalyst.[13] When the division was deactivated in late October 1947, Sapp was offered a similar position in the newly-formed Central Intelligence Agency, which was to continue monitoring communications in Germany.[14] He declined this offer and returned to Cambridge with Norma the following month to resume his musical career.

3. A RETURN TO HARVARD, 1947-58

BEGINNING WITH THE SPRING TERM IN FEBRUARY 1948, Sapp began work on an A.M. degree in composition at Harvard University. He quickly renewed contacts there and became Piston's assistant in his orchestration course.[1] During his graduate work he served as a teaching fellow in the Music Department, assisting the faculty in various courses including Orchestration (Walter Piston and Randall Thompson), Elementary Harmony (Richard French), and Tonal Counterpoint (Irving Fine).[2] Norma Sapp also resumed her graduate studies and was employed as a teaching fellow by Archibald T. Davison in his Survey of Music History.

The spring of 1948 began a period of intensive composition for Sapp, following a period of relative inactivity (since the *Piano Sonatina* of late 1945) during which he was preoccupied with his administrative work in the army's Civil Censorship Division in Germany. The first major work to be completed was the *Violin Sonata II* (W54), which was awarded the 1948 George Arthur Knight Prize at Harvard. Later in the year he also composed the *Viola Sonata* (W55) and a cantata for his sister Nancy's wedding, *A Song of Marriage* (W98).

During the summer of 1948, Sapp began a serious personal study of the music of the late Middle Ages and the Renaissance. Perhaps due to his immersion in cryptanalysis during the previous five years, Sapp was particularly intrigued by the coded elements of this ancient music, especially isorhythmic techniques and musical games and puzzles. He immediately put isorhythmic technique to work in the last movement of the *Viola Sonata*. This was the beginning of a very important change of technique for the composer, branching out from the *grand ligne* approach of Boulanger toward more complex, multi-layered organizational structures.

The trend toward a greater technical complexity in his music continued during the following year, when Sapp made a rigorous study of selected works by Schoenberg, Webern, and Berg. Their music was generally outside the accepted Harvard curriculum up to this time;[3] but Sapp's work began to shed more light upon this new area.[4] His most ambitious efforts were extensive analyses of Schoenberg's *Wind Quintet* (op. 26) and *Klavierstücke* (op. 33), on which he delivered presentations in Davison's Seminar in Music History[5] and Piston's Seminar in Composition. Howard Pollack stated that Sapp's "'decodings' of such Schoenberg works as the *Third Quartet* won the respect of Piston, who by then had used the method himself, but was rather quiet about it. Sapp's analyses may have helped spur the interest of such older friends as Copland, Fine, Binkerd, and Middleton in the technique."[6]

Influence is very difficult to measure, but one cannot dispute Pollack's observation that Sapp "anticipated [serialism's] vogue in America."[7]

Sapp first employed serial technique in the fourth movement of his *Suite for Piano* (W14), composed in 1949. It opens with a rather basic application in which only the melodic line is in a twelve-note cycle (twice forward, once retrograde, with its accompaniment freely composed); beginning in measure 12 both melody and accompaniment are ordered by the series (see MUSICAL EXAMPLE 3.1, mm. 1-15). In his next work, *Piano Trio* (W56), Sapp used some form of serial treatment in each of the four movements, in varying degrees of plasticity and rigor. Nearly all of his works since 1949 have employed some form of serial technique.[8] He soon developed a very sophisticated use of serial method, but usually maintained a tonal orientation within his works; this was achieved by employing tone rows which served to emphasize tonal centers rather than to obscure them. One of his most blatantly tonal serial works is the *Piano Sonata III* (W19), composed in 1957. The opening of the first movement boldly presents A minor in a rocketing arpeggiated figure, with triads featured prominently in the accompaniment throughout (see MUSICAL EXAMPLE 3.2). The tone row (A - C - Db - Eb - B - G♯ - Gb - F - E - D - Bb - G) contains a minor triad at the close of each hexichord.[9]

With this strong reaffirmation of the importance of tonality in his compositions, Sapp's reasons for adopting serial technique were obviously very different from those of the composers of the Second Viennese School.

> [Through my] analysis of the Schoenberg *Wind Quintet* . . . I became aware of the fact that [his] processes were very similar to the processes that I'd been using in my own composing, ever since I first started writing. They weren't systematic and they weren't serial in the sense of that obligatory quality that was so much a factor in early serial writing. But the discovery of what was going on in that music was very similar to the process of encrypting and decrypting, which I had spent so much time doing in the war. That tied in immediately with the notion of some sort of linguistic statement which was then encoded in various ways. . . . I discovered that there was a first theme and second theme and third theme, and they were all in different, what I call, modes. Different proto-keys. And I was carried along by that idea and felt that I had sufficient evidence to demonstrate it. And also to prove to myself that the composer was the master of the process, not the reverse. The tenor around Cambridge at that time was that if you were in the serial camp, you just generated this mechanical stuff and that you had no artistic control. Well, this is untrue, of course. It settled me into a firm understanding that the user of serial music was at all times perfectly able to make happen in the realm of melody and harmony and sonority exactly what he wanted. The control was only a corollary of the skill and the technique and the command of the musical medium of the composer. . . .
>
> The Schoenberg canon said don't use triads because they'll sound sort of key-like. And, of course, I completely rejected that and wrote a lot of triads and seventh chords and so on. Whether it's successful or not from a technical standpoint somebody else is going to have to decide. But the conscious effort in those two sonatas [*Piano Sonatas III* and *IV*] was to compose serial music which would, by any serious analysis, fit the canon of serial writing, but to a listener and a performer would appear to be sort of advanced 20th century music in tonal style.[10]

After completing his A.M. at Harvard in June 1949, Sapp remained there the following year as a Teaching Fellow and took additional courses toward a doctorate. On 23 January 1950, Sapp was offered an appointment as Instructor in the Harvard Music Department.[11]   Although this would mean abandoning his pursuit of the doctorate, Sapp accepted the position with alacrity, responding that he was "more interested in the appointment as annual instructor in the Music Department than anything else. To continue on, teaching at Harvard, has been the ambition I have cherished ever since entering as an undergraduate in 1939."[12] Shortly after his appointment to the faculty, Sapp was also appointed Tutor in Music at Kirkland House, one of the campus residences with an active co-curricular education and social program. In addition to his regular meetings with music students, he produced many concerts there, including several performances of his own works. He enjoyed interacting with the other members of the "common table" at Kirkland House, including such eminent Harvard professors as John Fairbank (Chinese scholar), Mason Hammond (classicist, and Master of Kirkland House), and Reginald Phelps (German scholar, and Chairman of the Commission on Extension Courses).[13]

Sapp was warmly welcomed by the senior faculty, and formed especially close relationships with the newest faculty members, Randall Thompson (joining in 1948) and Otto Gombosi (joining in 1951). Thompson's influence on the younger composer is evidenced by Sapp's production of several choral and solo vocal works in the early 1950s:

Choral
Five Landscapes (W100; 1950)
American Fantasies (W101; ca. 1952)
The Little Boy Lost (W102; 1953)
A Birthday Piece for A.T.D. (W103; 1953)
A Prayer for Commencement (W104; 1954)

Solo vocal
The Bridal Song (W84; 1951-52)
Nursery Rhymes (W85; ca. 1952)
Seven Epigrams (Both Sweet and Sour) (W86; 1952)
The Lady and the Lute (W87; 1952, rev. 1957)

Prior to his contact with Thompson, he had written only one choral work, the cantata *A Song of Marriage* (1948), and had not written any works for solo voice. It should be noted that Piston, Sapp's primary mentor in the prior decade, wrote almost no music for voice during his career.[14]   However, Piston's influence can be strongly detected in Sapp's instrumental music of this period, particularly in his *String Quartet I* (W57; 1951) and *Second Suite for Orchestra* (W113; 1952-56).

The class which gave Sapp the most joy during his Instructorship was Analysis of Musical Form (Music 102), a course he inherited from Merritt for the 1950-51 academic year.[15] Sapp had many gifted students in that course who went on to have distinguished careers, including Howard M. Brown, Bathea Churgin, and Peter Westergaard. In addition to the study of forms from the ancient to modern, Sapp led the students in performances of works studied in class, with the culmination of study for each composition being a carefully made recording of the work. During the next two years, Sapp taught Elementary Harmony (Music 51) and Orchestration (Music 153).

In the early 1950s Sapp helped to found the Creative Concerts Guild, together with Paul Des Marais, Claudio Spies, Robert Middleton, and Morton and Diane Margolis.   The Guild gave several important concerts in the early 1950s, commissioning and premiering such works as Luigi Dallapiccola's *Goethe-Lieder*, Irving Fine's song cycle *Mutability*, and Andrew Imbrie's *String Quartet No. 2*. These concerts also featured works by such composers as Sessions, Bartók, Goeb, Haieff, Piston, Smit, and Stravinsky, intermingled with standard chamber music works of the eighteenth and nineteenth centuries.   After only a few seasons, the Guild, unfortunately, ceased operations when Middleton, Des Marais and Spies left Boston for other positions after finishing their work at Harvard.[16]

WGBH-FM in Boston began broadcasting on 6 October 1951; one week later, Sapp initiated a weekly radio series of one-hour programs on that station, "Music of the Baroque" (see B5).   Later that season Sapp also became the on-air program annotator of the Boston Symphony Orchestra broadcasts.[17]   During the 1952-53 season, he began another series of weekly broadcasts, "Music of Our Time" (see B7). Although the live symphony broadcasts were at that time heard only on WGBH-FM, Sapp's two weekly series were recorded and distributed throughout the country by the National Association of Educational Broadcasters.[18] Sapp discontinued regular work for WGBH in 1953 when his faculty duties at Harvard became too pressing, but he was occasionally called upon by the station to substitute for his Harvard colleague, G. Wallace Woodworth, on the Boston Symphony's preview program, "Tomorrow's Symphony."

Sapp was promoted to Assistant Professor at Harvard in March 1953. He was immediately given a leadership role, serving as Acting Chairman of the Music Department for two summer sessions, 1953 and 1954. His most significant acts were to plan and direct two successive summer conferences, each featuring symposia and concerts. Sapp chose as the theme of the 1953 conference "The American Composer and Choral Music" and was able to engage Elliott Carter, Virgil Thomson, and Irving Fine to participate.[19] The success of this conference led to Sapp's being asked to repeat as Acting Chairman in the summer of 1954, this time directing a conference on "Music in the Church."

In the autumn, Sapp was appointed to the university's influential Committee on Educational Policy, which was both an honor and a harrowing experience for the young professor:

> There is a tradition at Harvard that a junior, non-tenured member is appointed to the Committee on Educational Policy. The CEP was in fact the steering committee of Harvard University. It was the committee chaired by the Dean of the Faculty of Arts and Sciences, which represented the policy making and determinative executive council of the University. . . . I received a call from a McGeorge Bundy,[20] who was the Dean, asking me if I would join this group. And I didn't know what it really was, but I was very flattered. . . . So I became a member of this illustrious committee. No sooner had I begun to attend the meetings than I was appointed secretary, because the junior member becomes the secretary. So I had the onerous job for those years . . . of serving as the committee secretary in the most brilliant conclave that I ever expect to be in: George Kistiakowsky, one of the people who worked on the atomic bomb; Douglas Bush, the great English scholar; Fred [B. F.] Skinner, . . . one of the world's leading psychologists; . . . and [other]

people of that eminence. There was poor little me [laughter] sitting there in this group! . . . The discussions were curricular, budgetary and everything else, chaired by this incredibly brilliant Mac Bundy, who was really one of the most brilliant men I ever expect to know. Well, this was overwhelming. Just writing the minutes [of the meetings] . . . was very, very onerous and not only time consuming, but a tremendous emotional strain. These issues were so far away from the parochialities of the Music Department."[21]

In the summer of 1954, Sapp was invited to teach at the Salzburg Seminar on American Studies. Some of the other notable teachers at the seminar were political scientist Max Lerner (Brandeis University), historian Avery Craven, (University of Chicago), and novelist Ralph Ellison. Sapp's teaching in Salzburg focused on recent American music, that of Piston, Copland, and Gershwin, among others. Impressed by Sapp's lectures, Craven arranged to have Sapp invited to give a series of lectures on "The Search for Language in American Music" as part of the Walgreen Lectures[22] series at the University of Chicago during the fall of 1955 (see B12).

As mentioned earlier, Sapp formed a close friendship with the renowned Hungarian musicologist Otto Gombosi. Along with Davison, Gombosi had on several occasions urged Sapp to become active as a scholar. Sapp assisted Gombosi in preparations for his summer 1953 seminar on the music of Bartók; when Gombosi became seriously ill, Sapp took over the teaching of this seminar.[23] After a leave of absence Gombosi returned to teaching in the spring term of 1954 but suffered more serious health problems during the summer. Although still very frail, he once again attempted to teach a seminar on Bartok in the 1954-55 academic year. Gombosi died on 17 February 1955, and Sapp once again took over his seminar.

As the preceding paragraphs illustrate, Sapp was quite overburdened in these first few years of his career. The heavy load took its toll. He became seriously depressed in the summer of 1954, and began consultation with a psychiatrist. During the following academic year his condition worsened, and upon the recommendation of his psychiatrist Sapp admitted himself into the Ring Sanitarium in nearby Arlington on 8 April 1955.[24] Dean Bundy granted Sapp a leave of absence for the remainder of the term.[25] Sapp remained at the sanitarium for approximately three weeks, then checked out and remained on leave, recuperating in seclusion at home for the remainder of the term.

During the summer of 1955, Sapp turned down another invitation to teach at the Salzburg Seminar, since he felt that would be too much of a strain after his ordeal; instead, he and his family[26] retreated to the summer home of Robert Middleton's father-in-law in Kennebunkport, Maine. The following academic year, Sapp returned to Harvard and resumed a normal teaching load, but without the extra burden of administrative and committee work. He taught two courses that year, Analysis of Musical Form and History and Literature of Music: 1600 to 1900. Following his Walgreen Lectures at the University of Chicago in November, Sapp once again began to write music, making progress on his *Piano Sonata II* (W16) and *Second Suite for Orchestra* (W113).

In March 1956, Sapp was awarded the Howard Foundation Fellowship from Brown University, which allowed him to travel to Rome for a sabbatical leave.[27] Sapp left with his family for Europe immediately following the academic year in June 1956, and remained there for over a year, returning in time to start the 1957-58 academic year. "The express mission was to see whether I could retrieve any spark out of my creative energy or if my creative ability was gone forever. . . . I was pretty demoralized and pretty weak in spirit.   But I did not lack courage altogether; I thought that this could all be salvaged.   Certainly my ability to write music was something that was too precious to me to just write off."[28]

After touring France and Northern Italy via automobile during the summer, the Sapp family arrived in Rome in September 1956.   They rented an apartment on an aptly named street for a professor on sabbatical, Via Madonna del Riposo; "I thought any street named 'Our Lady of Rest' would do just fine!"[29]   Sapp declined an invitation to use studio space at the American Academy in Rome, and instead rented an upright piano from Ricordi's for his apartment study.   Finding his way back to writing was very difficult at first: "The first month was just terrible.   I couldn't write; nothing was working.   I was writing junk and I couldn't seem to get started. . . . I began to get really quite despairing as to whether I was ever going to get anything back."[30]   Finally he produced a set of *Seven Bagatelles for Piano* (W15) in October.   The pump now primed, he began one of the most prolific periods of his career, creating eight major compositions during the next year:

Seven Bagatelles, piano (W15)	14 min.
Four Impromptus, piano (W17)	9 min.
Piano Sonatina II (W18)	11 min.
Piano Sonata III (W19)	17 min.
Piano Sonata IV (W20)	17 min.
Six Ricercare, viols (W59)	12 min.
String Trio (W60)	12 min.
The Double Image, orchestra (W114)	12 min.

In addition, he finished the orchestration of his *Second Suite for Orchestra*; began work on another composition for large orchestra (*The Heptagon*, W127); and made substantial revisions to the *Piano Sonata II*, composing an entirely new third movement and completing the fourth movement.[31]

In the evenings the Sapps were drawn into the social circles of the fellows of the American Academy in Rome, many of whom were friends and colleagues from Harvard.   Mason Hammond, former Master at Kirkland House during Sapp's affiliation as Tutor and now head of the academy's School of Classical Studies, warmly welcomed the Sapps shortly after their arrival in Rome.   Among the composers at the academy that year were Alexei Haieff and Billy Jim Layton.   Haieff and Sapp met on several occasions to examine each other's music.   Haieff was especially complimentary of Sapp's *Second Suite for Orchestra*.   The younger composer recalled that Haieff "was very encouraging at a time when I could have certainly used some encouragement."[32]   Sapp also spent a great deal of time with Leon Kirchner, who was also living in Rome that year on leave from Mills College. The evening gatherings at the academy also offered these composers the opportunity to interact with other prominent artists and scholars—not only Americans, but also celebrated Italian figures, including composers Luigi Dallapiccola, Bruno Maderna, and Luigi Nono.   The Sapps also befriended the cultural attaché of the American Embassy, George Picard, and his wife Ilse, to whom the *Seven Bagatelles for Piano* are dedicated.

In December 1956 Sapp received a letter from Randall Thompson bearing the sad but not entirely unexpected news that he had not been awarded tenure and promotion at Harvard.[33]   Thompson offered no explanation, but perhaps one factor was Sapp's period of illness in 1954-55, and the resultant lack of significant production of new compositions or major performances since his promotion to Assistant Professor in 1953. It is ironic that this letter arrived just as Sapp was in the middle of one of the most productive and highly inspired phases of his career. Fortunately, this news did not have an adverse effect on Sapp's creativity; if anything, it had the opposite effect. Thompson, who was very close to Sapp, almost predicted this reaction: "I hope that your year has gone happily and productively and that this letter, which I have written with a heavy heart, will not darken it in any way; rather, from some mystical source, release you for the fuller exercise of your powers and the fuller enjoyment of your months of freedom."[34]

Sapp returned for his final year of teaching at Harvard in September 1957. He again taught a mixture of theory and history courses in 1957-58: Tonal Counterpoint, Studies in American Music, and The Classical Period: 1750 to 1820. In addition to teaching, he premiered the *Piano Sonata III* (a work he composed specifically for himself to perform) in Philadelphia on 24 February 1958. Several other Boston area performances followed later in the year. Norma Sapp premiered the other two Roman *Piano Sonatas* (*II* and *IV*) during that academic year.

In the spring of 1958, Sapp was offered a three-year lectureship appointment at Wellesley College, which he accepted. He had been solicited by a number of different colleges and universities,[35] but he chose Wellesley so that he and his wife could maintain their musical and educational contacts and activities within the Boston metropolitan area.[36]

Sapp's final day as a faculty member at Harvard was a memorable one. Following the final lecture in his course The Classical Period, his large "non-concentrator" (i.e., non-music major) class of nearly 200 gave him a standing ovation.[37] It was a sweet ending to a somewhat bitter period.

4. WELLESLEY COLLEGE, 1958-61

WHEN HUBERT LAMB, Chairman of the Music Department at Wellesley College, became aware that Sapp's appointment at Harvard was coming to an end, he offered Sapp a three-year Lecturer appointment to begin in the autumn of 1958.[1] Sapp accepted and relocated his family near the Wellesley campus.

Sapp's courses at Wellesley ranged from Introduction to Music, essentially a music fundamentals course in basic music theory and ear training, to survey courses intended for juniors and seniors, including The Symphony and The String Quartet.[2] Sapp's gift as a teacher within a broad liberal arts environment is illustrated by Hubert Lamb's remarks to President Margaret Clapp in the letter proposing his appointment to the Wellesley College faculty:

> He is . . . a very idealistic and sympathetic person, deeply devoted to music and to teaching. . . . His warm interest in people should make [Introduction to Music] . . . far more than a dry study of basic techniques. . . . He has been spectacularly successful at Harvard, as I learn from Mr. [A. Tillman] Merritt, in just this kind of teaching. Merritt speaks of his gift for arousing the interest of the non-major student and for leading such a student to do really solid work as reminiscent of Dr. [Archibald T.] Davison's similar gift. Mr. Sapp has made very valuable contributions in extra-curricular projects at Harvard. . . . He enjoys arranging things that will interest and enlighten.[3]

Sapp's undemanding teaching duties at Wellesley provided him with ample time for composing. Seven concert works and incidental music for three plays were produced during those three years. Two of these works were composed for the 17 April 1960 dedicatory program for the college's Jewitt Arts Center. *A Maiden's Complaint in Springtime* (W105), a cantata setting of the eleventh century anonymous Latin poem, "Levis exsurgit Zephyrus," was conducted by then faculty colleague Howard Mayer Brown. Brown, a former student of Sapp's at Harvard, also conducted another of Sapp's premières, the *Five Landscapes* (W100) for mixed chorus, in 1951. Also performed on the dedicatory program were the *Six Variations on the Hymn-Tune "Durant"* (W61), based on the Wellesley College hymn. Each variation satirized one of his faculty colleagues: "I thought it was important at such an occasion not to be relentlessly solemn."[4]

Sapp also composed incidental music for three Greek plays produced by students at Wellesley under the direction of Barbara McCarthy, Professor of Greek. These plays were Euripides' *The Trojan Women*, Aristophanes' *The Frogs*, and Sophocles' *The Women of Trachis* (see W136, W138, and W139). This was a return to the type of quasi-improvised incidental music that Sapp had enjoyed creating for the Harvard Dramatic Club productions some twenty years earlier. While the music for *The Trojan Women* was fairly conventional instrumental music,[5] the other two plays received two of Sapp's most experimental efforts. Since *The Frogs* was to be quite unconventionally "staged" at Wellesley's natatorium, Sapp decided to compose a two-track tape work rather than an instrumental score.   Just as McCarthy's production superimposed a modern interpretation upon the Classical Greek text, Sapp's incidental music superimposed his modern musical idiom upon Baroque and Classical chamber music in an Ivesian fashion. For *The Women of Trachis*, Sapp composed another experimental tape work, this one largely a recording of his improvisation upon various percussion instruments.[6] These two works are the only known examples of Sapp compositions which exist only on tape.

Across town, Sapp continued to be active in the wider musical life of Boston and Cambridge. Performances of his Roman *Piano Sonatas* were especially plentiful, the composer himself performing *Sonata III* no less than seven times in three years. Sapp was active with the Cambridge Composers' Forum, and in 1959-60, along with John Biavicci, created the "Nova Concerts," a new music series similar to his earlier effort with the Creative Concerts Guild in the early 1950s. The following season, the Boston Fine Arts Chamber Orchestra premiered two works by Sapp, his *Overture to "The Women of Trachis"* (W115, totally unrelated musically to his later tape-recorded percussion incidental music) and *June* (W116) for wind quintet and string orchestra.

Sapp's classes at Wellesley were very popular, and he did have some very talented students, most notably musicologist Bonnie Blackburn. However, he missed the challenge of graduate level teaching. With this in mind, Sapp was receptive to pursuing his career elsewhere following his three-year appointment.

Through Sapp's continued association with Reginald Phelps of the Harvard Extension Courses, he kept informed of large-scale national discussions of trends in higher education and occasionally attended conventions as a representative of the Commission on Extension Courses.[7] Phelps was the first person to inform Sapp of the recently founded State University of New York (SUNY) system.   Having absorbed many of the state's private colleges and universities, SUNY was touted as being potentially on the level of the University of California system. Perhaps through Phelps' intervention, Sapp was soon thereafter contacted by Myles Slatin,[8] Assistant Dean of the College of Arts and Sciences at the University of Buffalo, and asked to consider taking the position of Chairman of the Music Department.

> I thought "Well, I don't know anything about Buffalo." Buffalo was like the end of the world to me. Typical Easterner, you know. . . . [I] hardly knew where it was. . . . I went through the place and I had meetings with various people and came back. It didn't seem to be very much—seemed to be okay, but not that interesting. Then I began to get some urgent telephone calls from [Dean Milton C.] Albrecht, [Slatin's] superior, saying that this was a real situation and [asking me to] come up again. So I went back, and this time was formally offered the job as chairman of music there, and an enormous increase in salary and rank. So I took it. And the whole rationale was that I was going to have a free hand to build upward."[9]

Musicologist Frank D'Accone, who had joined the UB faculty the previous year, had served as a teaching assistant to Sapp at Harvard. He remembers "saying loudly and clearly that if Allen were willing to come to Buffalo, we couldn't find a better candidate for the post."[10]

5. FROM COMPOSER TO ADMINISTRATOR: BUFFALO, 1961-68

UPON HIS ARRIVAL IN BUFFALO, Sapp began the most publicly active period of his life, surpassing even his first years on the Harvard faculty. These activities took the form of serving not only as an academic administrator, but also as a director on numerous boards of artistic institutions and foundations at the local, state, and national levels.[1]   During this period, he made major contributions to these institutions and to the artistic careers of many individuals as well. This period of administrative activity would span the next two decades of his life and would reach such an extreme level of commitment of his time that his activity as a composer came almost to a complete halt between 1964 and 1979, with the exception of a few minor works and sketch fragments.[2]

Allen Sapp was introduced to Buffalo and the university community as the Slee Professor of Composition for the autumn semester of 1961. He gave three lecture-recitals, entitled "Three Modes of Musical Communication" (see B17a-c). The first of these, "The Personal Gesture," featured the composer performing his *Piano Sonata III* (W19) and his wife, Norma Bertolami Sapp, performing *Piano Sonatas II* and *IV* (W16 and W20), the set of sonatas completed in Rome in 1957. John Dwyer wrote in the *Buffalo Evening News* that he "enjoyed some frankly romantic passages in the old nostalgic manner, but with fresh notions of voicing and coloration. . . . For all the dynamic contrasts, the works seemed to have a rather even emotional set, at the base, as if an able essayist were involved with the skilled and leisurely turnings of his own mind. The performances were excellent."[3]   The noted Metropolitan Opera mezzo-soprano Jennie Tourel assisted Sapp with performances during the second lecture, "The Lyric Impulse," and the Bel Arte Trio (Joseph Silverstein, violin, Joseph de Pasquale, viola, and Samuel Mayes, violoncello) performed on the third, "The Corporate Experience," which included a performance of Sapp's *String Trio* (W60).[4]

Sapp's impact in the artistic community actually began several months earlier in the summer of 1961, when he was introduced to the Board of Directors of the Buffalo Philharmonic Orchestra. He volunteered to personally search for an Assistant Conductor for the orchestra, and recommended Ronald Ondrejka for the position. The Board was very pleased with Sapp's work, and immediately appointed him as a director. He served as Chairman of the Music Advisory Committee, consulting Music Director Josef Krips on his programming decisions.[5] The following year, Sapp played the key role in hiring Lukas Foss as successor to Krips.[6]

Sapp also made immediate and cordial contact with Gordon Smith, Director of the Albright-Knox Art Gallery, and with Seymour H. Knox, an investment banker and Buffalo's leading arts benefactor, who was President of the Buffalo Fine Arts Academy and later Chairman of the New York State Council on the Arts. Through these associations Sapp was appointed Music Advisor to the gallery and elected an Honorary Member of the Buffalo Fine Arts Academy.[7] That Sapp impressed these men was evident when he was inducted into the city's most exclusive club, the Thursday Club, whose members included many of the city's most powerful and wealthy people, among them Knox, Smith, and Clifford Furnas, President of the University. Sapp's involvement with this group would pay rich dividends for the artistic life of Buffalo and the University in the coming decade, especially in the planning and funding of the 1965 and 1968 Buffalo Festivals of the Arts Today.

At the University, Sapp inherited a small and rather unfocused Department of Music, founded only nine years earlier by Cameron Baird.[8] The son of a wealthy Buffalo industrialist and himself the former head of a sewer pipe company, Baird also had a consuming interest in music, with impressive training for a non-professional. He studied composition and viola with Paul Hindemith and Bernard Heiden, and conducting with Felix Weingartner and Bruno Walter, although he apparently never completed an academic degree in music.[9] His parents were also very interested in music, and frequently hosted chamber music concerts by such prominent groups as the Budapest Quartet.[10]

Baird modeled the department after a conservatory, using mostly part-time instructors from the Buffalo Philharmonic Orchestra. When Sapp arrived in the summer of 1961, the continuing full-time staff of the Department consisted of a handful of instrumental and vocal instructors and ensemble directors, a music education professor of national repute (Dr. Irving Cheyette), and a promising young musicologist (Dr. Frank D'Accone), for a total of eight regular faculty positions.[11] The undergraduate music education program accounted for ninety percent of enrolled students by 1960.[12] The department was considerably enriched in its nebulous stage through a major bequest by Frederick Caldecott Slee. It allowed for the visitation of "a musician equal to high rank of the Paris Conservatoire and master-teacher of Harmony, Counterpoint and Fugue."[13] This bequest also established the Slee Beethoven Cycle,[14] which provided funds for the complete series of Beethoven string quartets, to be played on campus each year by well known professional quartets. This allowed for significant student and faculty interaction with figures such as Aaron Copland, the first Slee Professor in 1957, and the Budapest Quartet, who performed the first Slee Beethoven Cycles (1955-1964).[15]

Sapp's charge was to transform the University of Buffalo Music Department into a strong unit of the western anchor of the new State University of New York (SUNY) system; the other major university centers were located in Stony Brook, Albany, and Binghamton. Sapp immediately assessed the situation in Western New York and became aware that the State University College at Fredonia had a more developed program of teaching applied music and music education at the undergraduate level and was only an hour's drive southwest of Buffalo. He also took into account that an hour east of Buffalo stood the Eastman School of Music which, although it was independent of the SUNY system, still provided a comprehensive high-quality performance oriented school which attracted many of the best student performers from Western New York.

Backed by considerable state and private resources which allowed for rapid addition of high caliber faculty, Sapp's development plan made an almost complete reversal of the existing emphasis of the department, choosing to focus on the missing links in the region. The plan he put in place and began to develop over its first seven years remains the current structure of the Music Department today. He set out to build a department with these guidelines:

> There would be no major music education sector. That was being handled by Fredonia; there was no reason to have it. We would have a graduate [music education] program eventually,[16] which would concentrate on national problems and so on, but there would be a small staff. We would have an emphasis on serious musicology and music history study. We would build a sector there of great strength, the best people we could find. That went along, of course, with the building of the [Music] Library. The Library was nothing in those days. . . . [Another] decision was to build an emphasis throughout the whole place on contemporary music. We would become known as a place to come where the study of 20th century music and advanced music and music of our times, so to speak, would be emphasized and would be a thematic element. This would differentiate us from other elements in the state system and would give Buffalo a link to the international community and to the serious community of composers and build on the Slee Chair, which was the visiting chair. . . . [In addition] we would build a small number of sectors of strength in the instrumental area. That is, a better piano area of instruction. I mean, the pianist we would have would be the best we could find. There would be a small number of chamber music groups. That was the idea, that there would not be a large orchestra.[17]

His masterstroke in the chamber music area was negotiating the Budapest Quartet onto the faculty in 1962.[18] This immediately put the SUNY at Buffalo Music Department into the international spotlight. Why would the Budapest Quartet come to Buffalo?

> Well, there are several reasons. One of the interesting connections Mr. Baird had started was a program with the Library of Congress, with the Music Division whose head at that time was Harold Spivacke. Harold and I administered jointly certain activities of the [Library of Congress] Music Division, which had been financed by Mr. Baird and his family. . . . This was the end . . . of the Budapest as the resident group there.[19] . . . There was a graceful understanding between Spivacke [and me]. There wasn't any need for fencing or anything. . . . I proposed this extremely complex scheme,[20] which I must say I still feel very proud of, in which [Joseph] Roisman would come with no teaching responsibility, [Boris] Kroyt and Alexander Schneider would come with limited teaching responsibility, and Mischa Schneider would come with full teaching responsibility. And the professorial appointments were all set up that way. So instead of a contract with the quartet as a quartet, it was a contract with the four men individually as a quartet, but with the understanding that there would come a time in which the quartet would cease its professional life.[21]

The quartet members were also familiar with Sapp from their visits to Harvard during the previous two decades, and they were already quite familiar with Buffalo from their long association with the Baird and Slee families. As noted earlier, they had been the first quartet to perform the Slee Beethoven Cycle. In addition to playing several quartet concerts each year, some of the members performed solo recitals at the university.[22] They also held an annual institute for young string players during the university's spring break.[23]

Sapp also strengthened the keyboard studies area with the appointments of the pianist and composer Leo Smit and the harpsichordist, organist, and music historian David Fuller. Smit first came as the Slee Professor in autumn 1962 but was added as a regular faculty member the following year, being drawn away from a position at UCLA. Fuller joined the faculty in the 1963-64 academic year. These appointments significantly added to the strong foundation in performance studies provided by the full and part-time faculty from the Buffalo Philharmonic. A *Buffalo Evening News* music critic remarked of a faculty chamber music recital featuring Fuller, Alexander Schneider, and many Philharmonic members, that the concert "would have been the envy of any major music center in the country."[24]

In the music history area, the faculty already possessed a quality junior member in Frank D'Accone. Sapp and D'Accone initially wanted to hire an eminent American musicologist but were unsuccessful. "There are simply only about one-half dozen first class senior musicologists in the country. They are at Chicago, Harvard, Berkeley, and Illinois at present, and we think we would have quite a time dislodging them."[25] One of the major problems was the poor state of the library's music collection in the early 1960s. Sapp began to rectify this situation in the first year by nearly quintupling the annual acquisition of music books and scores and subscribing "to practically all the new periodicals."[26] In 1964, Sapp also acquired portions of the fine personal library of the eminent music librarian and musicologist Otto Kinkeldey for the university.[27]

Abandoning attempts to attract one of the top senior musicologists, Sapp was able to lure several very promising young musicologists to the faculty, all of whom have had distinguished careers: David Fuller, Herbert Kellman,[28] and Jeremy Noble. Sapp wanted to assemble a musicology faculty with specialization in each major national tradition in music: D'Accone for Italian, Fuller for French, Kellman for German, and Noble for English.[29] Unfortunately, Kellman left to take a position at the University of Illinois after just three years; however, he was replaced by an equally promising young musicologist, James McKinnon, in autumn 1966. In addition, the tradition of inviting senior visiting professors of musicology began in autumn 1965 with the appointment of Claudio Sartori, and continued in autumn 1967 with the appointment of Howard Mayer Brown.

To support this budding program, Sapp continued to aggressively develop the university's music collection. In the summer of 1964 he contracted Frank Campbell of the New York Public Library to serve as an acquisitions consultant.[30] Most importantly, Sapp hired two prominent music librarians in 1967. "The appointment of [James B.] Coover was the final triumph, because I did something which was almost unique. That is the appointment as a full professor in the academic departmental situation and as a major person in the [Libraries] . . . at the same time.[31] He had equal status in both. . . . He had equal power and equal authority."[32] Sapp then arranged for an appointment through the University Libraries for Coover's colleague at Vassar College, Carol June Bradley.

Sapp's role in strengthening the emphasis in the department on contemporary music began with the recruitment of Lukas Foss to Buffalo. As mentioned earlier, Sapp was Chairman of the Music Advisory Committee of the Buffalo Philharmonic Orchestra, charged with recommending a new Music Director to the Executive Committee. Even two months before the committee submitted its recommendations, Sapp wrote to Dean Albrecht that he thought it desirable to "find a conductor of the orchestra who might be even closer to the University than Dr. Krips. You may be sure that although my first aim in that sector will be to get the best qualified man in the world whom we can attract here, I shall have not far from the forefront of my mind the desirability of a man who will cooperate fully with the University in its new role."[33]

The hiring of Foss was certainly one of the best possible choices for the development of the contemporary music scene in Buffalo and for establishing a close relationship with the university. Foss greatly expanded the number of contemporary works performed by the Buffalo Philharmonic,[34] including many works by the university's visiting Slee Professors. More importantly, Foss and Sapp jointly conceptualized and established the SUNY at Buffalo Center of the Creative and Performing Arts. Following its first season, Sapp described in a report that

> The principal objective of the Center is to bring together, in an atmosphere devoted to study and performance, the most talented young musicians and composers. These "Creative Associates" study new music and new notational procedures, perform publicly in area concert halls, and occasionally teach. They communicate their enthusiasm for new music in frequent recitals: during the academic year they present, with special guidance from Lukas Foss, "Evenings for New Music" in concerts open to the public. Several of these "Evenings" are recreated at Carnegie Recital Hall.[35] In addition to these programs, the Center presents a Creative Associates Recital Series and numerous joint concerts with staff and students.[36]

The development of the Center began while Foss was serving as a consultant to the newly-established Rockefeller Foundation Cultural Development Program in 1963. Asked how they could best aid musical culture, Foss responded with a concept to support

> the young professional musician in general and the performer in particular [who] needs musical guidance and financial help at the critical moment when he is just out of school, lest he lose himself in a commercial situation. . . . Once out of school the young musician, who had thought until that moment of serving music, finds himself in a situation where he must think of music serving him. He often has a family to support and we can hardly blame him if his sole concern from one moment to the next becomes a search for a well paying job. I could name here dozens of extraordinarily gifted men who never enjoyed the fruits of their labor, who never "found themselves," who sold out to . . . the commercial situation. Thus I came to the conclusion that foundations should give *priority over all other forms of music support* to the young professional in the years following his musical education, put him on a sound financial basis, so that he may have leisure, concentration, facilities and outlets for such professional activities as would help him to find himself, viz. chamber music, new music, experimental music, which rarely yield remuneration. It should be clear that such activity

would be of the greatest importance not only to the young musician but also to the community, the University scene, and to the cause of music in general.[37]

Foss also remarked that another reason for this program was to help develop the newer forms of experimental musical expression.

> You see, we have many composers now who are creating a totally new kind of music, but so few musicians know how to play it. This music is terrifically difficult too—more difficult than any music has ever been before. We really need to have the performer work with us in creating it. . . . The whole point was to take people who were mature musically—real virtuosi—and conquer them for our cause.[38]

Foss conferred with Sapp, who "immediately saw that this fit in with the idea of the research institute, which would be staffed by special performers."[39] For these musicians, Sapp adopted the term "Creative Associates," by analogy to the research associates employed in the areas of science and medicine at many universities.[40] The formal proposal was prepared and submitted by Sapp to the Rockefeller Foundation, which decided to fund the project beginning in autumn 1964. The Center was the first of its kind in the United States, and its success spawned the establishment of similar groups around the country, including ones at the University of Chicago, Rutgers, the University of Iowa, Mills College, the University of Pennsylvania, and the Cleveland Institute of Music.[41]

In the first season there were nineteen Creative Associates;[42] in each of the next four seasons there would be no less than fifteen.[43] Foss and Sapp recruited many of these musicians from their personal contacts but also held open auditions occasionally in New York and other cities.[44] Following the reports of the initial success of the Center, most new members were hired from the voluminous applications and from the referrals of current Creative Associates.[45]

Sapp's role was primarily managing the relationship of the Center to the University and the Rockefeller Foundation, but he more than occasionally assisted Foss with key artistic matters, such as hiring and programming decisions.[46] The relationship between the Center's Creative Associates and the Music Department Faculty proved to be tenuous at times, since the more conservative members of the Faculty had little use for the activities of the Center. Renee Levine, who served as Coordinator of the Center, remembers at one point that Foss wrote to Alexander Schneider of the Budapest Quartet to ask him for recommendations of string players who might be recruited to the Creative Associates; Schneider responded rather tersely, apparently remarking "'Why would he send a good musician to work on music where the ink wasn't even dry on the page yet?,' . . . implying that there could be no worse waste of time."[47] This and many other instances would require Sapp to soothe the ruffled feathers of the musicians in both camps.

The Creative Associates ranged in age from the twenty-one year old Paul Zukofsky to the thirty-five year old George Crumb. Among the other early Creative Associates who proceeded to have notable professional careers were Sylvano Bussotti, Richard Dufallo, Don Ellis, Frederic Rzewski, and David Tudor. Some individual Creative Associates were later offered faculty positions at SUNY at Buffalo, most notably percussionist Jan Williams and soprano Sylvia Brigham-Dimiziani. Their appointments further enriched the performance studies area of the Music Department.

The Rockefeller Foundation provided most of the funding for the Center. The first two-year start-up grant of $200,000,[48] issued 1 March 1964,[49] was the fourth largest Rockefeller Foundation Cultural Development Grant that year.[50]   A supplementary grant of $10,000 was awarded in 1965 to support performances by the Creative Associates at Carnegie Recital Hall through May 1966.[51]   A $150,000 extension grant for the 1966-68 seasons was awarded in September 1966;[52] by this time, the state was beginning to take over the "hard money" funding of a large part of the Center's costs. In the 1967-68 season, 4.5 positions were supported through the Rockefeller Foundation renewal grant, while the state supported 11 positions; this was the highest level of state support the Center would ever receive.[53]   In the middle of that season, Sapp reported at a departmental faculty meeting that the Rockefeller grant would end in May 1968 and that the program would be taken over by the state at that point; he predicted the state would eventually expand the Center to 25 positions by 1973.[54] However, just the opposite happened: by the end of the 1967-68 academic year, the budget tide had turned, and the central administration in Albany was no longer sympathetic toward state-funded research centers with non-teaching positions, such as those held by the Creative Associates. In order to save the Center from total elimination, Sapp managed to shift the funding for these positions to the Slee Endowment and to other private funds as they became available.[55] The Center would remain active until 1980 but would never enjoy the level of funding of its first four seasons.

Two of the most exciting artistic events of the 1960s were the 1965 and 1968 Buffalo Festivals of the Arts Today. These festivals were organized around the theme of presenting works created within the past decade in the fields of music, visual art, poetry, dance, theater and film. Originally conceived by Lukas Foss,[56] the idea of a festival placing the city's new and more established arts organizations in an international spotlight appealed greatly to Seymour Knox, who, besides being Buffalo's leading benefactor of the arts, was chairman of the New York State Council on the Arts. Knox decided to subsidize the 1965 festival himself through his foundation rather than seek national foundation support;[57] the 1968 festival was also funded largely through local patronage, but also by the New York State Council on the Arts.[58] Sapp was one of the most significant players in the shaping of both festivals, particularly in coordinating the efforts of the major arts organizations and the university. The steering committee consisted of Sapp, Foss, Knox, businessman Max Clarkson, and Albright-Knox Art Gallery Director Gordon M. Smith, who served as chairman.

The first of these festivals (February 27-March 13, 1965) was planned around the opening of a new wing of the Albright-Knox Art Gallery, a modern art collection perhaps second in reputation only to the Museum of Modern Art in New York. Attendance at the festival was astonishing: Gordon Smith reported that 130,943 persons visited the gallery in just the first eight days of the festival, whereas the recent average *annual* attendance had been 140,000;[59] approximately 3,000 attended the U.S. premières of four Eugene Ionesco one-act plays,[60] and 6,500 attended the concerts,[61] from which many prospective attendees had to be turned away.[62] This festival also helped to showcase the Center of the Creative and Performing Arts during its inaugural season, as well as the Buffalo Philharmonic, with its new emphasis on contemporary music. Among the composers performed during the festival were Babbitt, Berio, Boulez, Bussotti, Cage, Feldman, Foss, Kagel, Ligeti, Penderecki, Pousseur, Sapp, and Varese.[63] The gallery featured kinetic sculpture and optic art works by Nicholas Schoffer and Len Lye, along with works by dozens of other living artists. Recent films by Andy Warhol, Jonas Mekas, Stan Brakhage, and ten other film makers were screened. Dance performances by the companies of Merce Cunningham and the Judson Art Theater were also featured. Poetry readings and a panel discussion featured poets Robert Creeley, Robert Graves, W. D. Snodgrass, and David Posner.

The first festival received considerable press coverage, including reporters from *Time, Life, The New Yorker, The New York Times*, and crews from the ABC and NBC television networks.[64] The success of this festival firmly established Buffalo as an international center for the contemporary arts.[65] The *Time* article summed up the festival as "perhaps the most all-encompassing, hip, with-it, avant-garde presentation in the U.S. to date."[66] *Life* went even farther, stating that it was "bigger and hipper than anything ever held in Paris or New York."[67]

The second festival (2-17 March 1968) was on a smaller scale, but with equally impressive featured artists. Poet Robert Creeley, who had recently joined the SUNY at Buffalo faculty, remembers "sitting in an audience for a performance of Merce Cunningham, and there of course was Cage, Jasper Johns (who had done one of the sets), he was sitting right there [along with] Marcel DuChamps. . . . I remember Allen Ginsberg was reading. . . . They performed pieces like Andy Warhol's set for Merce Cunningham which had these pillows which kept floating into the air [because they] were impregnated with helium.[68] . . . It was just this incredible star-studded yet intimate, terrific group of people. It was just a fantastically active and various confluence of people in a very classic Buffalo setting, and it was delicious."[69] Cunningham's company performed on three consecutive nights (8-10 March 1968). In addition to those mentioned above by Creeley, these performances also featured collaborative efforts of artists Frank Stella, Beverly Emmons, Stan Van Der Beek, and Robert Rauschenberg, and composers Gordon Mumma, David Tudor, LaMonte Young, and David Behrman.

The main musical event of the 1968 festival was the performance of three sections of Henri Pousseur's *Votre Faust*, a "fantasy in the manner of an opera," performed by the Creative Associates. Other concerts at the 1968 festival included performances of works by Tadeusz Baird, Harry Somers, Brock McElheran, Lukas Foss, John Cage, David Rosenboom, Luciano Berio, Yannis Xenakis, Yuji Takahashi, Jon Hassell, Robert Moran, and Carlos Roqué Alsina.[70]

Sapp was able to attract several prominent composers to serve as Slee Professor of Composition during his tenure. In addition to their interaction with students, faculty, and the public through their concerts and lectures, the later Slee Professors served especially well as senior mentors for the Creative Associates. Following Sapp in autumn 1961 as Slee Professor were Alexei Haieff (spring 1962 and autumn 1964), Leo Smit (autumn 1962), Virgil Thomson (spring 1963), David Diamond (autumn 1963), George Rochberg (spring 1964), Mauricio Kagel (spring 1965), Henri Pousseur (spring 1966 through autumn 1967), and Lejaren Hiller (spring 1968).[71]

As noted earlier, Sapp had little time for composing during this hectic period of his life. Only three compositions of any considerable length were forthcoming, and those were all written during his first two years in Buffalo.[72] However, he was able to enjoy several high quality performances of his music from the previous two decades. Boris Kroyt, violist in the Budapest Quartet, performed Sapp's *Viola Sonata* several times, including a performance at the Library of Congress on 4 March 1966 with pianist Arthur Balsam. Carol Plantamura, accompanied by George Crumb on harpsichord, performed *The Lady and the Lute* at the 1965 Buffalo Festival of the

Arts Today and at Carnegie Hall the following week. Lukas Foss conducted the Buffalo Philharmonic in the premières of two of Sapp's orchestral works, *The Double Image* (1957) and *Second Suite for Orchestra* (1952-56). Foss prepared the orchestra in a third work, *Colloquies I* (1963) for piano and string orchestra, but unexpectedly handed the baton to Sapp at the performance so he could accompany his wife, Norma Bertolami Sapp, as soloist.[73] Norma performed his solo piano works on several other occasions.

Because of his success in quickly building a quality department of music at Buffalo, and perhaps more notably establishing the Center of the Creative and Performing Arts, Sapp's notoriety as an arts administrator was on the rise, and he was increasingly called to serve as consultant or board member for foundations, councils, universities, and arts institutions around the country.[74] These included such important organizations as the New York State Council on the Arts, Composers Recordings, Inc. (CRI), the Danforth Foundation, Duke University, the University of California at San Diego, and the University of Minnesota. He was one of thirty-one prominent American musicians invited by President John F. Kennedy's Office of Science and Technology and the Office of Education of the Department of Health, Education, and Welfare to be a participant in the June 1963 Yale Seminar on Music Education.[75] In 1968, Sapp was commissioned to write a report recommending policies for the newly-formed National Endowment for the Arts on how it could best support musical activities in the country.[76]

Sapp became increasingly involved in the central administration of the university as the years progressed. In the spring of 1965, retiring President Clifford C. Furnas named him Head of the Division of Languages, Literature and the Arts of the soon to be obsolete College of Arts and Sciences.[77] Although this was not an interim appointment, it was understood that there would be major changes in the organization of the University with the appointment of a new president, and that the College of Arts and Sciences should be reorganized in order to cope with the major growth of the previous decade.[78] When the College of Arts and Sciences was officially dissolved in the spring of 1967, Sapp then became Acting Provost of Arts and Letters until the arrival of Provost Eric Larrabee in autumn of that year.[79]

In the autumn of 1966 Sapp moved into the upper strata of university administration upon the arrival of the new university president, Martin Meyerson. Sapp had been very active in recruiting Meyerson from his position as Acting Chancellor at the University of California at Berkeley, meeting with him in California[80] and hosting him during his Buffalo visit in January 1966.[81] Meyerson promoted Sapp to the cabinet-level post of Director of Cultural Affairs. This position essentially made him a "minister with special portfolio," and Meyerson employed Sapp as an advisor on several key issues, including the innovative academic restructuring plans, the high-level budget committee, and the planning sessions for the new campus.[82] Meyerson also appointed him as the first Chair of the Council of College Masters, making him the key advisor on the establishment of the collegiate system.[83] Sapp shared President Meyerson's wishes to emulate the British collegiate system at such institutions as Cambridge and Oxford, and in 1968 Sapp was granted an administrative leave to study the current forms of the system at several universities in England.

The mid-1960s was a time when ambitious, almost utopian plans for the university where thought to be achievable, and this sentiment was amplified with the coming of the Meyerson regime. Stellar faculty and administrators from the best universities were recruited to Buffalo with the temptation of "unlimited money, a

$650,000,000 new campus, bold and new organizational ideas, . . . the staggering number of new faculty and administrators to be added, [and] the romance of taking a mediocre up-state university and creating—well—*the Berkeley of the East.*"[84] University officials spoke of plans not only to have free tuition for all New York State students at SUNY institutions, but also to pay for courses at any university in the world, and offer them support stipends.[85]   Chairs of departments were given so much support for new faculty positions that they would occasionally not be able to fill them in the allotted time.[86]

With this level of confidence in the continued generosity of the state, it is no wonder there was a feeling of deep disappointment as this support waned by the end of the decade.   Indeed, by 1968, the state legislature began to pare the budget.[87] Particularly painful for Sapp was having to scale back plans to expand the Creative Associates program, as noted earlier.   The promised new campus, which had already been delayed for several years due to wrangling over site proposals, was further delayed by a lengthy labor union dispute.   Meanwhile, a high monitary inflation rate significantly eroded the value of the allocated construction funds, thus compromising some of the earlier plans.[88]   Consequently, the highly prized new faculty members remained for years (or until they left for greener pastures) in cramped, shared offices, some in temporary Quonset hut units.   Vice President Warren Bennis, in summing up the disillusionment felt by the faculty, said that "Inadvertently, we had cooked up the classic recipe for revolution as suggested by Aaron Wildavsky: 'Promise a lot; deliver a little.   Teach people to believe that they will be much better off, but let there be no dramatic improvement.'"[89]

For much of his last two years as Chair of the Music Department, Sapp was serving simultaneously on several different levels of university administration.   In order to devote his energies to the pressing needs of the central administration, Sapp felt it necessary to relinquish his chairmanship of the Music Department.   The department had become very large and somewhat complex in structure and required more attention than he could give.[90]

During the summer of 1967 Sapp discussed with incoming Provost Eric Larrabee the possibility of stepping down as chair in the near future and being replaced by a rotating, non-permanent, or "weak" chairmanship such as several of the other departments had recently adopted.[91]   An era of rapid development and generous funding was drawing to a close, and now the department needed attentive management from a leader with fewer distractions.   When Sapp announced his resignation at the Music Department faculty meeting on 23 May 1968, Provost Larrabee remarked to the faculty that Sapp's unique qualifications were making him much in demand with many national organizations.[92]   Relinquishing control of the Music Department would also allow him to focus his energies on his higher administrative positions at the university.   Sapp's shaping of the department has endured to the present day: a unique balance of strengths in graduate music scholarship, contemporary music, and selected areas of solo and chamber music performance.

6. UNIVERSITY AND NATIONAL ARTS LEADERSHIP: BUFFALO, 1968-75

DURING THE 1968-69 ACADEMIC YEAR, Sapp was given administrative leave to go to England to examine the current state of the British collegiate system, particularly at the newer universities such as York, Kent, and Warwick. By adopting such a system, the Meyerson administration hoped to create a new dimension of student affiliation, particularly one that would help students cope with the feelings of alienation inherent at a large university. Central to the collegiate system was "the idea of the wholeness of the educational process: the horizontal and vertical involvement of the student, the faculty member, the administrator and the community at large in the educational program of the college."[1]   Sapp was a member of Meyerson's advisory committee which recommended this reform in the fall of 1966, and in June 1968 was appointed Master of College B (the college focusing on the arts) and first Chair of the Council of Masters.[2]

The year in London was also a respite after seven years of intense administrative work at Buffalo. The Sapps rented an apartment in the Kensington borough of London, and they frequently enjoyed the concert and theatre life of the city. The first part of the year was taken up with finishing a commissioned report for the National Endowment for the Arts, a policy "blueprint" on how best to federally fund musical programs in the United States.[3] Sapp was also busy personally copying the parts for the première of his *Second Suite for Orchestra* by Lukas Foss and the Buffalo Philharmonic Orchestra. He attended the première on 8 December 1968, returning to London in time for the holidays.

During the winter and spring of 1969, Sapp made study visits to several of the new post-war British universities.

> It was clear that the collegiate system of old was pretty much gone. You couldn't staff it properly and have tutors anymore who wanted to live [with the students]. . . . So there were vestiges and one became a member of a college, but it didn't have the significance socially or academically that it had had earlier. The British system was approaching much more the American system; [the collegiate-tutorial system] seemed increasingly anachronistic. Still, I had very close and happy memories of the collegiate system as Harvard has managed it and wanted to re-institutionalize something like that [at Buffalo]."[4]

Upon his return to Buffalo in September 1969, Sapp shared the knowledge gleaned from his analysis of the contemporary British colleges with the other College Masters, and they began to establish this new layer of organization and student affiliation at the university. However, he was frustrated by the slow progress in the construction of the new campus, which necessitated the establishment of the new colleges within off-campus buildings and in the already tight quarters of the old campus.

The collegiate system at Buffalo consisted of the six original colleges created in June 1968 and ten additional colleges established during the following year. Each had a unique theme or discipline orientation; they were simply given a letter designation at first so that the naming of the college could develop naturally out of the program. For instance, Sapp's College B was eventually named Black Mountain College after the short-lived North Carolina experimental arts college of the 1950s where poet Robert Creeley and several other Buffalo faculty had taught. Some colleges focused on rather traditional subject areas, such as College D on the natural sciences. Other colleges were more radical, such as College A, which, with its theme of "community improvement," fast became a center of activism against the U.S. role in the Vietnam War.

College B, which encompassed a wide range of study areas in the arts from music and theater to arts management and philosophy, became one of the more successful colleges on campus. Beginning in the 1968-69 academic year, it was one of the first to offer both credit and non-credit courses. It was also one of the first to have an on-campus "living-learning center" with its own dormitory space in Macdonald Hall on the old Main Street campus.[5] In the Fall of 1973, it became one of the first occupants of residences in the new Amherst Campus buildings specifically designed for the Colleges, known as Governor's Complex.[6] College B also had off-campus affiliate locations. One was Oakstone Farm, the rural residence of Associate Master Jonathan Ketchum, which served as an off-campus "living-learning center" during the early years of the college. Another affiliate was Domus Theater, near downtown Buffalo, where courses and workshops in creativity and performance research were occasionally held.

The Colleges were viewed as ideal locations for developing new experimental courses, and Sapp initiated several of these for College B in its early years. Among the innovative courses taught by Sapp were the following:[7]

CB102 Hearing and Listening in Music (4 credits) Sapp W: 4-6

Sound and silence, the nature of aural experience, elements of listening, varieties of sonic experiences, noises and antinoise, mechanical systems including electronics of tone generation, rhythmic analysis from simple to complex idioms with graphic and oscilloscope projections. The course tries to build up a theory of hearing and listening by abolishing preconcepts about sound and reconstructing it in modes of entertainment, ritual or objective study. Inductive study of sound; acoustics (somewhat denatured); medical and scientific study of hearing and listening; objective--to help us hear without blockage, without filters.

CB104 Diction and Process in Music (4 credits) Sapp W: 2-4

Music as a coded language; music as a prototype of space-time. The experience will concentrate on twelve works of music attempting to induct from them principles of musical diction and of the processes which generate movement, and create affect. The music will be made to gain breadth of stylistic experiences; the objective of the course is depth and variety of listening by learning the music rhetorics of the significantly different periods and persons of the 1300-current era. Listening, reports, discussion, analysis will be included in the program. Designed for the advanced or the beginning student of music; the intermediate knows too much.

In addition to curriculum planning, Sapp also began the "Encounter" concert series for College B, which featured brief residencies of artists such as violinist Rafael Druian, pianist Leonid Hambro, and composers Daniel Pinkham and Zygmunt Krauze. In addition to formal recitals, this series also provided opportunities for informal interactions between the artists and the students, faculty, Buffalo Philharmonic musicians, and community members.

In January 1970, only months after Sapp's return from England, Martin Meyerson resigned as President of SUNY at Buffalo to assume the presidency of the University of Pennsylvania;[8] his Executive Vice President, Peter F. Regan, was named Acting President. Meyerson's resignation was deeply disappointing for the administration and faculty, who believed in his academic reforms and his dream to build a truly distinguished university. At that time, approximately seventy-five percent of all faculty had been appointed under his brief tenure of three and a half years.[9] Meyerson's departure, together with rapidly declining financial resources and a growing level of campus disruption caused by anti-war protests, caused some of the best-known faculty members to leave shortly afterward.[10]   It was clear that the administration's idealistic dreams of creating "the Berkeley of the East" would not be coming to fruition anytime soon.

Sapp remained as Director of Cultural Affairs and Master of College B under the succeeding administration of President Robert L. Ketter, but he was no longer involved with the inner circle of advisors. Ketter appointed his own new circle of more conservative-minded administrators. With his role on campus somewhat diminished, Sapp became more active in arts institutions outside of Buffalo.

Sapp was invited to speak to the National Council of the Arts in Education in November 1970. His presentation to this group was very favorably received, which led him to be selected as the director of one of their leading projects, "Arts/Worth." Sapp was granted a two-year leave of absence from the university beginning in February 1971 in order to fulfill this role, and soon thereafter he established the project office in New York City.

Funded by the National Endowment for the Humanities, Arts/Worth had the ambitious goal of bringing the arts "into a more central place in the educational system in this country,"[11] in an attempt to "reorient our society to the values of the arts."[12]   The scope of the project encompassed all educational levels, from preschool through graduate school, including adult continuing education. The initial phases of the program focused on community arts organizations and model curricula in pilot school districts throughout the country.

In June 1972, Sapp was elected executive director of the parent organization of Arts/Worth, the American Council for the Arts in Education (ACAE). This was a federation of more than 20 national organizations and successor to the National Council of the Arts in Education,[13] representing a total membership of approximately 100,000 educators, artists, and administrators.[14]   Later that month, ACAE sponsored a week-long conference in Los Angeles entitled "Community Arts and Community Survival" (19-23 June 1972), with Sapp serving as conference director. Billed as the first national conference on community arts, the program focused on the relationship between urban art centers and the public education system. More than 200 representatives of schools, arts councils, museums, and foundations attended workshops and meetings at the Studio Watts Workshop, the Inner City Cultural Center, and several other Los Angeles arts centers. Conference speakers included Dr. Abbott Kaplan, President of the State University of New York; dancer Katherine Dunham; and John Hightower, former director of the Museum of Modern Art and Executive Director of the New York State Council on the Arts.[15]

Sapp's position with Arts/Worth made him in demand as a public speaker, addressing arts councils and conventions of artists and educators all across the country. Sapp had envisioned his role from the start as involving a "good deal of evangelical work."[16] In particular, Sapp stressed the importance of the arts in higher education.

> I considered that the major task of Arts/Worth was to change the relationship of major universities, private and public, toward the arts. I felt that the real problem of the lack of an audience [for the arts], for example, was because universities, which were training an elite leadership component, whether they be engineers or nurses or whatever, were failing to give any sense of the value and importance of arts in modern life. I believe that was the correct assessment of the job of Arts/Worth. The worth of the arts meaning "How do we change public attitude within the system of education?" So I concentrated during my time at Arts/Worth on trying to see the executive vice presidents and provosts and the academic leadership [of universities].   I became involved in organizations like the American Association of Colleges, the American Association for Higher Education, the American Association of University Professors, and all those kinds of organizations.   I gave major speeches at their conventions about the importance and value of the arts, which were very widely applauded. In fact, I know I had an important role in changing some leadership attitudes.[17]

In the course of his work with ACAE and Project Arts/Worth, Sapp became deeply involved as a fund raiser and administrator in several other related organizations in New York City.   He served as Chairman of the New York Foundation for the Arts, the Creative Artists Public Service Program, and the Review Committee of the New York State Council on the Arts; as a director and later as Chairman of New York Museums Collaborative; and as a director of the Dance Notation Bureau. Sapp also became a director of "Space," a converted Manhattan "garment district" church used as rehearsal and performance space by the Alvin Ailey American Dance Theater and several other arts organizations. In addition to his New York activities, he also served in many administrative posts with national organizations during this time, including the National Guild of Community Schools of the Arts, the National Music Council, and the College Music Society.[18]

Upon returning from his leave of absence, Sapp remained active outside of Buffalo with ACAE and Arts/Worth, as well as with a new position as Senior Research Scholar at the Metropolitan Museum of Art.[19] Yet Sapp felt that his continued absence was causing College B to carry on without the aggressive and imaginative leadership which it required.[20]   In Sapp's opinion, the Ketter administration never properly funded the colleges, and he himself had not been able to attract outside financial resources for the innovative programs of College B.[21]

On 13 January 1974, Sapp resigned as Master of College B, leaving himself without any administrative post at the university for the first time since his arrival in Buffalo in 1961.[22]

Sapp remained on the Music Department faculty, teaching composition students as well as courses in orchestration and advanced music theory. Like many of the other faculty from the Meyerson era, he was uninspired by the new conservative climate at the university. He felt that he had "run out of mountains to climb" at Buffalo and was "spending more and more time away . . . doing consulting work to the point in which [he would come] back on the plane just in time to teach classes, and then get on another plane, and that [was] a bad sign."[23]

The following autumn, an opportunity arose for a new administrative position. From 29 Sept. to 2 October 1974, Sapp gave a series of lectures at Florida State University's School of Music on the topic "American Music in the 1920s."[24] This invitation came from Professor Marilyn Gombosi,[25] a former friend from his Harvard days and widow of the eminent Hungarian musicologist Otto Gombosi. That Sapp's lectures were well received is evidenced by the fact that his name was put forward as a candidate for Florida State University's newly-created position of Provost for Communication and the Arts. He interviewed for the position in July 1975 and several weeks later was offered the job. The decision to leave Buffalo was arrived at with great difficulty: after long consideration, Sapp first declined the offer, then changed his mind and telephoned a few days later to accept it.[26] His resignation from SUNY at Buffalo was announced in September 1975, to take effect in December of that year.[27]

Many in Buffalo were saddened to see Sapp leave, for he had been an innovative and enthusiastic catalyst both in the artistic community and at the university. He is recognized as one of the leading figures in the shaping of the modern University at Buffalo. He was invited to give the 1981 dedication address[28] at the opening ceremonies of Baird and Slee Halls, the music buildings within the new Fine Arts Complex, toward the establishment of which he had worked since his arrival at the university in 1961. Sapp was also honored the following year by the Music Department for his sixtieth birthday with a concert of his music, and a decade later by both the department and the Buffalo Philharmonic for his seventieth birthday.[29]

7. A DISAPPOINTING DETOUR: FLORIDA STATE UNIVERSITY, 1976-78

THE ANNOUNCEMENT OF ALLEN SAPP'S APPOINTMENT as Provost for Communications and the Arts at Florida State University was made in September 1975, and he began work at his new post in January 1976. Sapp was the third of three provosts appointed by President Stanley Marshall, who had established a multiple provost administration of three divisions (Social Sciences, Natural Sciences, and Communications and the Arts) to function in a role analogous to the former vice president for academic affairs position.[1]

His first months there were inauspicious indeed. The acting provost had spent nearly the entire annual budget, leaving only a few hundred dollars for the remainder of the year.[2] Furthermore, Sapp inherited a constituency of deans who were seemingly territorial and antagonistic toward each other; cooperation was out of the question, and mediation was his primary role. Even his sparsely furnished office, at first consisting of only a secretarial desk and a solitary metal chair, without even a second chair for guests, seemed to evince a discouraging situation.[3]

A severe blow occurred just ten weeks after Sapp's arrival at Florida State: Stanley Marshall announced his resignation as President.[4] The faculty had been increasingly disgruntled with Marshall, who apparently offended them by his lack of consultation, particularly over the new multiple provost reporting structure established on his order several years earlier.[5] One of the outcomes of the change in administration was a return to the former vice president for academic affairs unified reporting structure and the elimination of the three new provost positions. Marshall's successor, the former Executive Vice President Bernard Sliger, appointed Sapp to a new portfolio in 1977, that of Special Assistant to the Vice President for Academic Affairs and Director of Cultural Affairs.[6]

Clearly this unfortunate event was disheartening to Sapp, but he set out to make the best of his new position. In addition to his involvement in the usual academic and cultural committee work at the university, he became active in the local and statewide arts scene, serving as Chairman of the State Theater Board[7] and interacting closely with Florida Secretary of State Bruce Smathers.[8] At the request of U.S. Senator Richard Stone, Sapp prepared a 23-point position paper and plan of action for reshaping national cultural policy and funding initiatives (see B38). To help alleviate a severe university budget problem, Sapp also took responsibility for music history and analysis courses for faculty on leave.

Perhaps the best outcome of Sapp's stay in Tallahassee was his return to composition, albeit at a slow pace. His *Nocturne for Solo Violoncello* (W65) was composed in March 1978 for FSU cellist Roger Drinkall and premiered by him the following month. Sapp also enjoyed several other expert performances by FSU faculty of his earlier compositions, including the *Viola Sonata* (W55), the *String Trio* (W60), and the *Suite for Piano* (W14).

Feeling under-utilized in his position at Florida State, Sapp consulted Howard Klein of the Rockefeller Foundation about the possibility of a personal travel grant. Klein had been a close contact of Sapp's at the Foundation since his period as Co-Director of the Center of the Creative and Performing Arts at SUNY at Buffalo. Although Klein was unable to offer a travel grant at that time, this initiative eventually did pay a dividend: a short time later, Walter Levine, first violinist of the LaSalle Quartet, contacted Klein for recommendations for a new dean of the University of Cincinnati College-Conservatory of Music. Klein recommended Sapp, and before long Sapp was invited to Cincinnati for an interview. Sapp received the unanimous recommendation of the Decanal Search Committee, and UC Provost John McCall offered him the job, which he accepted on 18 June 1978.[9]

Sapp could now look forward to a challenging leadership position at a highly respected school of music, as well as an active role in Cincinnati's well-developed musical environment. "I came to Cincinnati on the positive impulse that it was very important for me to get back among a musical tribe. . . . It was time for me to face the issue of whether I was going to be an administrator for the rest of my days, or whether I was going to be in some way more connected to making music."[10]

8. THE MUSE RETURNS: CINCINNATI, 1978 TO PRESENT

THE UNIVERSITY OF CINCINNATI College-Conservatory of Music (CCM) was the result of a 1955 merger of two separate private institutions: the Cincinnati Conservatory of Music, established in 1867, and the College of Music of Cincinnati, established in 1878. The unified school was absorbed by the University of Cincinnati in 1962.[1] One of the country's largest music teaching institutions, CCM had a student enrollment in excess of 1,000 in autumn 1978.[2] For decades, CCM and its predecessors had been a great source of pride for the city, and once it became part of the university it was held in a favored position with the administration.

However, in the spring of 1978 it appeared that the school's fortunes were at least temporarily on the decline. During Sapp's interview visit at CCM, he met with outgoing CCM Dean Eugene Bonelli. "He gave me a very discouraging picture. I guess he didn't feel there was any need to be anything but candid with me. He more or less told me 'You're coming into a lot of trouble. Are you sure you know what you're doing?'" In spite of this warning, Sapp accepted the position; but it was clearly going to be a different situation than he had faced in Buffalo in 1961. This was an established institution which would require a skillful mediator more than an inspiring visionary.

Indeed, there were several problems confronting the new dean upon his arrival. He was inheriting a demoralized faculty, the result of several years of stringent budgets. Several top faculty were lost to other institutions, to retirement, or to ill health or death, and had not been replaced. The total size of the faculty declined from 132 in 1976 (fourth largest in the nation)[3] to 116 in 1978 (sixth largest).[4] Two resident chamber music groups, the LaSalle String Quartet and the Blackearth Percussion Group,[5] were wrestling with legal problems stemming from the replacement of personnel. There were long-standing and open disagreements within and between some of the major divisions of the school, which "had been allowed to fester to a point which was inimical to the institution."[6] Also, the school building had water leaks, insufficient sound insulation, and other structural problems that had not been repaired.

In the first several months of his tenure Sapp spent a considerable amount of time meeting with faculty so that he could begin to address their concerns. He was successful at resolving several of the lingering faculty disputes, while at least mollifying others. Unfortunately, the CCM budgets were very lean in the late 1970s, which left Sapp with little in the way of funds to address problems requiring financial commitments.

CCM's budget problems were compounded by the central administration's restrictions on Sapp's ability to raise private funds or otherwise develop the college's new fund raising arm, Friends of CCM.[7] "President [Henry Winkler] has indicated to me that I must not do any fund raising, because the capital drive of the university was about to start and all the energies were going to that."[8] This was especially disheartening to Sapp, who felt that one of his best qualities as an administrator was his ability to attract private donations.[9]

He was able to proceed with a number of searches to fill key faculty vacancies. The piano faculty had suffered the most devastating losses: three professors, one associate professor, and one assistant professor between 1976 and 1979.[10] Brought onto the piano faculty during Sapp's tenure were pianists Bela Siki and Eugene Pridonoff at the rank of professor, and Frank Weinstock at the assistant professor rank. There was also a critical need to recruit more viola students to staff the two orchestras, so the distinguished violist Donald McInnes was added to the faculty in 1980.[11]

Sapp also launched an ambitious new recruiting effort:

> I had come with the philosophy that the way of energizing the conservatory was to create international connections. I was on the board of the National Music Council. I had been assigned by Gunther Schuller, its incoming president, as the chairman of the international sector. So I planned to fuse that assignment with my wish to establish special relationships with certain countries and the cultural apparatus so we would start having exchange programs with professors, senior students, research scholars and so on. And I had chosen, kind of arbitrarily, Australia, Israel, South Africa, and Sweden.[12]

Sapp placed Norman Dinerstein, then Head of the Division of History, Theory and Composition, in charge of this new project. Dinerstein succeeded Sapp as Dean in 1981, and was able to continue to make successful cultural liaisons with these countries. The program enabled CCM to attract some of the best young musicians of these countries for graduate study.

Assistant Dean Harold Laster explained that Sapp extended this initiative to the faculty as well:

> One of the things that Allen, I think, really tried to deal with was to get the faculty to see themselves outside an insular situation. . . . CCM certainly is one of the very very top schools of the arts in the nation, and Sapp wanted to make sure that the faculty felt that. He felt that . . . even though we were very good, not a lot of people knew about it. And he really tried to, I think, do more of the internationalization of CCM, or to get that impetus started. I know that when I suggested to him that I go to the Banff Music Festival in Canada to recruit, he was all for it. He said that that is the kind of visibility we need to continue to explore."[13]

During his tenure as Dean, Sapp concurrently held an endowed professorship, the Thomas James Kelly Chair. Kelly (1870-1960) was a distinguished and long-serving member of the voice faculty of the Cincinnati Conservatory of Music; Mr. and Mrs. Louis Nippert, patrons of the University, established the chair in Kelly's honor to recognize the dean's professorship at CCM. Sapp, in turn, honored the chair by giving two series of lecture-concerts, patterned after his Slee lectures in Buffalo nearly two decades earlier.

During the second year of his tenure, Sapp became increasingly frustrated with his financial limitations. The second and third year budgets remained too restrictive to encourage new faculty initiatives to any great extent or to address many of the preexisting institutional problems. Sapp's budget difficulties were intensified by other factors stemming from communication problems between his office and that of the provost.[14] Meanwhile, Sapp was not sufficiently cautious in making verbal and written commitments.

> I began to be increasingly unhappy with all the management functions. I didn't mind trying to solve problems and work with people creatively, and I certainly tried to give leadership and to provide a sense that the conservatory was back on track . . . but I was having a great deal of trouble really enjoying myself. . . . My early Buffalo days were light years away. I mean, this was not an expanding thing, this was a contracting thing. So, obviously, I had to adopt a different style. But I began to get pretty restive. And I began to particularly feel the same problem that many a dean feels, that is the sense that you don't have any important work to do. You're just shuffling papers around all the time. You're not making any real decisions. And so I tried to support some faculty people who had ambitious schemes of one sort or another. And I was particularly and naturally attracted to faculty members who had ideas and who came to see me and said "Gee, this will be a great idea, if we can only do it." Well, I reacted too strongly to some of those faculty people and made commitments to them in excess of what I should have. I take full responsibility for that. And this stemmed from an honest desire to improve the situation.[15]

The result was a review of CCM's accounts and commitments ordered by Provost John McCall at the beginning of the autumn 1980 academic term. This revealed an overdraft of $8,000, and additional proposals in excess of the college's budget by $88,000.[16] These proposals were mostly part-time appointments to fill teaching vacancies. McCall stated that he accepted Sapp's letter of resignation on 6 November 1980 but did not request it; "He gave his resignation. . . . The problems were such it was very difficult to proceed."[17] He added that there "was not a problem with Dean Sapp's role as an academic planner and as a leader, but with his role as a fiscal planner and manager."[18] Sapp said that he and McCall "agreed that it would be better if I resigned. It was not a dismissal, but it was certainly clear that if I didn't do something myself that he was going to take some action. So I resigned."[19]

Sapp decided to remain on the CCM faculty as Professor of Composition; McCall also arranged for him to serve as Associate Dean for Special Projects.[20] He did not entertain for a moment the idea of moving to another position. "It seemed that the only solution for me was to remain here and maximize the good things that we had and to do an honest and conscientious job of teaching and working closely with people, and giving all my experience to them and supporting them. And also to be writing music."[21] Sapp taught composition seminar and private students for the remainder of the 1980-81 academic year, but in future years he would teach a full load of courses ranging from analysis and counterpoint to graduate seminars on the history of music theory and an interdisciplinary course in expressionism.

The fall of 1980 was clearly the beginning of a difficult time for Sapp personally. As might be expected, he experienced bouts of extreme depression during this period.[22] Fortunately, his light teaching load permitted him to immerse himself in composing. "I turned to the writing of music as a salvation and as a personal sense of a need to find my way back."[23] But at the same time he wondered

> Was there anything of substance that I had to say? Did I have any craft left? Were all these years of avoiding the writing of music years of retreat because of really lack of confidence, or merely that I was good at the other things and enjoyed those too? These were all problems that could only be settled by just sitting down and working.[24]

Sapp had actually begun composing smaller works by 1978, the year he completed *Nocturne* for violoncello solo (W65) and the first version of *Colloquies II* (W71).[25] But he had not composed a major work since *Colloquies I* (W117) in the summer of 1963. Sapp's desire to return to composing became evident in the summer of 1980 when he completed *Piano Sonatas V* and *VI* (W23-24).[26] A torrent of major compositions then came forth following his resignation as Dean of CCM in November; eleven more works would be completed by the following summer. In a letter Sapp wrote to Robert Middleton just months after this fertile period, the composer commented on his sudden rebirth as a composer following nearly two decades of inactivity:

> I wrote a few things in the 1960-80 period, but they were *pieces d'occasion*, things which showed technical skill and craft but which lacked the urgency and concern and commitment good writing needs. I worked very hard during this time and have much to show for it, but it was a period of divorcement from real composing. Buffalo, where I felt it was important to develop a center of experimental and *avant garde* music as a matter of service and institutional survival and growth, was devastating to me since all that music proved to be pretty alien to my own convictions. . . . The year of [composing] work [1980-81] was awful at first—like cleaning out some corroded sewer. But after a while I got going and feel very good about the results. . . . I am at a time when I write what I please, no longer worrying about anything except the working out of problems which interest me and ideas which preoccupy me.[27]

As with the long list of works Sapp composed in Rome in 1956-57 (see p. 19), the list of 1980-81 works contain some of his most highly regarded compositions:

Piano Sonata V (W23)	13 min.
Piano Sonata VI (W24)	15 min.
Piano Sonata VII (W25)	18 min.
Five Toccatas, harpsichord (W26)	12 min.
Four Hand Piano Sonata II (W44)	13 min.
Four Hand Piano Sonata III (W45)	12 min.
String Quartet II (W66)	15 min.
Taylor's Nine, percussion ensemble (W67)	20 min.
Violin Sonata IV (W68)	21 min.
String Quartet III (W69)	15 min.
String Quartet IV (W70)	12 min.

Imaginary Creatures, harpsichord
    and chamber orchestra (W118)   17 min.
Colloquies III, piano and ten winds (W128)   17 min.

This amounts to an astounding 200´minutes of music, all composed in the space of one year. His productivity remained very high throughout the decade and into the next. In all, Sapp composed over 60 works between 1980 and 1993.

In recognition of the quality of his recent compositions, Sapp was awarded the 1986 George Rieveschl Award for Distinguished Creative and Scholarly Works at the University of Cincinnati. Several of his Cincinnati, Buffalo and Harvard colleagues commented upon his compositions in their letters of nomination and support for this award. Discussing Sapp's *Piano Sonata V*, Robert Middleton described it as "an impressive work. It should have wide recognition, and a place in the repertoire. It has drama, strength, variety, logical shape, is expertly written for the instrument, and is very expressive."[28] Jan Williams offered the following remarks on *Taylor's Nine*: "As a percussionist and conductor, I have conducted and coached countless new works for the percussion idiom and must rank this piece as one of the strongest additions to the repertoire that I have seen recently. It exhibits not only complete control of technique but, more importantly, a highly individual and innovative style. The performance garnered much critical acclaim and confirms for me Allen's reputation as a composer to be respected, admired and sought after."[29] Referring to the "astonishing number of works" from the early 1980s, Jonathan Kramer observed that "most of them are of major proportions, all are finely crafted, all are beautiful, and many are original. This last aspect is what is amazing and unique about Professor Sapp. Although some of the recent works return to his concerns, methods, and style of the 1950s and '60s, some of them are extraordinarily fresh and innovative."[30]

Many of the works build upon his Boston style of "absolute music." Perhaps the most noticeable difference from Sapp's earlier neoclassic and serial works is a greatly expanded emotional and dramatic range, both between and within movements of works. Sustained from his earlier period in many of these works are uses of classical formal elements, lyrical melodic lines in both homophonic and contrapuntal settings, and his innovative usage of serial technique which actually focuses attention on tonal centers but within a sophisticated harmonic environment. Howard Pollack has stated that "there were few works of the 1980s that seemed to carry forth Piston's kind of elegance and craftsmanship so convincingly" as Sapp's works from this decade, noting especially the piano sonatas and the *Violin Sonata IV*.[31] The strikingly beautiful closing passage from the latter work is a fine illustration of Sapp's mature lyrical style (see MUSICAL EXAMPLE 8.1).

This example also illustrates another feature carried over from his Boston period, that of periodic sustained use of complex meters, in this case an exotic and undulating 13/16, accentuated in groups of three, four and six. In fact, the entire second movement features a gradual expansion of rhythmic environment, beginning in 9/16, then expanding in roughly even sections by one sixteenth note (10/16, 11/16, 12/16, 13/16).

Sapp's lifelong love for French music, literature and culture is made manifest in some of his compositions. Some references are overt, such as his song cycle *Dix chansons sphériques* (W95, a setting of eight different French Renaissance poets), and the two sets of works for two pianos with movements inspired by the poetry of Verlaine, *Aquarelles* (W46) and *Eaux-Fortes* (W47). Other references are more subtle, such as the composer's preference for light, economical and pure scoring in his orchestral works, even when writing for large forces, as in the etherial opening of *Xenón Ciborium* (W121; see MUSICAL EXAMPLE 8.2). Sapp also occasionally evokes a lighter, wittier and more engaging style, showing particularly his admiration of that vein in French chamber music of the late nineteenth and early twentieth centuries. While glossy on the outer surface, works such as the *Four Hand Piano Sonata II* (W44) are no less rigorously constructed than his more serious works (see MUSICAL EXAMPLE 8.3, opening of the third movement).

Two of the most innovative works produced during this period are *Imaginary Creatures: A Bestiary for the Credulous*, for harpsichord and chamber orchestra (W118), and the percussion ensemble composition *Taylor's Nine* (W67). *Imaginary Creatures* is one of the first works in which Sapp moved away from "absolute music" titles[32] in favor of evocative captions more suitable to his new highly dramatic and imagistic style. The movements of *Imaginary Creatures* are titled after mythical hybrid animals: "Halcyons," "Basilisk," "Unicorn," Phoenix," and "Centaurs." Expanding upon the hybrid theme, Sapp experimented with fusing two different types of harmonic languages in each movement. For example, in the "Unicorn" movement (see MUSICAL EXAMPLE 8.4), a sustained pianissimo E Phrygian texture of strings (all in "white" notes, omitting only D) supports slow triadic block chordal progressions in the harpsichord; meanwhile, a lyric dodecaphonic melody is played over this texture; later, the Phrygian texture is momentarily contrasted by dodecaphonic chordal progressions in the woodwinds. The effect is typical of Sapp's orchestral writing, marked by dramatic contrasts and light scoring in pure orchestral colors.

Taylor's Nine begins with an extremely sparse, pointillistic texture followed by a dramatic twenty-minute slow crescendo of rhythmic activity within a steady meter and pulse (see MUSICAL EXAMPLES 8.5 and 8.6). In order to better understand the striking character, intricate multifaceted construction, and personal significance of this composition, a long excerpt from Sapp's program note for the work is reprinted below. Not only does this program note indicate the type, depth and extent of precompositional planning indicative of many of his later works; it also gives a particularly good example of Sapp's colorful and engaging verbal communication style:

> *Taylor's Nine* is a piece of memories, influences and impressions of my Cambridge years as a college student, a young teacher and a youthful composer in 1939-58. It is the only frankly autobiographic work I have ever written. . . . I started with the idea of a fairly extended (but not really very long) work in which I would use instruments of the bell-like families. This was a conscious decision to exclude the many fascinating percussion instruments which cover the stage in any concert of new music. It is part of my fundamental philosophy as a composer to use restricted means where I can. The notions of working through the years of my growing up came slowly as I started thinking of the sonorities and designs I wanted for this work. Bells took me back to my work as a bell-ringer in Lowell House where I formed part of a small group which rang the great Russian bells atop the tower.[33] It was a shattering experience, rising to a great climax in which gradually larger and larger bells were added in new rhythmic shapes to patterns already established, building up layers of sonorities until the sounds suddenly ceased and the whole rhythmic pyramid tumbled down.
>
> My concerns of these years (and during the war) were much related to mathematics, of which I was and remain a serious student. The focus of

my interest was number theory, particularly the work of Dickinson, Minkowski, Birkhoff and Hancock.   I was able to use much of this in my work as a cryptanalyst in military service.   Brook Taylor's fundamental theorem producing Taylor's Series was one of the earliest openings to this field.   My interest in bells—and my unquenchable thirst for good mysteries—lead me to Dorothy Sayres' great series of Peter Whimsey stories. . . . Her most stimulating novel was for me *The Nine Taylors*, a work in which the great bells of this name played a great role.   The novel is a veritable textbook on another kind of bell ringing: change bell, as practiced in the English churches.   *Taylor's Nine* has a goodly number of applications of "the change" and of precise usages of change technique.

The work is designed as a structure of layered isometric periods (of course there are nine of them and the meter is nine), designed for nine players.   It has a basic sound-shape rising from the idea of beginning with dispersed, extremely scattered sonorities and gradually consolidating or fusing them into increasing patterns more and more dense until by the ninth period a kind of frantic squeezing of rhythmic values and figures has replaced the thin atmosphere of the beginning.   Imagine if you can a closed chamber in which the gaseous atmosphere is extremely thin at first, hardly breathable, at the top of Mt. Everest and then gradually the pressure rises until it is hundreds of meters below the surface of the sea, unbearably intense.

As the pressure rises and the apparent speed increases and the tension mounts, the unfolding of several series takes place.

The scoring supposes that there will be a group of four virtuoso players and a group of attentive but much less skilled players, much as in the hierarchical structure of gamelan organizations which move from the . . . amateur to the consummate professional.

The materials of the work are very simple, two sequences of notes, one of seven tones and one of eleven tones. The cycles and permutations of these short sequences form the essential sound bias of the work.

There were other Taylors important in my life then.   The great historian of medieval history and governments, Charles Henry Taylor, who was my most important mentor from whom I learned to appreciate the outlook of the composers of isorhythmic music.   He was crazy about baseball, and had in fact a group of players which we affectionately called Taylor's Nine.   I say nothing of such malignant influences as Old Taylor and Taylor Porkroll however much I may have enjoyed them at this period.   The word "nine" recalls not only baseball but is in fact the number symbol for I (the ninth letter) and has special relevance to an autobiographic work.   It is also a homonym for "nein"—and in that period as in this I have experienced more than a usual share of the negative.

The work has a fairly intricate and complex construction, but I trust that it will reach an audience as a piece in which the sounds of celesta and electric piano and marimba and bell all combine sometimes in repetitive rhythmic patterns and sometimes in clusters of cascading chords to attempt to penetrate through the present to a time past—and perhaps a time future?[34]

Sapp's extended hiatus from composition may have been caused by his incredibly busy schedule as an administrator during much of the 1960s and 1970s. However, his relationship to much of the experimental music that was being performed in Buffalo during this period (an artistic atmosphere that he had helped to create) was apparently another negative influence on his creativity. "I think I could have written more music in Buffalo, but that whole avant-gardistic ethic and style was then and now inimical to me. Not that I don't understand or support it or feel that it's worthwhile, but it isn't me. And so rather than try to sit there and be miserable I decided I would disconnect."[35]

Another serious consequence of his focus on administrative work for two decades was his increased disregard for promotion of his music. Indeed, Jonathan Kramer observed that Sapp "felt a professional conflict of interest. He believed, quite rightly, that he could not actively promote his own works at the same time he was charged with promoting the activities of his faculty composers. Thus his compositional career suffered."[36] Unfortunately, Sapp continued this disdain of self-promotion in his post-administrative period, focusing exclusively on composing works rather than actively seeking performance or distribution personally or through an agent. The result is a surprising number of major works that remain unpublished, unrecorded, and even unperformed, most notably the three 1981 *String Quartets* (W66, W69 and W70). Thanks to the interest and devotion of several current and former faculty colleagues and students, his music began to see performance beyond his area of residence. Also contributing to his wider recognition was the publication of Howard Pollack's 1992 book, *Harvard Composers*, which devoted half of a chapter to Sapp and his music (see B143).[37] In 1995, dozens of scores from both his later and earlier periods were made available through American Composers Alliance, and recordings of a few works were finally accessible to the general public.

In 1989, Sapp was honored once again by his University of Cincinnati colleagues, who elected him Faculty Representative to the Board of Trustees and subsequently Chair of the Faculty Senate from 1990 to 1992. Sapp welcomed the challenge of university leadership once again. Although these important roles required a heavy commitment of time and energy, Sapp maintained his productivity as a composer, unlike his previous experiences in university leadership.

Sapp officially retired from the CCM faculty in 1993. Concerts celebrating his retirement and his seventieth birthday were given by the Buffalo Philharmonic Orchestra, the Music Department at SUNY at Buffalo, and the University of Cincinnati College-Conservatory of Music. Sapp was also honored that year by the Cincinnati Chamber Orchestra, which commissioned him to write a work to celebrate the orchestra's twentieth anniversary. Keith Lockhart conducted the première of the *Concerto for Chamber Orchestra: The Four Reasons* (W122) on 20 March 1994, which was followed by a lengthy standing ovation for the composer.

The highlights of 1993 were quickly tempered by the illness of his wife Norma. Her final public performances were given at the two celebration concerts in Buffalo and Cincinnati in the winter and spring of 1993 (see P41a-b). Shortly thereafter, a combination of maladies including arthritis and anemia made it impossible for her to perform. This was especially tragic because, for the first time in her career, she was planning to make studio recordings intended for commercial release, including recordings of Sapp's *Piano Sonatas II-IV* (W16, W19, and W20) and *Fantasy III: Homage to Mendelssohn* (W41). She was diagnosed with leukemia in the spring of 1995. Norma Bertolami Sapp died on 5 June 1995 while undergoing hospital treatments.

Composing became very difficult for Sapp during this period. The commission for the Cincinnati Chamber Orchestra was originally planned to be an entirely new work, but after a long period of frustration the composer decided to orchestrate four movements of earlier compositions[38] to fulfill the commission in time for the orchestra's anniversary concert. Sapp was not able to complete another commission, this one from Gerhard Samuel for a large orchestral work intended for performance in spring 1995 by the University of Cincinnati Philharmonia Orchestra.[39] He spent a great deal of time caring for Norma at home and had little energy or desire for composing.

1995 also brought more overdue recognition for Sapp, including an Individual Artist Fellowship from the Ohio Arts Council and a recording grant from the Aaron Copland Foundation. These two awards came in support of a CRI recording project, scheduled for autumn 1996, featuring Keith Lockhart conducting the Cincinnati Chamber Orchestra, in the *Concerto for Chamber Orchestra: "The Four Reasons"* (W122), *Imaginary Creatures* (W118, with Eiji Hashimoto as harpsichord soloist), and the *Overture to "The Women of Trachis"* (W115).

While Sapp's official retirement from the University of Cincinnati College-Conservatory of Music took place in 1993, he has continued as a part-time faculty member, mostly teaching private lessons in composition. He is currently working on a four-movement work for large orchestra (the work commissioned by Gerhard Samuel in 1994). He is also composing two more piano sonatas and continues work on two operas, *The Death of Anton Webern* and *Philoctetes*.

MUSICAL EXAMPLES

Sound recordings corresponding to these MUSICAL EXAMPLES are available via the *Allen Sapp Home Page* (B149) on the world-wide web at the following URL address:

http://muslib.lib.ohio-state.edu/sapp/index.htm

Example 3.2: *Piano Sonata III* (1957), opening of first movement.

Example 8.1: *Violin Sonata IV* (1957), closing passage.

Violin Sonata IV (cont.)

Violin Sonata IV (cont.)

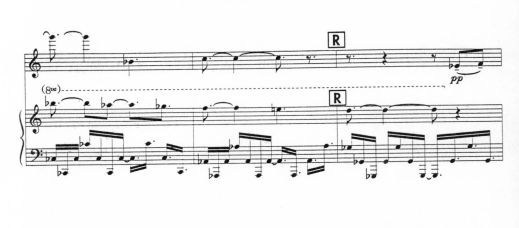

Example 8.2: *Xenon Ciborium* (1982-85), opening.

Example 8.4: *Imaginary Creatures* (1981), opening of "Unicorn" movement.

II. WORKS AND PERFORMANCES

THIS CATALOG WAS COMPILED BETWEEN December 1989 and November 1995, and is based primarily on direct observation of holographs and photocopies of works in the composer's home. It includes all known works excluding only the composer's juvenilia (works written prior to Sapp's enrollment at Harvard in autumn 1939). Many concert programs, letters, resumés, and other documents giving information about performances were also found and examined at the home of the composer and in various libraries, archives, and private collections. All approximate dates of compositions or concerts which are not explained by endnotes were supplied by the composer. Dates of composition are given in ranges when more than one time indication is given in the holograph, e.g., a range of dates on the title page, and a completion date at the colophon.

All compositions currently available through the American Composers Alliance (ACA) bear this information in the "Publisher" field. Works without this field are currently unavailable for purchase as of this writing; however some of these works (mostly recent works in pencil score) will become available soon as fair copies and computer typeset editions are prepared for ACA. Make inquiries to the following address:

American Composers Alliance
170 West 74th Street
New York, NY 10023
(212) 362-8900
Fax: (212) 362-8902
E-mail: 75534.2232@compuserve.com

In many cases, the composer has chosen to give a work a different title than the one originally written on the title page or caption of the holograph; these are the titles given at the head of each entry. In almost all cases these alterations are very slight, and most are only for the sake of consistency within the catalog, e.g., the sonatas. The original title from the holograph is given in a separate field in each entry, with cross references in the alphabetical title index. Where alternate titles exist, e.g., in concert programs or documents of the composer's authorship, they are given in a separate line of the catalog entry and cross referenced in the alphabetical title index (see Appendix C).

Initial verbal tempo indications for each movement of a work (when present) are given in parentheses following the titles of the movements; metronome markings are only given when there is neither a verbal tempo indication nor a movement title in the holograph. In most cases, only the initial tempo marking for each movement is given; exceptions are single-movement works which are clearly divided into sections by tempo changes, in which cases all major tempo changes are indicated.

The main body of the catalog consists of a chronological listing of the compositions of the composer within each of eleven categories of works: Keyboard Solo (W1-W41, mostly for piano, but also including one work each for organ and harpsichord); Piano Duet (W42-W47); Chamber and Instrumental (W48-W83); Solo Vocal (W84-W96); Choral (W97-W109); Orchestral (W110-W122); Orchestral, Unfinished (W123-W127); Wind Ensemble (W128-W132); Dramatic (W133-W139); Works Written under a Pseudonym (W140-W142); and Missing Work (W143). Within each entry, known performances of the work are labeled with corresponding numbers preceded by an upper case "P" (Performance) and followed by lower case alphabetic characters placing them in chronological order. For example, the first performance of Sapp's *Violin Sonata IV* (W68) is assigned the label P68a, the second performance P68b. Bibliographic citations pertaining to the works are assigned labels in the same manner, with "WB" (Works Bibliography) used as the prefix. Most of the "WB" entries are reviews, but the remainder are concert previews and analytical works.

ABBREVIATIONS

Alto	chorus (A)
Baritone	Bar.; chorus (B)
Bass	chorus (B)
Bass Clarinet	B. Cl.
Bass Drum	B. Dr.
Bass Trombone	B. Tbn.
Basso continuo	B. C.
Bassoon	Bn.
Celesta	Cel.
circa	ca.
Contrabass	Cb.
Contrabass Clarinet	Cb. Cl.
Contrabassoon	C. Bn.
Cymbals	Cym.
English Horn	E. H.
Euphonium	Euph.
Flute	Fl.
Glockenspiel	Glock.
Harp	Hp.
Harpsichord	Hpscd.
Horn	Hn.
Marimba	Mar.

minute(s) . . . . min.
number . . . . no.
Oboe . . . . Ob.
page(s) . . . . p.
Piccolo . . . . Picc.
Saxophone . . . . Sax.
Snare Drum . . . . S. Dr.
Soprano . . . . Sop.; chorus (S)
Tambourine . . . . Tamb.
Tenor . . . . Ten.; chorus (T)
Timpani . . . . Timp.
Trombone . . . . Tbn.
Trumpet . . . . Tpt.
Vibraphone . . . . Vib.
Viola . . . . Va.
Violin . . . . Vn.
Violoncello . . . . Vc.
Xylophone . . . . Xyl.

KEYBOARD SOLO

W1. Piano Sonata I

Title on holograph: *Sonata for Piano*
Medium: Piano solo.
Composition date and location: 13 March 1941, in Cambridge, Mass.
Dedication: "To Robert Middleton"
Location of holograph: The composer.
Duration: 11 min.
Score: 13 p.
Movements: I. Andante -- II. Allegro

First performance:

P1a.   Ca. late March-early May (not later than 3 May) 1941,[1] Irving Fine, at a meeting of the Harvard and Radcliffe Music Clubs at the home of Prof. Edward Ballantine, 18 Trail Street, Cambridge, Mass.

W2. January Eighth

Medium: Piano solo.
Composition date and location: 8 January 1943; no location given in holograph, but the composer was living in Bryn Mawr, Pa. during this period.
Location of holograph: The composer.
Duration: 2 min.
Score: 2 p.

1 movement: Allegretto
Notes: No performances.

W3. Two Short Moods for Piano

Medium: Piano solo.
Composition date and location: 11 January 1943; no location given in holograph, but the composer was living in Bryn Mawr, Pa. during this period.
Dedication: "For my angel"
Location of holograph: The composer.
Duration: 4 min.
Score: 4 p.
Movements: I. Lassitude (Slowly) -- II. Mighty Lak a Piece Named Toccata by a Certain M. Ravel (Allegro molto possible)
Notes: Composed for Norma Bertolami previous to her marriage to the composer. No performances.

W4. Four Scenes in One Act

Medium: Piano solo.
Composition date and location: 19-22 January 1943, in Bryn Mawr, Pa.
Dedication: "For my angel"
Location of holograph: The composer.
Duration: 6 min.
Score: 10 p.
Movements: I. Gray Day (Andante) -- II. Washington: Union Station (Presto) -- III. Praeludium (Allegro non troppo) -- IV. End (Andante molto)
Notes: Composed for Norma Bertolami previous to her marriage to the composer. No performances.

W5. Two Etudes

Medium: Piano solo.
Composition date and location: 10 February 1943; no location given in holograph, but the composer was living in Bryn Mawr, Pa. during this period.
Dedication: "For my angel"
Location of holograph: The composer.
Duration: 4 min.
Score: 4 p.
Movements: I. Not slowly -- II. Fast
Notes: Composed for Norma Bertolami previous to her marriage to the composer. No performances.

W6. "21"

Medium: Piano solo.
Composition date and location: 7 April 1943, "VHFS" (Vint Hill Farms Station, Warrenton, Va.).
Dedication: "To Richard Herr"
Location of holograph: The composer.
Duration: 2 min.
Score: 2 p.
1 movement: Briskly
Notes: No performances.

W7. Pigeons

Medium: Piano solo.
Composition date and location: 19 May 1943, "VHFS" (Vint Hill Farms Station, Warrenton, Va.).
Location of holograph: The composer.
Score: 4 p.
1 movement: [No tempo indication in holograph]
Notes: No performances.

W8. Prelude and Finale

Medium: Piano solo.
Composition date and location: 11-13 August 1943, "VHFS" (Vint Hill Farms Station, Warrenton, Va.).
Location of holograph: The composer.
Duration: 5 min.
Score: 6 p.
Movements: I. Quarter note = 100 -- II. Andante
Notes: No performances.

W9. Anniversary

Medium: Piano solo.
Composition date and location: 31 May 1944; no location given, but the composer was stationed in Bexley (near London), England on this date.
Location of holograph: The composer.
Duration: 3 min.
Score: 1 p.
1 movement: Slowly
Notes: No performances.

W10.   *Pearl*

Medium: Piano solo.
Composition date and location: 31 May 1944; no location given in holograph, but the composer was stationed in Bexley (near London), England on this date.
Location of holograph: The composer.
Duration: 1 min.
Score: 1 p.
1 movement: Very rapidly
Notes: No performances.

W11.   *Novelette*

Medium: Piano solo.
Composition date and location: 21 February 1945; no location given in holograph, but the composer was stationed in Belgium (near Namur or Verviers) on this date.
Location of holograph: The composer.
Duration: 3 min.
Score: 3 p.
1 movement: Allegretto
Notes: No performances.

W12.   *Piano Sonatina I*

Title on holograph: *Sonatina for Piano.*
Medium: Piano solo.
Composition date and location: July-1 September 1945, in Pullach bei München, Germany.
Dedication: "To 'DD'" [Dèdè Barbier]
Publisher: New York: American Composers Alliance, 1995.
Location of holograph: The composer.
Duration: 6 min.
Score: 10 p.
Movements: I. Allegro -- II. Allegretto -- III. Allegro

First performance:

P12a.   Ca. 1950, Norma Bertolami Sapp, at Paine Hall, Harvard University.

Other known performances:

P12b.   17 May 1953, Norma Bertolami Sapp, at Kirkland House Junior Common Room, Harvard University.

P12c.   19 August 1953, Norma Bertolami Sapp, at Paine Hall, Harvard University.

P12d.   10 March 1954, Norma Bertolami Sapp, at a concert of the Cambridge Musical Club, Cambridge, Mass.

W13.   Three Piano Pieces

Medium: Piano solo.
Composition date and location: 1941-46
Location of holograph: Unknown.
Notes: The only information known about this set is the title and composition dates, obtained from the program for the concert cited below. The individual titles and tempo indications were not printed in the program.

First performance:

P13a.   17 May 1953, Norma Bertolami Sapp, at Kirkland House Junior Common Room, Harvard University.

W14.   Suite for Piano

Medium: Piano solo.
Composition date and location: 1949, in Arlington, Mass.
Dedication: "To Aaron Copland"
Publisher: New York: American Composers Alliance, 1952.
Location of holograph: American Composers Alliance, 170 West 74th Street, New York, NY 10023.
Duration: 11 min.
Score: 12 p.
Movements: I. Allegro -- II. Adagio -- III. Allegretto -- IV. Andante -- V. Allegro Molto
Recording: See D24a-b (recording of P14g); D34 (excerpt).

First performance:

P14a.   19 December 1949, Norma Bertolami Sapp, at Paine Hall, Harvard University.

Other known performances:

P14b.   9 October 1950, Edith Stearns, piano, at Jordan Hall, New England Conservatory of Music, Boston.

P14c.   17 May 1953, Norma Bertolami Sapp, at Kirkland House Junior Common Room, Harvard University.

P14d.   6 July 1965, the composer, at Norton Union Conference Theatre, State University of New York at Buffalo.

P14e.   20 July 1965, the composer, at Norton Union Conference Theatre, State University of New York at Buffalo.

P14f.   4 October 1977, Edward Kilenyi, at Rudy Diamond Auditorium, Florida State University.

P14g.   12 November 1985, Norma Bertolami Sapp, at Patricia Corbett Theatre, University of Cincinnati College-Conservatory of Music.

Bibliography:

WB14a.   Dwyer, John. "At Norton Hall: Duo Makes Bright 'Family Musicale' out of UB Concert." *Buffalo Evening News*, 7 July 1965. "Composer Sapp played his 1949 *Suite for Piano*, a romantic strain running through light touches of deep colors, with an unusual Andante in free recitative, dances with a throwaway beat and an Adagio of sheer textures in transition."

WB14b.   Cook, David. "Kilenyi Performs Dohnanyi's Music." *Tallahassee Democrat*, 6 October 1977. "[Sapp's *Suite*] is marked by a rather classical approach, lean and spare. . . . Considerable applause indicated the audience which packed Rudy Diamond Auditorium liked what it heard."

W15.   Seven Bagatelles for Piano

Medium: Piano solo.
Composition date and location: October 1956, in Rome.
Dedication: "For George and Ilse Picard"
Publisher: New York: American Composers Alliance, 1995.
Location of holograph: The composer.
Duration: 14 min.
Score: 12 p.
Movements: I. Allegretto -- II. Con anima -- III. Non troppo allegro -- IV. Allegro -- V. Andante -- VI. Largo -- VII. Agitato
Notes: No performances.

W16.   Piano Sonata II

Title on holograph: *II Piano Sonata*.
Medium: Piano solo.
Composition date and location: 1954-56, in Cambridge, Mass.; revised 1957, in Rome.
Publisher: New York: American Composers Alliance, 1995.
Location of holograph: The composer.
Duration: 16 min.
Score: 19 p.
Movements: I. Larghetto -- II. Allegro molto -- III. Andantino -- IV. Allegro

Notes: According to the composer's remembrances,[2] the 1956 "version" consisted of movements I and II as they appear in the 1957 score, the third movement "Adagietto" from the *Suite for Orchestra, No. 2* (in piano score), and a performance from the sketches from the "Allegro" fourth movement (partially improvised), with much of the material that eventually took final form in the 1957 score. The completion of the fourth movement, and an entirely new third movement were composed in Rome in 1957.

Recording: See D16a-b (recording of P16e).

First performance of original 1956 version:

P16a.   17 May 1956, the composer, at Paine Hall, Harvard University.

First performance of revised 1957 version:

P16b.   Ca. autumn 1957, Norma Bertolami Sapp, at Paine Hall, Harvard University.

Other known performances of revised 1957 version:

P16c.   19 October 1961, Norma Bertolami Sapp, at Butler Auditorium, Capen Hall, University of Buffalo.

P16d.   25 February 1988, Frank Polansky, at "Festae Sappiana," Ewing Fine Arts Auditorium, Copiah-Lincoln Junior College, Wesson, Mississippi.

P16e.   3 November 1988, Norma Bertolami Sapp, at Patricia Corbett Theatre, University of Cincinnati College-Conservatory of Music.

Bibliography:

WB16a.   Baldwin, Bertram C.   "The Music Box: Composer's Laboratory." *Harvard Crimson*, 23 May 1956. "There is an intensity about it that commands attention. Something is being said that is worth listening to, particularly in the faster movements, where brilliant figurations and subtle rhythms sustain a motion that has few lapses. . . . The Sonata in E-flat has sincerity and strength."

WB16b.   Dwyer, John.   "Magic is Essential Power of Composer, Says Slee Professor." *Buffalo Evening News*, 20 October 1961. "I enjoyed some frankly romantic passages in the old nostalgic manner, but with fresh notions of voicing and coloration. . . . For all the dynamic contrasts, the works[3] seemed to have a rather even emotional set, at the base, as if an able essayist were involved with the skilled and leisurely turnings of his own mind. The performances were excellent."

See also: WB19b.

W17.   Four Impromptus for Piano

Medium: Piano solo.
Composition date and location: February 1957, in Rome.
Publisher: New York: American Composers Alliance, 1995.
Location of holograph: The composer.
Duration: 8 min.
Score: 7 p.
Movements: I. Adagio -- II. Grazioso -- III. Andante -- IV. Agitato
Recording: See D10 (recording of P17a).

First performance:

P17a.   8 May 1970, Norma Bertolami Sapp, at Baird Hall, State University of
New York at Buffalo.

Other known performance:

P17b.   16 November 1970, Norma Bertolami Sapp, at the Central Library
Auditorium, Buffalo and Erie County Public Library.

Bibliography:

WB17a.   Dwyer, John. "Central Library: Soloists Give Fine Performance."
Buffalo Evening News, 17 November 1970. "The Impromptus, shaped
and grouped like a Sonata da Chiesa, were played with that sort of
graceful refinement."

W18.   Piano Sonatina II

Title on holograph: *Sonatina II.*
Medium: Piano solo.
Composition date and location: 3 March 1957, in Rome.
Location of holograph: The composer.
Duration: 11 min.
Score: 8 leaves in pencil sketch.
Movements: I. Allegro giocoso -- II. Larghetto -- III. Piacevole

First performance:

P17a.   30 March 1995, David Curtin, at Corbett Auditorium, University of
Cincinnati College-Conservatory of Music.

W19.   Piano Sonata III

Title on holograph: *III Piano Sonata.*
Medium: Piano solo.

Composition date and location: 15 March 1957, in Rome.
Publisher: New York: American Composers Alliance, 1995.
Location of holograph: The composer.
Duration: 17 min.
Score: 20 p.
Movements: I. Allegro molto -- II. Adagio -- III. Agitato
Recordings: See D17 (recording of P19i); D18a-b (recording of P19n); D35 (excerpt).

First performance:

P19a.   24 February 1958, the composer, at the Philadelphia Art Alliance Auditorium, Philadelphia.

Other known performances:

P19b.   19 March 1958, the composer, at Paine Hall, Harvard University.

P19c.   3 August 1958, the composer, at Cummington School of the Arts, Cummington, Mass.

P19d.   13 November 1958, the composer, at Exhibition Hall, Brookline (Mass.) Public Library.

P19e.   22 February 1959, the composer, at the Radcliffe Graduate Center, Radcliffe College.

P19f.   14 October 1959, the composer, at Dunster House Junior Common Room, Harvard University.

P19g.   19 October 1960, the composer, at a concert of the Cambridge Composers' Forum, at the home of Mr. Thaddeus Beal, Cambridge, Mass.

P19h.   19 October 1961, the composer, at Butler Auditorium, Capen Hall, University of Buffalo.

P19i.   23 April 1965, the composer, at Butler Auditorium, Capen Hall, University of Buffalo.

P19j.   24 February 1975, Norma Bertolami Sapp, at Mason Recital Hall, SUNY College at Fredonia.

P19k.   28 January 1980, Norma Bertolami Sapp, at Patricia Corbett Theatre, University of Cincinnati College-Conservatory of Music.

P19l.   31 January 1980, Norma Bertolami Sapp, at Patricia Corbett Theatre, University of Cincinnati College-Conservatory of Music.

P19m.   27 March 1980, Norma Bertolami Sapp, at Patricia Corbett Theatre, University of Cincinnati College-Conservatory of Music.

P19n.   14 May 1984, Norma Bertolami Sapp, at Corbett Auditorium, University of Cincinnati College-Conservatory of Music.

P19o.   30 May 1992, the composer, at a concert of the music of Allen Sapp produced by the Cincinnati Composers' Guild, at the Contemporary Arts Center, Cincinnati.

Bibliography:

WB19a.   Singer, Samuel L.   "Art Alliance Hears 5 Modern Composers." *Philadelphia Inquirer*, 25 February 1958.   "Sapp's cyclical Sonata explored sonorities of the piano but seldom in a clangorous way."

WB19b.   Pollack, Howard. *Harvard Composers: Walter Piston and His Students from Elliott Carter to Frederic Rzewski.* Metuchen, N.J.: Scarecrow Press, 1992. "It was regrettable that [*Piano Sonatas II, III*, and *IV*, and *Double Image* for orchestra] did not find their way into print, for they were of a high order of craftsmanship and imagination. . . . *Piano Sonatas Nos. 3* and *4* . . . were big works, and had more the feel of repertory status. . . . They represented . . . a continued expansion of the composer's chromatic adventurousness, but they retained a fundamental tonal bearing, and often came to rest on triads. . . . The opening movement of No. 3 had a crystalline formal neatness that included a thoroughly classical development of its dynamic and syncopated first theme. . . . The slow movement . . . had a hymn-like, four-voice first theme, and a march-like contrasting theme that eventually submitted to Pistonian contrapuntal development. . . . The swirling last movement . . . was an act of dissolution, like the ending of the Chopin *Sonata* in B♭ minor."

See also: WB16b.

W20.   *Piano Sonata IV*

Title on holograph: *IV Piano Sonata.*
Medium: Piano solo.
Composition date and location: August 1957, in Rome.
Publisher: New York: American Composers Alliance, 1995.
Location of holograph: The composer.
Duration: 17 min.
Score: 21 p.
Movements: I. Decisively -- II. Slowly -- III. Theme and variations (fluently)
Recording: D19a-b (recording of P20g).

First performance:

P20a.   21 July 1958, Norma Bertolami Sapp, at Sanders Theatre, Harvard University.

Other known performances:

P20b.   22 February 1959, Norma Bertolami Sapp, at the Radcliffe Graduate Center, Radcliffe College.

P20c.   5 April 1959, Norma Bertolami Sapp, at the Longy School of Music, Cambridge, Mass.

P20d.   19 October 1961, Norma Bertolami Sapp, at Butler Auditorium, Capen Hall, University of Buffalo.

P20e.   30 January 1974, Stephen Manes, at Baird Recital Hall, State University of New York at Buffalo.

P20f.   17 November 1976, Norma Bertolami Sapp, at Lee Scarfone Gallery, University of Tampa (Florida).

P20g.   4 November 1986, Norma Bertolami Sapp, at Patricia Corbett Theatre, University of Cincinnati College-Conservatory of Music.

P20h.   21 February 1987, Norma Bertolami Sapp, at Slee Concert Hall, State University of New York at Buffalo.

Bibliography:

WB20a.   Putnam, Thomas.   "Manes' Thoughtful Piano Commands Full Attention." *Buffalo Evening News*, 31 January 1974. "The Sapp Fourth Piano Sonata releases its rhythmic tension with controlled activity, and its lyricism is expressed in a single, drifting line (the first movement) or in harmonious intervals (the movement marked "Slowly"). The third and last movement, a theme and variations, seems to be an outgrowth of a repeated-note figure in first movement, with denser harmonic material, in massed sònorities, or fluid, tangling lines. The sonata was composed in 1958 [*sic*], and is described by the composer as "like most of my music, tonal but totally serial," which explains the overall consonant feeling, the logical growth, and the stimulating if relieved abrasiveness.

WB20b.   Parris, Roger.   "Nostalgia Links 'Parade' Segments." *Buffalo News*, 22 February 1987. "Sapp's Piano Sonata No. 4 from 1957 got a very strong and probably definitive performance by Norma Bertolami Sapp. It was more notable for rhythmic thrust than melody."

See also: WB16b, WB19b.

W21.   Fantasy I: "The Pursuers"

Title on holograph: *Fantasy for Piano, "The Pursuers"*
Medium: Piano solo.

Composition date and location: 6 July 1960, in Wellesley, Mass.
Dedication: "To Lily Dumont"
Publisher: New York: American Composers Alliance, 1995.
Location of holograph: The composer.
Commissioned by: Lily Dumont.
Duration: 5 min.
Score: 10 p.
1 movement: Allegro feroce

First performance:

P21a.   12 October 1995, Daniel E. Mathers, at Nippert Studio, University of Cincinnati College-Conservatory of Music.

W22.   Untitled [four preludes for piano]

Medium: Piano solo.
Composition date and location: No date given in score; the composer estimates 1972 or 1973, in Buffalo.
Location of holograph: The composer.
Duration: 5 min.
Score: 5 p.
Movements: I. Slowly -- II. Lively -- III. Slowly -- IV. Quickly
Notes: No performances. A fifth sheet of manuscript paper labeled "V", consisting of 29 empty measures, a time signature 6/8, and the tempo indication "Moderately" was found with the other movements. No other sketches for this movement have been located.

W23.   Piano Sonata V

Medium: Piano solo.
Composition date and location: 26 August 1980, in Cincinnati.
Dedication: "To Norma Bertolami"
Location of holograph: The composer.
Duration: 13 min.
Score: 21 p.
1 movement: Violently
Recordings: See D20a-b (recording of P23a); D21 (recording of P23c).

First performance:

P23a.   2 November 1982, Norma Bertolami Sapp, at Patricia Corbett Theatre, University of Cincinnati College-Conservatory of Music.

Other known performances:

P23b.   13 November 1982, Norma Bertolami Sapp, at "Forum82," a festival sponsored by Composers' Forum at Symphony Space, 95th St. and Broadway, New York, N.Y.

P23c.   10 December 1982, Norma Bertolami Sapp, at a concert in honor of the composer's 60th birthday, at Slee Concert Hall, State University of New York at Buffalo.

Bibliography:

WB23a.   Putnam, Thomas. "Sapp Returns to Play His Music." *Buffalo News*, 11 December 1982. "[This work] is not unpleasant when it is aggressive; notes punched out have shape and an energy that is not riotous." See also: WB44a, WB68a, B126.

W24.   Piano Sonata VI

Title on holograph: *Sixth Sonata for Piano*
Medium: Piano solo.
Composition date and location: 28 September 1980, in Cincinnati.
Dedication: "To Frances and Joseph Poetker in affectionate appreciation"
Location of holograph: The composer.
Duration: 15 min.
Score: 20 p.
Movements: I. Allegro -- II. Allegro
Recording: See D22a-b (recording of P24a).

First performance:

P24a.   14 January 1982, Norma Bertolami Sapp, at Patricia Corbett Theatre, University of Cincinnati College-Conservatory of Music.

W25.   Piano Sonata VII: "Conversations with Friends"

Medium: Piano solo.
Composition date and location: 18 December 1980, in Cincinnati.
Location of holograph: The composer.
Duration: 18 min.
Score: 36 p.
Movements: I. Introspectively -- II. Violently -- III. Playfully -- IV. Seriously -- V. Brightly[4]

Notes: The composer recounted to the author the "friends" with which he was "conversing" in this work: I - Aaron Copland; II - Charles Rosen; III - Virgil Thomson; IV - Walter Piston; V - Irving Fine.[5]

First performance:

P25a.   14 March 1993, Stephen Self, at a concert of the Central Ohio Composers Alliance, at Huntington Recital Hall, Capital University, Columbus, Ohio.

W26.   Five Toccatas for Solo Harpsichord

Medium: Harpsichord solo.
Composition date and location: 1 July 1981, in Cincinnati.
Location of holograph: The composer.
Duration: 12 min.
Score: 13 p.
Movements: I. Lively -- II. Tempo rubato -- III. Quarter note = 84 -- IV. Brilliantly -- V. Eighth note = 80

First performance:

P26a.   Movements I, III, and V performed on 11 May 1987, Janet Lopinski, at Patricia Corbett Theatre, University of Cincinnati College-Conservatory of Music. The complete work remains unperformed.

W27.   For Debbie

Medium: Piano solo.
Composition date and location: December 1981, in Cincinnati.
Location of holograph: Deborah Hucke, Cincinnati.
Duration: 1 min.
Score: 1 p.
1 movement: Brightly
Notes: No performances.

W28.   For Vicky

Medium: Piano solo.
Composition date and location: December 1981, in Cincinnati.
Location of holograph: Victoria Conley, Cincinnati.
Duration: 1 min.
Score: 1 p.
1 movement: Lively
Notes: No performances.

W29. Five Inventions for Piano

Medium: Piano solo.
Composition date and location: 1983, in Cincinnati.
Location of holograph: The composer.
Duration: 4 min.
Score: 5 p.
Movements: I. Rapidly -- II. Expressively -- III. Smoothly -- IV. Andante -- V. Crisply
Notes: No performances.

W30. Up in the Sky

Medium: Piano solo.
Composition date and location: 1983-84, with slight revision in 1985, in Cincinnati.
Commissioned by: Gloria Ackerman, American Music Scholarship Association.
Publisher: New York: American Composers Alliance, 1985.
Location of holograph: The composer.
Duration: 33 min.
Score: 21 p.
Movements: I. Companion Stars (Fast) -- II. Waltz of the Dwarf Stars (Gracefully) -- III. Galactic Storm (Anxiously) -- IV. March of the Planets (Aggressively) -- V. Cassiopeia (Very slowly) -- VI. Mercury on a Trip (Bouncily) -- VII. A Giant Red Star (Steadily and firmly) -- VIII. Interstellar Dust (Sadly) -- IX. Cosmic Particles in a Rush (Full of life) -- X. The Big Bear Constellation (Lively) -- XI. Cold Space beyond Pluto (Expressively) -- XII. Harmony of the Spheres (Not too slowly) -- XIII. Comet with a Long Tail (Quickly) -- XIV. Moonshine (Gracefully) -- XV. Andromeda (Briskly) -- XVI. Black Holes (Moderately) -- XVII. Galaxy's End (Smoothly) -- XVIII. After the Nova (Dancing) -- XIX. Saturn's Rings (Not too fast) -- XX. Meteorite (Steadily) -- XXI. Arcturus (Brightly)
Notes: This is a set of pieces intended for young student pianists at the intermediate level.

First performance:

P30a.   29 April 1984, Norma Bertolami Sapp, Cynthia Lazo, alternating solo pianists, at the Cincinnati Art Museum.

W31. Piano Sonata VIII

Medium: Piano solo.
Composition date and location: 10 July 1985, in Cincinnati; revised 4 July 1986, in Cincinnati.
Dedication: "For Norma in love"
Publisher: New York: American Composers Alliance, 1995.
Location of holograph: The composer.

Duration: 24 min.
Score: 53 p.
Movements: I. Moderately -- II. Iridescently -- III. Vehemently

First performance:

P31a.   26 April 1989, Norma Bertolami Sapp, at Patricia Corbett Theatre, University of Cincinnati College-Conservatory of Music.

W32.   *Epithalamium*

Medium: Organ solo.
Composition date and location: January-20 April 1986, in Cincinnati.
Dedication: "For Anthony and Denise on their Wedding Day, May 24, 1986" [Anthony Collin Sapp and Denise Kathleen Powell, son and daughter-in-law of the composer].
Location of holograph: The composer.
Duration: 10 min.
Score: 28 p.
1 movement: Lively

First performance:

P32a.   24 May 1986, Dorothy Papadakos, at St. James Chapel, The Cathedral Church of St. John the Divine, New York, N. Y.

W33.   *In Memoriam: R. F.*

Medium: Piano solo.
Composition date and location: 17 January 1987, in Cincinnati.
Dedication: "Composed in memory of a dear friend, Robert Fryxell"
Location of holograph: Marjorie Fryxell, Cincinnati.
Duration: 2 min.
Score: 3 p.
1 movement: Semplice

First performance:

P33a.   31 May 1987, the composer, at the home of the Fryxell family, Cincinnati.

W34.   *Piano Sonata IX*

Medium: Piano solo.
Composition date and location: 12 April 1989, in Cincinnati.
Location of holograph: The composer.

Duration: 20 min.
Score: 16 p.
Movements: I. After a Sermon of Donne (Fast and ferocious!) -- II. Scherzo (Presto) -- III. Nocturne (Intimately) -- IV. Rondeletto (Agreeably but rapidly!)

First performance:

P34a.   27 April 1992, Karol Sue Reddington, at Patricia Corbett Theatre, University of Cincinnati College-Conservatory of Music.

Other known performance:

P34b.   30 May 1992, Karol Sue Reddington, at a concert of the music of Allen Sapp produced by the Cincinnati Composers' Guild, at the Contemporary Arts Center, Cincinnati.

W35.   Piano Sonata X

Medium: Piano solo.
Composition date and location: Spring 1989, in Cincinnati.
Location of holograph: The composer.
Duration: 15 min.
Score: 14 p.
Movements: I. Quarter note = 84-88 -- II. Semplice con espressione -- III. Allegro molto
Notes: No performances.

W36.   Rose Petals Falling

Medium: Piano solo.
Composition date and location: October 1989, in Cincinnati.
Dedication: "For Nurit"
Location of holograph: The composer.
Duration: 1 min.
Score: 1 p.
1 movement: Moderately
Notes: Dedicated to Nurit Parker, a piano student of Norma Bertolami Sapp. No performances.

W37.   A Bestiary: 25 Preludes for Piano

Medium: Piano solo.
Composition date and location: 30 October 1989, in Cincinnati.
Dedication: "To Hyeon-Ju Heo"
Location of holograph: The composer.
Duration: 35 min.

Score: 24 p.
Movements: I. Apteryx -- II. Basilisk -- III. Centaur (lively) -- IV. Dog (frisky) -- V. Elephant (moderately) -- VI. Fox (craftily) -- VII. Giraffe (gracefully) -- VIII. Halcyon (furiously) -- IX. Ibex (slowly) -- X. Jaguar (dangerous and fierce) -- XI. Koala (gentle, delicate) -- XII. Lion (with royal pace) -- XIII. Mouse (terrified!) -- XIV. Nightingale -- XV. Owl (with a fine solemnity and wise restraint) -- XVI. Porcupine -- XVII. Quail (prestissimo) --XVIII. Rhinoceros (mysteriously) -- XIX. Spider -- XX. Tiger -- XXI. Unicorn -- XXII. Vampire (violently) -- XXIII. Whale (gracefully, with dignity) -- XXIV. Yak (coarsely, lumbering) -- XXV. Zebra (quickly)
Notes: No performances.

W38.　　The Farewell

Medium: Piano solo.
Composition date and location: 1 June 1990, in Cincinnati.
Dedication: "For Jonathan Kramer as he leaves Cincinnati"
Publisher: New York: American Composers Alliance, 1995.
Location of holograph: The composer.
Duration: 3 min.
Score: 3 p.
1 movement: Nostalgically
Notes: No performances.

W39.　　Fantasy II: "A Piece of the Rach"

Medium: Piano solo.
Composition date and location: Spring-8 July 1990, in Cincinnati.
Dedication: "For Elizabeth Pridonoff"
Location of holograph: The composer.
Duration: 10 min.
Score: 13 p.
1 movement: Moderato

First performance:

P39a.　　26 April 1993, Elizabeth Pridonoff, at a concert in honor of the composer upon his retirement from the University of Cincinnati College-Conservatory of Music, at Patricia Corbett Theatre, University of Cincinnati College-Conservatory of Music.

W40.　　Five Impromptus

Medium: Piano solo.
Composition date and location: 24 April 1990-23 April 1991, in Cincinnati.
Publisher: New York: American Composers Alliance, 1995.

Location of holograph: The composer.
Duration: 7 min.
Score: 12 p.
Movements: I. Adagietto -- II. Vivace -- III. Andante -- IV. Sostenuto --
V. Andantino
Notes: No performances.

W41.   *Fantasy III: "Homage to Mendelssohn"*

Medium: Piano solo.
Composition date and location: Summer-21 September 1992, in Cincinnati.
Dedication: "To Norma with Love"
Publisher: New York: American Composers Alliance, 1995.
Location of holograph: The composer.
Duration: 9 min.
Score: 16 p.
1 movement: Andante - Vivace - Tempo I° - Vivace

First performance:

P41a.   16 February 1993, Norma Bertolami Sapp, at a concert in honor of the composer's 70th birthday,[6] at Slee Concert Hall, State University of New York at Buffalo.

Other known performances:

P41b.   26 April 1993, Norma Bertolami Sapp, at a concert in honor of the composer upon his retirement from the University of Cincinnati College-Conservatory of Music, at Patricia Corbett Theatre, University of Cincinnati College-Conservatory of Music.

PIANO DUET

W42.   *Four Hand Piano Sonata I*

Title on holograph: *Four Hand Sonata*
Medium: Piano duo, 2 performers, 1 piano.
Composition date and location: February 1944, in Namur, Belgium.
Publisher: New York: American Composers Alliance, 1952.
Location of holograph: American Composers Alliance, 170 West 74th Street, New York, NY 10023.
Duration: 10 min.
Score: 29 p.
Movements: I. Allegro ma non troppo -- II. Lento - Allegro molto
Recording: See D8a-b (recording of P42d).

First performance:

P42a.   [Between February and July?], 1945, René and Lucienne Barbier, at the Conservatoire de Musique, Namur, Belgium.

Other known performances:

P42b.   16 December 1945, Hans Rosbaud and Martin Piper, at the Prinzregententheater, Bayerische Staatstheater, München; concert under the direction of Karl Amadeus Hartmann.

P42c.   10 March 1948, Norma Bertolami Sapp and Robert Middleton, at Paine Hall, Harvard University.

P42d.   11 April 1950, Norma Bertolami Sapp and Allen Sapp, at Adams House Lower Common Room, Harvard University.

P42e.   17 May 1953, Norma Bertolami Sapp and Allen Sapp, at Kirkland House Junior Common Room, Harvard University.

P42f.   19 August 1953, Norma Bertolami Sapp and Allen Sapp, at Paine Hall, Harvard University.

P42g.   14 October 1959, Norma Bertolami Sapp and Allen Sapp, at Dunster House Junior Common Room, Harvard University.

W43. *Four Dialogues for Two Pianos*

Medium: Piano duo, 2 performers, 2 pianos.
Composition date and location: 1953-55, in Cambridge, Mass.
Dedication: "To Robert and Polly Middleton"
Publisher: New York: American Composers Alliance, 1995.
Location of holograph: The composer.
Duration: 8 min.
Score: 17 p.
Movements: I. Adagietto -- II. Con anima -- III. Comodo -- IV. Vivace
Notes: Although the title page of the score gives the composition dates "1954-55," the composer recalls that there were no significant changes between that fair score and the draft score that was performed at the first performances on 10 December 1953 and 25 May 1954.[7]

First incomplete performance:

P43a.   10 December 1953, Norma Bertolami Sapp and the composer, at Kirkland House Junior Common Room, Harvard University. The title on the program for this concert gives the title as *Three Dialogues for Two Pianos (December 4, 5, & 6, 1953)*; movement titles given in the program match those of movements I, II, and III given above.

First complete performance:

P43b. 25 May 1954, Norma Bertolami Sapp and the composer, at Kirkland House Junior Common Room, Harvard University. Broadcast on WGBH-FM as part of a series of discussion concerts, "New Trends in Contemporary Music."

Other known performances:

P43c. 28 February 1960, Susanna Carter and June Aiken, during a concert of the Philadelphia Festival, at Community Chamber Music Groups (136 Radnor Road), Bryn Mawr, Pa.

P43d. 16 April 1962, Norma Bertolami Sapp and the composer, at Baird Recital Hall, University of Buffalo.

P43e. 25 October 1963, Joseph Rollino and Paul Sheftel, at Baird Recital Hall, State University of New York at Buffalo.

P43f. 6 July 1965, Norma Bertolami Sapp and the composer, at Norton Union Conference Theatre, State University of New York at Buffalo.

P43g. 20 July 1965, Norma Bertolami Sapp and the composer, at Norton Union Conference Theatre, State University of New York at Buffalo.

P43h. 18 April 1968, Frina Arschanska Boldt and Kenwyn Boldt, at the Albright-Knox Gallery Auditorium, Buffalo, N.Y.

Bibliography:

WB43a. Dwyer, John. "Concert Features 'Old Grads' among UB Slee Composers." *Buffalo Evening News*, 17 April 1962. "The piece itself [is] full of the patterns and pleasures of the baroque suite. Strikingly so, in fact. This listener was inclined to send Dr. Sapp straight back to the drawing board, to open out the latent but urgent pianism of the first three movements—a stately Sinfonia, fleet and graceful Courante and reflective Sarabande. The final Toccata-Gigue, an admirable, syncopated two-step against a drum-roll in the bass, confirmed the essential keyboard-dance nature of his inspiration."

WB43b. Gill, Kenneth. "Baird Hall Program is Well Done." *Buffalo Courier-Express*, 17 April 1962. Sapp's composition "brought quick applause to the composer and his wife, Norma Bertolami, performers of the pieces. The abstraction of the tonal ideas was well emphasized in sharp and angular effects with the double keyboard work well timed and matched."

WB43c. Dwyer, John. "At Norton Hall: Duo Makes Bright 'Family Musicale' out of UB Concert." *Buffalo Evening News*, 7 July 1965. "The composer's *Four Dialogues* for two pianos completed the program, this set inclining more to the baroque model with an American accent, easy minded syncopations, a limpid 'Comodo' and an inventive drum-roll finale. We've heard this before, and it wears well."

WB43d.   Dwyer, John.   "Seven UB Composers Offer Moments of Art, Pleasantry." *Buffalo Evening News*, 19 April 1968. An "enjoyable and balanced reading of this intimate exchange. . . . The Comodo movement seems most effective and unusual, a kind of amorous adagio-chorale."

W44.   Four Hand Piano Sonata II

Medium: Piano duo, 2 performers, 1 piano.
Composition date and location: 1981, in Cincinnati.
Location of holograph: The composer.
Duration: 13 min.
Score: 26 p.
Movements: I. Allegro semplice -- II. Andante -- III. Allegro assai
Recording: See D9 (recording of P44a); D38 (excerpt).

First performance:

P44a.   10 December 1982, Frina Arschanska Boldt and Kenwyn Boldt, at a concert in honor of the composer's 60th birthday, at Slee Concert Hall, State University of New York at Buffalo.

Other known performance:

P44b.   26 April 1993, Jae Hyang Koo and Nancy Larson, at a concert in honor of the composer upon his retirement from the University of Cincinnati College-Conservatory of Music, at Patricia Corbett Theatre, University of Cincinnati College-Conservatory of Music.

Bibliography:

WB44a.   Putnam, Thomas. "Sapp Returns to Play His Music." *Buffalo News*, 11 December 1982. "Sapp's Piano Sonata No. 4 [*sic*] for Four Hands . . . is music of neoclassical clarity. . . . There is consonant activity in the sonata, a good sense of harmonic space, and largely a sense of peace. The coda to the lighthearted finale is a bracing slammer, a rug pulled from under the ears." See also: WB23a, WB68a, B126.

W45.   Four Hand Piano Sonata III

Medium: Piano duo, 2 performers, 1 piano.
Composition date and location: 1981, in Cincinnati.

Location of holograph: The composer.
Duration: 12 min.
Score: 26 p.
Movements: I. Chorales (Flowing) -- II. Scherzo (Roughly) -- III. Chorales II
Notes: No performances.

W46.   *Aquarelles*

Medium: Piano duo, 2 performers, 2 pianos.
Composition date and location: 1984, in Cincinnati.
Location of holograph: The composer.
Duration: 11 min.
Score: 29 p.
Movements: I. Beams -- II. A Poor Young Shepherd -- III. Streets (A lively jig-time!) -- IV. Green (The tempo of an early tango from an early film) -- V. Child Wife (Very slowly) -- VI. Spleen (Piano I: Petulantly, irritably; Piano II: Languorously, sensuously)
Notes: Additional information from the title page: "...after the poems of Paul Verlaine (1873)"; "A companion piece to *Eaux-Fortes.*"

First performance:

P46a.   4 April 1985, Janet Lopinski and Dolors Cano, at Corbett Auditorium, University of Cincinnati College-Conservatory of Music.

Other known performance:

P46b.   21 February 1987, Lorraine Abbott and Maxine Berens-Bommer, at Slee Concert Hall, State University of New York at Buffalo.

Bibliography:

WB46a.   Parris, Roger. "Nostalgia Links 'Parade' Segments." *Buffalo News*, 22 February 1987. "Francophile Sapp's *Aquarelles* . . . constantly recalled spare Debussy and lush Ravel. . . . They were alive with light and shade."

W47.   *Eaux-Fortes*

Medium: Piano duo, 2 performers, 2 pianos.
Composition date and location: 10 January 1984, in Cincinnati.
Dedication: "For Peggy Kite and Sally Brown"
Publisher: New York: American Composers Alliance, 1995.
Location of holograph: The composer.
Duration: 15 min.
Score: 41 p.

Movements: I. Croquis de Paris (Très calme et expressif) -- II. Cauchemar (Tumultueux) -- III. Marine (Modéré et triste) -- IV. Effet de nuit (Animé) -- V. Grotesques (Langoureux)

Notes: A companion piece to *Aquarelles*. From title page: "...based on the poems of Paul Verlaine 1863-68." From preliminary page: "'vers la sensation rendue' (lettre à Mallarmé, 22 Novembre 1866)."

First performance:

P47a.   4 April 1985, Janet Lopinski and Dolors Cano, at Corbett Auditorium, University of Cincinnati College-Conservatory of Music.

CHAMBER AND INSTRUMENTAL

W48.   *Suite for Two Flutes and Piano*

Composition date and location: April 1940; no location given in holograph, but the composer was living in Cambridge, Mass. during this period.
Location of holograph: The composer.
Duration: 12 min.
Score: [28] p.
Movements: I. Prelude (Allegro molto) -- II. Sarabande (Adagio) -- III. Gigue (Allegro vivace) -- IV. Pavane (Moderato)

First Performance:

P48a.   Ca. April 1940, Robert Commanday and Gabriel Jackson, flutes, the composer, piano, broadcast on "The Crimson Network," WHRB, Cambridge, Mass., AM 800.

W49.   *Four Movements for Three Stringed Instruments*

Medium: String trio (violin, viola, violoncello).
Composition date and location: 1941; no location given in holograph, but the composer was living in Cambridge, Mass. during this period.
Dedication: "To Anne Flick"
Location of holograph: The composer.
Duration: 15 min.
Score: 27 p.
Movements: I. Allegro -- II. Lento -- III. Allegretto -- IV. Allegro molto
Notes: No performances.

W50.   *Sonata Movement for String Trio*

Medium: String trio (violin, viola, violoncello).

Composition date and location: Ca. 1941 (date not given in holograph, estimated by the composer; no location given in holograph, but the composer was living in Cambridge, Mass. during this period.
Location of holograph: The composer.
Duration: 9 min.
Score: 20 p.
1 movement: Allegro moderato
Notes: No performances. The holograph bears a caption title page with the phrase "George Arthur Knight Prize Competition" and the pseudonym "Spēs." This work was submitted for the Knight Prize Competition, but was not given the award.

W51.   Cello Sonata

Title on holograph: *Sonata for Piano and Cello*
Composition date and location: 1941-42; no location given in holograph, but the composer was living in Cambridge, Mass. during this period.
Dedication: "To Suzanne King"
Location of holograph: Harvard University Archives.
Duration: 14 min.
Score: [34] p.
Movements: I. Allegro -- II. Andantino -- III. Allegro
Notes: This composition, submitted under the pseudonym "Hezekiah Fundless," received the 1942 Bohemians Prize at Harvard University.

First Partial Performance:

P51a.   3 March 1941, Peter G. Swing, violoncello, Robert Middleton, piano, broadcast on "The Crimson Network," WHRB, Cambridge, Mass., AM 800 (movements I and II).

First Complete Performance:

P51b.   Ca. 1942, Peter G. Swing, violoncello, William W. Austin, piano, at Walter Piston's *Seminar in Composition* at Harvard University.

W52.   Violin Sonata I

Title on holograph: *First Violin Sonata.*
Medium: Violin and piano.
Composition date and location: January 1943, at Bryn Mawr, Pa.
Publisher: New York: American Composers Alliance, 1952.
Location of holograph: American Composers Alliance, 170 West 74th Street, New York, NY 10023.
Dedication: "To Miss Viviane Bertolami"
Duration: 14 min.
Score: 18 p.
Movements: I. Lento -- II. Allegro -- III. Andante

Notes: On title page: "1942"; at colophon: "Jan. 1943".
Recording: See D30a (recording of P52a).

First performance:

P52a. 21 January 1945, Viviane Bertolami, violin, Norma Bertolami Sapp, piano, City Center Chamber Music Hall, New York, N.Y., at a League of Composers concert. [An earlier private performance was given by these performers at a meeting of the Harvard Music Club earlier in January 1945.]

Bibliography:

WB52a. Schubart, Mark. "Composers League Offers New Works." *New York Times*, 22 January 1945. "Sergeant Sapp's Violin Sonata appeared to be the most immediately rewarding work on the program. Sergeant Sapp, 22, who is serving with the Signal Corps overseas, is strongly influenced by the music of Aaron Copland. His sonata showed workmanship and a sense of form and received a pleasing performance by Viviane Bertolami, violinist, and Norma Bertolami, pianist."

WB52b. Fuller, Donald. "Stravinsky's Visit; New Music in 1945." *Modern Music* 22 (March-April 1945): 179. "Most musical and promising was Sergeant Allen Sapp's Sonata for Violin and Piano. It achieves style without striving, and its emotions grow freely and naturally."

W53.   And the Bombers Went Home

Medium: Violin and piano.
Composition date and location: 15 January 1943; no location given in holograph, but the composer was living in Bryn Mawr, Pa. during this period.
Location of holographs: The composer.
Duration: 3 min.
Score: 2 p.
1 movement: Adagio
Notes: The fair copy holograph does not bear a composition date, but a sketch is dated 15 January 1943, just days before he enlisted in the army for service during World War II. A later fair copy bears a title page with the pseudonym "S. M. Sebbél" and the date April 1944; it was apparently submitted for the George Arthur Knight Prize Competition at Harvard University, but was not awarded the prize. Sapp was stationed in Bexley, England during this period and had graduated from Harvard in 1942, but the work may have been submitted on his behalf by his wife, Norma Bertolami Sapp.
Recording: See D2.

First performance:

P53a. 25 July 1995, Martin Gelland, violin, Lennart Wallin, piano, at Rödöns kyrka, near Östersund, Sweden.

W54.   *Violin Sonata II*

Title on holograph: *Second Violin Sonata.*
Medium: Violin and piano.
Composition date and location: February-April 1948, in Cambridge, Mass.
Dedication: "For James Schevill"
Publisher: New York: American Composers Alliance, 1952.
Location of holograph: American Composers Alliance, 170 West 74th Street, New York, NY 10023.
Duration: 16 min.
Score: 30 p.
Movements: I. Allegro ma non troppo -- II. Larghetto -- III. Presto
Notes: This composition won the 1949 George Arthur Knight Prize at Harvard University.
Recording: See D31 (recording of P54d).

First performance:

P54a.   23 February 1949, Joseph Leibovici, violin, Norma Bertolami Sapp, piano, at Paine Hall, Harvard University.

Other known performances:

P54b.   18 April 1949, Robert Ritzenhein, violin, Norma Bertolami Sapp, piano, at a Composers' Forum concert, McMillin Academic Theatre, Columbia University.

P54c.   12 June 1963, Willy Frey, violin, Kenneth Seitz, piano, at Baird Recital Hall, State University of New York at Buffalo.

P54d.   18 April 1968, Charles Haupt, violin, August Martin, piano, at the Albright-Knox Art Gallery, Buffalo.

P54e.   11 October 1977, Ruth Posselt, violin, Norma Bertolami Sapp, piano, at Opperman Music Hall, Florida State University, Tallahassee, Fla.

Bibliography:

WB54a.   Lewis, F. Bruce. "The Music Box: Music Club Concert at Paine Hall." *Harvard Crimson*, 24 February 1949. "The highlight of the evening for me was Allen Sapp's Second Violin Sonata. The dry-tang texture of the first movement, caused by the conflict of harmonies between violin and piano, combines with the many melodies to give a very striking effect. Perhaps the best moment in the piece comes in the carefully built-up climax of the second movement. Except for a few scattered parts, the writing throughout the Sonata is tight; the piece never seems too long for its contents."

WB54b.   A. V. B. "Composers Forum." *New York Herald-Tribune*, 19 April 1949. "There was ... a brief Americana episode that suddenly emerged in the Larghetto of the *Violin Sonata* and disappeared as suddenly. This seemed to carry a conviction that the pale and austere lines elsewhere rarely had. Inevitability in the succession of ideas and formal balance and proportion are also still problems Mr. Sapp has not quite resolved."

WB54c. Dwyer, John. "Many Styles, Moods Expressed Tastefully by Violinist Frey." *Buffalo Evening News*, 13 June 1963. "It is a young composer's lyric essay on romantic love, intricate and ingenuous, probably indebted to Hindemith for a certain rhetoric and interval relationship, but wholly its own in a natural expression of sonnet moods. It is inseparably violin-piano music, with thematics and colors relying as much on mixture as dialogue."

WB54d. Gill, Kenneth. "Frey Recital is Applauded by Audience." *Buffalo Courier-Express*, 13 June 1963. A favorable review of the performance, but no specific comments were made about Sapp's composition.

WB54e. Dwyer, John. "Seven UB Composers Offer Moments of Art, Pleasantry." *Buffalo Evening News*, 19 April 1968. A favorable review of the performance, but no specific comments were made about Sapp's composition.

See also: WB55b.

W55.   *Viola Sonata*

Title on holographs: *First Viola Sonata*
Medium: Viola and piano
Composition date and location: September 1948, in Brookline, Mass.
Publisher: New York: American Composers Alliance, 1952.
Location of holographs: The 1948 manuscript is held by American Composers Alliance, 170 West 74th Street, New York, NY 10023. The 1986 revised manuscript (see note below) is held by the composer.
Duration: 12 min.
Score: 24 p.
Movements: I. Comodo -- II. Adagio -- III. Allegro molto
Notes: This composition won the 1950 Bohemians Prize at Harvard University. The 1986 revised manuscript (written in ink on seven folios of Dayman 15016 paper) changes all 10/8 meters to 5/4 and all 4/8 meters to 2/4 from the original 1948 vellum and ink manuscript (written on 24 leaves of Maestro no. 109 14-plain vellum, Independent Music Publishers); no other significant variants were noted. The revised 1986 version is unpublished.
Recordings: See D26 (recording of P55c); D27 (Recording of P55d); D28 (recording of P55e); D29 (recording of P55i).

First performance of original 1948 version:

P55a.   18 April 1949, Philip Goldberg, viola, Norma Bertolami Sapp, piano, at a Composers' Forum concert, McMillin Academic Theatre, Columbia University.

Other known performances of original 1948 version:

P55b.   8 March 1953, Joseph De Pasquale, viola, Norma Bertolami Sapp, piano, at Sanders Theatre, Harvard University.

P55c.   19 April 1965, Boris Kroyt, viola, Norma Bertolami Sapp, piano, at Baird Recital Hall, State University of New York at Buffalo.

P55d.   4 March 1966, Boris Kroyt, viola, Arthur Balsam, piano, at Coolidge Auditorium, Library of Congress.

P55e.   29 March 1967, Boris Kroyt, viola, Murray Perahia, piano, at Baird Recital Hall, State University of New York at Buffalo.

P55f.   29 February 1976, Kari Gunderson, viola, Karyl Louwenaar, piano, in Opperman Music Hall, Florida State University, Tallahassee, Fla.

Known performances of revised 1986 version:

P55g.   29 October 1986, Pamela Ryan, viola, Sandra Rivers, piano, at Watson Hall, University of Cincinnati College-Conservatory of Music.

P55h.   10 November 1987, Pamela Ryan, viola, Robert Spano, piano, at Patricia Corbett Theatre, University of Cincinnati College-Conservatory of Music.

P55i.   29 March 1989, Pamela Ryan, viola, Robert Spano, piano, at Bryan Recital Hall, Bowling Green State University College of Musical Arts.

P55j.   8 November 1993, Brian Peshek, viola, Phillip Farris, piano, at Watson Hall, University of Cincinnati College-Conservatory of Music.

Bibliography:

WB55a.   A. V. B. "Composers Forum." *New York Herald-Tribune*, 19 April 1949. "His *Viola Sonata* . . . seemed mostly an expression of musical energy and integrity. He has not yet made the crucial step of adopting courageously the single direction that will bring, musically, the most out of him."

WB55b.   Harman, Carter. "Talma, Sapp Offer New Compositions." *New York Times*, 19 April 1949. "Mr. Sapp's music gave incomplete but undeniable evidence of talent, and had more moments of unaffected grace than Miss [Louise] Talma's. The slow movement of his Viola

Sonata used too many tenths in the bass, but took the curse off them with some charming harmonic resolutions, and there was a lilting moment of inspiration in the [Second] Violin Sonata. Otherwise his music music was contrapuntally contrived, lacked a definable style and seemed to reach its climaxes by sheer impetus rather than growth."

WB55c.   Roy, Klaus George. "American Music at Harvard." *Christian Science Monitor*, 9 March 1953. "Allen Sapp's Sonata for Viola and Piano (1948) is a work of beauty and immediate emotional appeal. It pays homage to Hindemith and Piston without being essentially derivative. There is a genuine lyric line and warmth of expression, carried by a real mastery of the polyphonic medium. Perhaps the final toccata somewhat overwhelms the finely spun first movement and the elegiac second, by sheer weight of activity; yet interest never flags. Who says the moderns can't write a melody?"

WB55d.   Dwyer, John. "Violist Kroyt Puts Magical Touches in Superb Recital: Budapest Quartet Member Includes Sonata by UB's Allen Sapp, Trios with Clarinet." *Buffalo Evening News*, 20 April 1965. "In three episodes varying widely in tempo but strongly related in thematics, each with a falling, plainsong coda, the work also suggests French influence in that ageless Gallic pairing of economy and grace, with an echo or two of impressionism in its fleecy innuendo. Searching out the viola's several tones of voice, the work is filled with fine keyboard detail in running figures, counterpoised by recurring chordal thrusts.   This was an excellent performance, Mr. Kroyt showing intensive preparation and commitment, and pianist Bertolami, who is the composer's wife, sensing the mood with easy intuition."

WB55e.   Hume, Paul. "Kroyt and His Viola a Delight to Hear." *Washington Post*, 5 March 1966. "The Sapp Sonata, now nearing the end of its second decade, is also a work wholly romantic in spirit, in the same way that Hindemith is.   Unusually attractive in ideas, its three movements combine the strengths of a vigorous and well ordered opening with a slow movement of great and unbroken eloquence in the most lyrical manner.   The finale is a brilliant affair of flying fingers that make sensible and striking music as they go."

WB55f.   McCorkle, Donald.   "Violist Kroyt Plays as Romantic Poet." *The Evening Star* (Washington, D. C.), 5 March 1966. "Sapp . . . seems to have something worthwhile to say as a composer. The Sonata, which is in three movements, is basically a neo-classic form, nicely and logically chiseled, well textured and sonorous.   A strong Bachian influence was detected in the middle adagio."

WB55g.   Dwyer, John. "Salon Gems Have Sparkle, Freshness in Kroyt Recital." *Buffalo Evening News*, 30 March 1967. "[Sapp's Viola Sonata] won this audience . . . and the composer was called for bows. A young work, it has an air for quickly-mended heartstring, and a sparkling fleetness and freshness in the finale, beautifully caught by the violist and the youthful pianist. The virtuoso home stretch was truly exciting."

WB55h.   Putnam, Thomas. "Recital at UB." *Buffalo Courier Express*, 30 March 1967. "[Kroyt and Perahia's] presentation . . . brought the composer to his feet with 'Bravos.' Kroyt motioned Sapp, chairman of the UB Music Department, to the stage to share the bows."

W56.   Piano Trio

Title on holograph: *Trio No. 1.*
Medium: Piano, violin, and violoncello.
Composition date and location: April 1949, in Brookline, Mass.
Dedication: "To Irving Fine"
Publisher: New York: American Composers Alliance, 1952.
Location of holograph: American Composers Alliance, 170 West 74th Street, New York, NY 10023.
Duration: 16 min.
Score: 37 p.
Movements: I. Lento -- II. Agitato -- III. Comodo -- IV. Allegro molto e sempre giocoso

First performance:

P56a.   14 November 1993, The Looking Glass Ensemble (Stephen Self, piano, Joyce Green, violin, and Deborah Wilson, violoncello), at a concert of the Central Ohio Composers Alliance, at Kenyon College, Gambier, Ohio.

Other known performances:

P56b.   15 November 1993, The Looking Glass Ensemble, at a concert of the Central Ohio Composers Alliance, at Huntington Recital Hall, Capital University, Columbus, Ohio.

P56c.   19 November 1993, The Looking Glass Ensemble, at a concert of the Central Ohio Composers Alliance, at Denison University, Granville, Ohio.

W57.   String Quartet I

Medium: 2 violins, viola, violoncello.
Composition date and location: 1951, in Cambridge, Mass.
Location of holograph: The composer (multilith master).
Duration: 16 min.

Score: 29 p.
Movements: I. Allegro -- II. Andantino -- III. Adagio - Allegro giocoso

First performance:

P57a.　　19 April 1953, the Stringart Quartet (Morris Shulik and Irwin Eisenberg, violins, Gabriel Braverman, viola, Hershel Gorodetzky, violoncello), at a League of Composers concert, at the Auditorium, Museum of Modern Art, New York, N.Y.

Other known performances:

P57b.　　3 August 1958, the Cummington String Quartet (Sonya Monosoff and Harris Monosoff, violins, Louise Rood, viola, Harold Sproul, violoncello), at the Cummington School of the Arts, Cummington, Mass.

P57c.　　5 April 1967, the Beaux Arts String Quartet (Charles Libove and Stephen Clapp, violins, John Graham, viola, Bruce Rogers, violoncello), at the Albright-Knox Gallery Auditorium, Buffalo, N.Y.

P57d.　　18 January 1968, the Hartwell String Quartet (Norma Auzin and Lorene Field, violins, Ascher Temkin, viola, Ronald Leonard, violoncello), at the Newman Oratory, SUNY College at Brockport.

Bibliography:

WB57a.　　A. B. "League of Composers." *New York Herald Tribune*, 20 April 1953. "Allen Sapp's *String Quartet* was perplexing, since the composer did not convince this listener that he was at home in the fairly advanced chromatic idiom at which he was aiming. Whether due to the execution or the work itself, the colors and curves that suit this idiom were too few, and the result was somewhat arch."

WB57b.　　Dwyer, John. "Convocation Works Played Admirably by Noted Quartet." *Buffalo Evening News*, 6 April 1967. "Sapp's work "develops a characteristic motif with serial implications, pursued right through to the incidental roulades in the fluent, three-beat courante, and on to the passacaglia figure in the Andantino. The brief, lovely adagio is a delicately veined leaf pressed into the American hymnal, and the finale romps lightly, in statements and reversals recalling the original set of intervals. The design is strong, the effect lyrical in the old tonal sense, the style a recollected one."

WB57c.　　Putnam, Thomas. "Beaux Arts Quartet Rated Quality Group." *Buffalo Courier-Express*, 6 April 1967. "There is nothing shocking about the music of [Robert] Washburn, Sapp, and [Karl] Korte. It's solid music made by composers who are craftsmen more than innovators."

W58.   *Chaconne for Violin and Organ*

Medium: Violin and organ.
Composition date and location: 1 August 1953, in Newtonville and Cambridge, Mass.
Publisher: New York: American Composers Alliance, 1995.
Location of holograph: The composer (multilith master).
Duration: 2 min.
Score: 4 p.
1 movement: Andante

First performance:

P58a.   16 August 1953, Robert Brink, violin, Daniel Pinkham, organ, live radio broadcast (9:30-10:00 A.M. on WEEI) from the Busch-Reisinger Museum, Harvard University.

Other known performances:

P58b.   31 July 1988, Cecilia Gelland, violin, Ann-Kristin Färnström, organ, at Gamla Kyrkan, Östersund, Sweden.

P58c.   24 April 1994, Cecilia Gelland, violin, Ann-Kristin Färnström, organ, at Birgittakyrkan, Sundsvall, Sweden.

W59.   *Six Ricercare for Viols*

Medium: Viol ensemble
Composition date and location: October 1956, in Rome.
Location of holograph: The composer.
Duration: 12 min.
Score: 9 p.
Movements: I. Slowly -- II. Vigorously -- III. Vigorously -- IV. Quite Slowly -- V. Moderately -- VI. Vigorously
Notes: No performances.

W60.   *String Trio*

Title on holograph: *Trio for Strings*.
Medium: Violin, viola, and violoncello.
Composition date and location: February 1957, in Rome.
Publisher: New York: American Composers Alliance, 1995.
Location of holograph: The composer.
Duration: 12 min.
Score: 28 p.
Movements: I. Allegro grazioso -- II. Andante -- III. Vivace

First performance:

P60a.   Ca. 1957, The Bel Arte Trio (Joseph Silverstein, violin, Joseph DiPasquale, viola, and Samuel Mayes, violoncello), at Sanders Theatre, Harvard University.

Other known performances:

P60b.   5 February 1962, The Bel Arte Trio, at Butler Auditorium, Capen Hall, University of Buffalo.

P60c.   29 October 1986, Le-yi Zhang, violin, Bruce Owen, viola, Drew Owen, violoncello, at Watson Hall, University of Cincinnati College-Conservatory of Music.

Bibliography:

WB60a.   "Bel Arte Trio Joins UB Music Head in Unusual Slee Event." *Buffalo Evening News*, 6 February 1962. Sapp's composition "fits the slender strings like a well-made sheath. And if it is not on the strongly assertive, impassioned or bond-breaking side, it has a wholeness and lyricism which seems to put the composer in his best light. The rather unusual contrapuntal opening, considering the sonata-allegro form, the spirit of 'continual flow,' the unremitting course of sound against brief motifs, the dexterous transmission of a chromatic obbligato in the slow movement into the dominant theme material in the close, all this bespeaks a resourceful musical mind."

W61.   Six Variations on the Hymn-Tune "Durant"

Title on holograph: *6 Variations on the Hymn-Tune "Durant"*
Medium: Flute, oboe, English horn, and bassoon.
Composition date and location: [Between 1 January and 17 April] 1960, in Wellesley, Mass.
Dedication: "To My Colleagues at Wellesley"
Location of holograph: The composer.
Duration: 9 min.
Score: 12 p.
Movements: [0]. Hymn-style, flat and plain -- I. H. H. (Fast, with rough and benevolent good humor) -- II. H. W. L. (Lively, with wit and precision) -- III. W. A. H. (Tempo identical to the hymn-tune) -- IV. A. D. S. (Allegro, alla maniera classica) -- V. H. B. (In rather a hurry but never imprecisely) -- VI. C. A. (Allegretto marziale)

First performance:

P61a.   17 April 1960, William Grass, Flute, Richard Summers, oboe, Dorothy Kidney, English horn, Ruth McKee, bassoon, at Jewett Arts Center, Wellesley College, Wellesley, Mass.

W62.   *Violin Sonata III*

Title on holograph: *Sonata III for Violin and Piano.*
Medium: Violin and piano.
Composition date and location: November 1960, in Wellesley, Mass.
Publisher: New York: American Composers Alliance, 1995.
Location of holograph: The composer.
Duration: 14 min.
Score: 28 p.
Movements: I. Allegro energico -- II. Adagietto -- III. Presto
Notes: The date of the first performance needs further investigation. The month and day of the performance was located by the composer in a diary from that period, but it did not supply the year.

First performance:

P62a.   3 August 1961, Sonia Monosoff, violin, Joel Spiegelman, piano, at the Cummington School of the Arts, Cummington, Mass.

Other known performances:

P62b.   21 July 1963, Sonia Monosoff, violin, Joel Spiegelman, piano, at the Cummington School of the Arts, Cummington, Mass.

P62c.   11 December 1964, Nancy Cirillo, violin, Joel Spiegelman, piano, in Slosberg Recital Hall, Brandeis University.

P62d.   30 January 1980, Mimi Bryant, violin, Pat Sinozich, piano, at Patricia Corbett Theatre, University of Cincinnati College-Conservatory of Music.

W63.   *Variations on "A solis ortus cardine"*

Medium: Oboe, horn, 2 violins, viola, violoncello, and contrabass.
Composition date and location: December 1962, in Buffalo.
Location of holograph: The composer.
Duration: 12 min.
Score: 25 p.
Movements: I. Cantus in bass (Andante) -- II. Canon at unison (Eighth note = 80) -- III. Canon at 7th (Bright and cheerful) -- IV. Cantus in all parts (Tempo di I) -- V. Canon at 5th (In moving quarters) -- VI. Canon at 6th -- VII. Cantus in alto (Allegretto) -- VIII. Cantus in bass [movement I without Va. and Cb.]

First performance:

P63a.   9 December 1962, Harry Taub, violin, Willy Frey, violin, Fred Ressel, viola, Dodia Feldin, violoncello, Thomas Coleman, contrabass, Ronald

Richards, oboe, Barbara Bloomer, horn, at Albright-Knox Art Gallery, Buffalo.

W64.   Irregular Polygon

Medium: String quartet
Composition date and location: 12 November 1973, in Buffalo.
Location of holograph: The composer.
Duration: 25 sec.
Score: 1 p.
1 movement: Eighth note = 160.
Notes: No performances.

W65.   Nocturne for Solo Violoncello

Medium: Violoncello alone.
Composition date and location: March 1978, in Tallahassee, Fla.
Commissioned by: Roger Drinkall.
Dedication: To Roger Drinkall.
Location of holograph: The composer.
Duration: 4 min.
Score: 3 p.
1 movement: Freely

First performance:

P65a.   2 April 1978, Roger Drinkall, Opperman Music Hall, Florida State University, Tallahassee, Fla.

P65b.   Ca. autumn 1978, Jack Kirstein, Patricia Corbett Theatre, University of Cincinnati College-Conservatory of Music

W66.   String Quartet II

Medium: 2 violins, viola, violoncello.
Composition date and location: 1981, in Cincinnati.
Location of holograph: The composer.
Duration: 15 min.
Score: 45 p.
Movements: I. Moderately -- II. Very fast -- III. Moderately
Notes: No performances.

W67. Taylor's Nine

Medium: Percussion ensemble.
Composition date and location: 1981, in Cincinnati.
Dedication: "For THE PERCUSSION GROUP of the College-Conservatory of Music in the University of Cincinnati"
Location of holograph: The composer.
Duration: 20 min.
Score: 32 p.
Instrumentation: 1 Xyl., 1 Glock., 1 Vib., 2 Mar., 1 Cel. or Electric Piano, Bells.
1 movement: Eighth note = 128
Note: Commissioned by WGUC-FM in Cincinnati in celebration of the station's twentieth anniversary.
Recording: See D25 (recording of P67b); D40-41 (excerpts).

First performance:

P67a.　13 October 1981, The Percussion Group (Allen Otte, James Culley, and William Youhass) with Jack Brennan, Tracy Davis, Mark Dayton, Eugene Novotney, and Peggy Richards, at Corbett Auditorium, University of Cincinnati College-Conservatory of Music.

Other known performances:

P67b.　10 December 1982, University at Buffalo Percussion Ensemble, conducted by Jan Williams, at a concert in honor of the composer's 60th birthday, at Slee Concert Hall, State University of New York at Buffalo.

P67c.　26 April 1993, The Percussion Group [with five other performers not named in the program], at a concert in honor of the composer upon his retirement from the University of Cincinnati College-Conservatory of Music, at Patricia Corbett Theatre, University of Cincinnati College-Conservatory of Music.

Bibliography:

WB67a.　Chute, James. "Music Peals Radio Milestone, but Allen Sapp Work Deserved Quieter Showcase." *Cincinnati Post*, 14 October 1981. "On paper, the work's inner logic and sense of proportion seem indisputable. From its first note, the piece builds in dynamics and in tempo.[8] Simply stated, it begins softly and very slowly, and ends loudly and very quickly. In performance, however, the personal nature and inner logic of *Taylor's Nine* failed to come across. . . . [It] is chamber in scale and demands an investment of concentration from the listener. So soft are the sounds at the beginning of the piece, that even the rattle of a chair or a folding of a paper in the auditorium seemed to violate the mood of the work, in which silence is meaningful. Unfortunately, despite the performance being broadcast live by WGUC to other National Public Radio stations and despite the fact a performance like this represents hundreds of hours of time on the part of the composer and the performers, one woman insisted on bringing a young child to the concert. The child's innocent jabbering destroyed the mood the Percussion Group attempted to create."

WB67b.   Palmer, Bob. "High Marks for Percussionists." *Cincinnati Enquirer*, 16 October 1981. *Taylor's Nine* "begins as a gossamer web of bell-like sounds and transparent structural silences. Though the pitch material is limited, the feather-light matrix of growing fibers ever-so-gradually thickens, congeals and finally bursts into bloom. The growing process is almost imperceptibly slow and quiet. For 15 of its 20 minutes, the sound doesn't exceed a whisper. . . . Considering its austere nature, the piece was surprisingly effective and curiously well received."

WB67c.   Holland, Bernard. "Music Notes: From Film Comedy to Offenbach." *New York Times*, 2 October 1983. Brief notice of Allen Sapp's commission from WGUC-FM (Cincinnati) for *Taylor's Nine*. Other composers who received commissions in celebration of the station's twentieth anniversary were Norman Dinerstein, Michael Gielen, Darrell Handel, Joel Hoffman, Scott Huston, and Jonathan Kramer.

W68.   Violin Sonata IV

Title on holograph: *Sonata IV for Violin and Piano.*
Medium: Violin and piano.
Composition date and location: 1981, in Cincinnati.
Publisher: New York: American Composers Alliance, 1995.
Location of holograph: The composer.
Duration: 21 min.
Score: 36 p.
Movements: I. Roughly -- II. Slowly
Recordings: See D32a-c (recording of P68a); D36 (excerpt).

First performance:

P68a.   10 December 1982, Thomas Halpin, violin, Norma Bertolami Sapp, piano, at a concert in honor of the composer's 60th birthday, at Slee Concert Hall, State University of New York at Buffalo.

Other known performances:

P68b.   20 February 1987, Cecilia Gelland, violin, and Janet Lopinski, piano, at Watson Hall, University of Cincinnati College-Conservatory of Music.

P68c.   23 April 1987, Cecilia Gelland, violin, and Janet Lopinski, piano, at Bryan Recital Hall, Bowling Green State University College of Musical Arts, Bowling Green, Ohio.

P68d.   30 May 1992, DeAnn Burger, violin, Norma Bertolami Sapp, piano, at a concert of the music of Allen Sapp produced by the Cincinnati Composers' Guild, at the Contemporary Arts Center, Cincinnati.

Bibliography:

WB68a.   Putnam, Thomas. "Sapp Returns to Play His Music." *Buffalo News*, 11 December 1982. "The first [movement] has a jaunty rhythm to start; changes of mood are composed smoothly. Tender reflection is an important quality in this music. The sonata's second movement is thoroughly beautiful; the singing violin and the piano seem to enjoy a relaxed relationship. There is a sense of agitation, but this sonata is determined to be contented." See also: WB23a, WB44a, B126.

W69.   String Quartet III

Medium: 2 violins, viola, violoncello.
Composition date and location: March 1981, in Cincinnati.
Location of holograph: The composer.
Duration: 15 min.
Score: 28 p.
Movements: I. Grazioso -- II. Adagietto -- III. Vivace -- IV. Agitato
Notes: No performances.

W70.   String Quartet IV

Medium: 2 violins, viola, violoncello.
Composition date and location: March 1981, in Cincinnati.
Location of holograph: The composer.
Duration: 12 min.
Score: 19 p.
1 movement: Slowly - Violently - Moderately - Violently - Slowly
Notes: No performances.

W71.   Colloquies II

Medium: Piano, flute, and viola.
Composition date and location: October 1978 in Cincinnati; revised 1982, in Cincinnati.
Publisher: New York: American Composers Alliance, 1995.
Location of holograph: The composer.
Duration: 4 min.

Score: 11 p.
1 movement: Vehemently
Notes: The 1978 version is scored for flute and viola only, is 73 measures in length on eight leaves of National manuscript paper. The 1982 version, written on Dayman 15016 manuscript paper, is expanded to 140 measures, and adds a piano part, thus becoming consistent with the other works in the Colloquies series which all involve the piano as one of the instruments.

First performance of 1982 revised version:

P71a.   24 October 1978, Rochelle Draizar, flute, Yizhak Schotten, viola, at Corbett Auditorium, University of Cincinnati College-Conservatory of Music.

First performance of 1982 revised version:

P71b.   5 November 1988, Judith Bently, flute, Pamela Ryan, viola, and Robert Spano, piano, in the Great Gallery of the Toledo Museum of Art, Toledo, Ohio, as part of the 1988 New Music and Art Festival, Bowling Green State University.

Other known performance of 1982 revised version:

P71c.   30 May 1992, Rebecca Malloy, flute, Riichi Uemura, viola, and Karol Sue Reddington, piano, at a concert of the music of Allen Sapp produced by the Cincinnati Composers' Guild, at the Contemporary Arts Center, Cincinnati.

W72.   *Five Pieces for Solo Violin in the Language of Flowers*

Medium: Violin solo.
Composition date and location: May 1983, in Cincinnati.
Dedication: Dana Hudgens Mader
Publisher: New York: American Composers Alliance, 1995.
Location of holograph: Dana Hudgens Mader, Freemont, OH.
Duration: 10 min.
Score: 5 p.
Movements: I. Heliotrope (Moderately) -- II. Cypress (Quickly) -- III. Azalea (Slowly) -- IV. Bougainvillea (Moderately) -- V. Rhododendron (Rapidly)
Notes: No performances.

W73.   *Sirius :: Stella Canis*
The Companion of Sirius :: The Serious Companion

Medium: Tuba and piano.
Composition date and location: 2 March 1984, in Cincinnati.

Dedication: "For Paul Conrad"
Publisher: New York: American Composers Alliance, 1995.
Location of holograph: The composer.
Duration: 7 min.
Score: 10 p.
Movements: I. Sirius :: Stella Canis -- II. The Companion of Sirius :: The Serious Companion
Notes: From preface: "These two works which revolve around each other as does the Brightest Star and its companion, the White Dwarf, may be performed in any order. The allusions to work of Stravinsky are deliberate and part of the serious tone of <u>SIRIUS</u> which is marked by a markedly episodic continuity and various realignments of memorable fragments." At the première, a recording of "The Companion" (movement II) was played on tape synchronous to the live performance of "Sirius" (movement I); then a recording of "Sirius" was played on tape synchronous to the live performance of "The Companion;" finally, a performance of "Sirius" was performed without a synchronous tape.

First performance:

P73a.   3 February 1985, Paul Conrad, tuba, Molly Knight, piano, at a concert of the Contemporary Music Ensemble of the College-Conservatory of Music in Corbett Auditorium, University of Cincinnati College-Conservatory of Music.

W74.   *Colloquies IV: "The Lament for Adonis"*

Title on holograph: *The Lament for Adonis*
Medium: Violoncello and piano.
Composition date and location: 12 July 1984, in Cincinnati.
Publisher: New York: American Composers Alliance, 1995.
Location of holograph: The composer.
Duration: 7 min.
Score: 8 p.
1 movement: Very slowly
Notes: Inspired by "The Lament for Adonis" by the pastoral poet Bion of Phlossa (fl. ca. 100 B.C.). A translation of this work appears on the verso of the title page of the holograph. *Colloquies IV* is listed in *Baker's Biographical Dictionary of Music and Musicians* (7th ed.) as being "for Orch.," but the orchestral work was never completed, and the series title has been reassigned to this work.
Recording: See D3 (recording of P74e).

First performance:

P74a.   14 May 1985, Katie Rietman, violoncello, the composer, piano, at Watson Hall, University of Cincinnati College-Conservatory of Music.

Other known performances:

P74b.   28 January 1986, Candace Wood, violoncello, May-Chee Chen, piano, at Patricia Corbett Theatre, University of Cincinnati College-Conservatory of Music.

P74c.   14 April 1987, Michael Daniels, violoncello, Kelley Coppage, piano, at Watson Hall, University of Cincinnati College-Conservatory of Music.

P74d.   24 May 1987, Drew Owen, violoncello, [pianist unknown], at Scarlet Oaks Chapel, Cincinnati.

P74e.   30 October 1988, Lee Fiser, violoncello, Kenneth Griffiths, piano, at Corbett Auditorium, University of Cincinnati College-Conservatory of Music.

P74f.   9 January 1989, Iris Schneider, violoncello, Beth Hull, piano, at Watson Hall, University of Cincinnati College-Conservatory of Music.

W75.   *A Garland for Anna*

Medium: Violin solo.
Composition date and location: 6 August 1984, in Cincinnati.
Dedication: "for Anna [Choi]"
Publisher: New York: American Composers Alliance, 1995.
Location of holograph: The composer.
Duration: 25 min.
Score: 12 p.
Movements: I. Quarter note = 126 -- II. [same] -- III. [same] -- IV. [same] -- V. Lively -- VI. Slowly -- VII. Waltz-Time -- VIII. Undulatory -- IX. Thoughtfully -- X. Espressivo (Intensely) -- XI. Harshly -- XII. As in a dream -- XIII. Petulant/Animated -- XIV. Very slowly - sadly -- XV. Warm/Sensuously -- XVI. Reflectively -- XVII. Tentatively -- XVIII. Moderately -- XIX. Moving along -- XX. Proud and happy
Notes: No performances.

W76.   *Thirteen Anti-Strophes*

Medium: Violoncello and piano.
Composition date and location: 1985, in Cincinnati.
Dedication: "To the Bloustein family"
Publisher: New York: American Composers Alliance, 1995.
Location of holograph: Missing.
Duration: 4 min.
Score: 4 p.
1 movement: Not too slowly
Notes: No performances.

W77.   *Romance for Solo Violin*

Medium: Violin alone.
Composition date and location: June-July 1985, in Cincinnati.
Publisher: New York: American Composers Alliance, 1995.
Location of holograph: The composer.
Duration: 6 min.
Score: 3 p.
1 movement: Flowing
Notes: No performances. A brief unattributed poem appears at the colophon:

> When I was but thirteen or so
>   I went into a golden land,
> Chimborazo, Cotopaxi
>   Took me my the hand.

W78.   *Fantasia: "Shiny Dumplings Rising Like Bubbles of Air, Clockwise"*

Medium: Violin and piano.
Composition date and location: 15 March 1986, in Cincinnati.
Publisher: New York: American Composers Alliance, 1995.
Location of holograph: The composer.
Duration: 8 min.
Score: 19 p.
1 movement: Fiercely
Notes: Subtitle quotation attributed to Sigrid Ottersten.

First performance:

P78a.   20 February 1987, Cecilia Gelland, violin, and Janet Lopinski, piano, at Watson Hall, University of Cincinnati College-Conservatory of Music.

Other known performance:

P78b.   23 April 1987, Cecilia Gelland, violin, and Janet Lopinski, piano, at Bryan Recital Hall, Bowling Green State University College of Musical Arts, Bowling Green, Ohio.

W79.   *Colloquies V: "The Cage of All Bright Knocks"*

Title on holograph: *Colloquy V: "The Cage of All Bright Knocks"*
Medium: Alto flute and piano.
Composition date and location: 10 October 1986, in Cincinnati.
Publisher: New York: American Composers Alliance, 1995.
Location of holograph: The composer.

Duration: 10 min.
Score: 13 p.
1 movement: Quarter note = 85

First performance:

P79a. 14 November 1986, Laura Kahler, alto flute, Nancy Vogelsang, piano, at Watson Hall, University of Cincinnati College-Conservatory of Music.

W80. *To Be Played Softly...*

Medium: Violin, viola, and violoncello.
Composition date and location: June 1987, in Cincinnati.
Dedication: "For Alan Green and Joyce Sympson, on the occasion of their marriage, June 13, 1987."
Publisher: New York: American Composers Alliance, 1995.
Location of holograph: Alan and Joyce Green, Columbus, Ohio.
Duration: 6 min.
Score: 16 p.
1 movement: Not too slowly
Notes: Ellipsis points are part of the composer's title; no words have been omitted from the title transcription above.

First performance:

P80a. 13 June 1987, Manami White, violin, Teresa Jansen, viola, and Iris Schneider, violoncello, at St. George Roman Catholic Church, Cincinnati.

Other known performances:

P80b. 21 February 1988, Manami White, violin, Teresa Jansen, viola, and Iris Schneider, violoncello, at Unity Center (1401 E. McMillan St.), Cincinnati.

P80c. 25 February 1988, Patrice Evans, violin, Leslie Woods, viola, and Norman Woods, violoncello, at "Festae Sappiana," Ewing Fine Arts Auditorium, Copiah-Lincoln Junior College, Wesson, Mississippi.

W81. *Colloquies VI: "Socrates and Phaedrus Speak of Love by the Banks of the Illisus"*

Medium: Oboe and piano.
Composition date and location: June-2 October 1988, in Cincinnati.
Dedication: "To Sally Bloom"

Publisher: New York: American Composers Alliance, 1995.
Location of holograph: The composer.
Duration: 10 min.
Score: 5 p.
1 movement: Eighth note = 72
Recording: See D4.

First performance:

P81a.   10 January 1990, Sara Lambert Bloom, oboe, and Elizabeth Pridonoff, piano, at Corbett Auditorium, University of Cincinnati College-Conservatory of Music.

Other known performance:

P81b.   26 April 1993, Sara Lambert Bloom, oboe, and Elizabeth Pridonoff, piano, at a concert in honor of the composer upon his retirement from the University of Cincinnati College-Conservatory of Music, at Patricia Corbett Theatre, University of Cincinnati College-Conservatory of Music.

Bibliography:

WB81a.   Lehman, Mark L. "Oboe Premieres." *American Record Guide* 58, no. 5 (September/October 1995): 262-63. Review of D4. "Its expansive, slow-moving dialog-like structure is more meditative than lyrical. . . . Sapp (who studied with Walter Piston) refuses to abandon the resources of traditional harmony, and *Colloquies IV* [*sic*]—despite some chromatic enrichment—pays homage to the allure of simple diatonic chords, ending with a calm C Major triad."

W82.   *Inscriptions and Commentaries*

Medium: Oboe, violin, viola, violoncello
Composition date and location: Spring-8 August 1991; no location given in holograph, but the composer was living in Cincinnati during this period.
Dedication: "For Robyn Dixon
Location of holograph: The composer
Duration: 10 min.
Score: 17 p.
1 movement: Quarter note = 96

First performance:

P82a.   1 November 1991, Robyn Lea Dixon, oboe, Yuko Tsujimoto, violin, Gina Calloway, viola, Rocio Mendoza, violoncello, at Watson Hall, University of Cincinnati College-Conservatory of Music.

W83.   *Polyhedra*

Medium: Woodwind quintet
Composition date and location: July-24 November 1992, in Cincinnati.
Dedication: "To The Antares Quintet"
Location of holograph: The composer.
Score: 17 p.
Duration: 17 min.
Movements: I. Tetrahedron (Moderately) -- II. Cube (Lively) -- III. Octahedron (Very slowly) -- IV. Icosahedron (Tempo di minuetto) -- V. Dodecahedron (Vivace)

   First performance:

P83a.   20 February 1993, The Antares Wind Quintet (Betty Douglas, flute, Alexandra Garcia-Trabucco, oboe, David Kirby, clarinet, Denise Smith, bassoon, Katie Humble, horn), at Little Theater, Dodge City Community College, Dodge City, Kansas.

SOLO VOCAL

W84.   *The Bridal Song*

Medium: Mezzo-soprano, flute, violin, viola, and violoncello.
Composition date and location: 1951-52; no location given in holograph, but the composer was living in Cambridge, Mass. during this period.
Dedication: "To Cynthia on the occasion of her marriage" [Cynthia Sweeny].
Location of holograph: The composer (pencil sketch).
First performance: At the wedding of Cynthia Sweeny, ca. 1952, near Boston.
Duration: 4 min.
Score: 10 leaves of Passantino no. 30 manuscript paper cut into half-sheets.
Vocal range: e′ - g′′
1 movement: "Cynthia, to thy power and thee we obey" (Allegro)
Notes: Text by John Fletcher. Composed for Cynthia Sweeny, a student of the composer at Radcliffe College.

W85.   *Nursery Rhymes*

Medium: Mezzo-soprano and piano.
Composition date and location: Ca. 1952 (date not given in holograph, estimated by the composer); no location given in holograph, but the composer was living in Cambridge, Mass. during this period.
Location of holograph: The composer (pencil sketch).
Duration: 5 min.
Score: 5 leaves of Passantino no. 30 manuscript paper cut into half-sheets.
Vocal range: c′ - e′′

Movements: I. "Ride a cock horse" (Fast) -- II. "Old Mother Hubbard" (Waltz tune) -- III. "Little Jack Horner" (Very slowly) -- IV. "Hickory dickory dock" (Fast)
Notes: No performances.

W86.   Seven Epigrams (Both Sweet and Sour)

Title on holograph: 7 Epigrams (Both Sweet and Sour)
Medium: Bass voice and piano
Composition date and location: 1952; no location given in holograph, but the composer was living in Cambridge, Mass. during this period.
Dedication: "To Morton and Diane Margolis"
Publisher: New York: American Composers Alliance, 1995.
Location of holograph: The composer.
Duration: 10 min.
Score: 10 p.
Vocal range: F♯ - d′
Movements: I. "Short epigrams relish both sweet and sour" (Allegro grazioso) -- II. "Treason doth never prosper" (Andante) -- III. "Weapons in peace grow hungry" (Feroce) -- IV. "Thy sins and hairs may no man equal call" (Comodo) -- V. "Thy flatt'ring picture, Phryne" (Pomposo elegamente) -- VI. "Who only in his cups will fight" (Andantino) -- VII. "Some men marriage do commend" (Animato)
Notes: Texts by Robert Hayman (I), Sir John Harrington (II), Thomas Bancroft (III and VI), John Donne (IV and V), and John Weever (VII).

First performance:

P86a.   25 April 1958, Robert Beckwith, bass, James Haar, piano, at Winthrop House, Senior Common Room, Harvard University.

Other known performance:

P86b.   18 January 1963, Clifford Chappman, bass-baritone, Leo Smit, piano, at Capen Hall, State University of New York at Buffalo.

W87.   The Lady and the Lute

Alternate title: Eight Songs to Texts of Robert Herrick[9]
Medium: Soprano and piano or harpsichord
Composition date and location: 1952, in Lincoln and Cambridge Mass.; revised in Rome, 1957.
Publisher: New York: American Composers Alliance, 1995.
Location of holograph: The composer.
Duration: 17 min.
Score: 18 p.
Vocal range: b - bb″

Movements: I. "So smooth, so sweet" (Con tenerézza) -- II. "Clear are her eyes" (Giocoso) -- III. "Her pretty feet like snails did creep" (Troppo serioso) -- IV. "Put up your silks" (Con passione) -- V. "When as in silks my Julia goes" (Voluttuosamente) -- VI. "A sweet disorder in the dress" (Astutamente) -- VII. "Goe, perjur'd man!" (Feroce) -- VIII. "When I thy singing next shall heare" (Con tenerézza)
Notes: Texts by Robert Herrick.
Recordings: See D12a-b (recording of P87a); D13 (recording of P87k).

First performance:

P87a.   Ca. late summer 1952, Jean Lunn, soprano, Norma Bertolami Sapp, piano, at Paine Hall, Harvard University.

Other known performances:

P87b.   18 April 1953, Jean Lunn, soprano, Norma Bertolami Sapp, piano, at Jordan Hall, New England Conservatory of Music, Boston.

P87c.   26 April 1953, Jean Lunn, soprano, John Davison, harpsichord, at Paine Hall, Harvard University.

P87d.   5 May 1955, Jean Lunn, soprano, Russell Woollen, piano, at Paine Hall, Harvard University.

P87e.   18 October 1957, Helene Rountree-Smith, soprano (pianist unknown), at the festival "Decade of the New American Music," l'Atelier—Rotonde, Palais des Beaux-Arts, Brussels, Belgium

P87f.   23 February 1958, Dorothy Crawford, soprano, John Crawford, piano, at Lowell House Junior Common Room, Harvard University.

P87g.   22 February 1959, Jean Lunn, soprano, Norma Bertolami Sapp, piano, at the Radcliffe Graduate Center, Radcliffe College.

P87h.   14 October 1959, Jean Lunn, soprano, Norma Bertolami Sapp, piano, at Dunster House Junior Common Room, Harvard University.

P87i.   2 November 1959, Jean Lunn, soprano, Norma Bertolami Sapp, piano, at Wellesley College, Wellesley, Mass.

P87j.   8 January 1960, Jean Lunn, soprano, Norma Bertolami Sapp, piano, at the Nova Gallery, Boston.

P87k.   4 March 1965, Carol Plantamura, soprano, George Crumb, harpsichord, at Albright-Knox Art Gallery, Buffalo, during the Buffalo Festival of the Arts Today (27 February-13 March 1965).

P87l.   9 March 1965, Carol Plantamura, soprano, George Crumb, harpsichord, at Carnegie Recital Hall, New York City.

P87m.   Ca. autumn 1979, Nelga Lynn Dinerstein, soprano, Norma Bertolami Sapp, piano, at Patricia Corbett Theatre, University of Cincinnati College-Conservatory of Music.

P87n.   25 February 1988, Cecelia Renfroe-Rassier, soprano, Carol Sparkman, piano, at "Festae Sappiana," Ewing Fine Arts Auditorium, Copiah-Lincoln Junior College, Wesson, Mississippi.

Bibliography:

WB87a.   Casler, Lawrence R. "The Music Box: Festival of Harvard Composers and Harvard-Radcliffe Orch." *Harvard Crimson*, 30 April 1953. "I found Allen Sapp's *Eight Songs to Texts by Robert Herrick* the most appealing part of the program. The music not only established an appropriate mood for each poem, but also vividly illustrated their meanings. I don't think I'll ever be able to read 'The Curse' [song VII, 'Goe, perjur'd man!'] again without thinking of Sapp's terrifying, almost screaming treatment of the opening words."

WB87b.   Buttenwieser, Paul A. "The Music Box: Contemporary Music." *Harvard Crimson*, 25 February 1958. "These songs exhibited a greater concern with the setting of the text than with the more idiomatic aspects of vocal writing."

WB87c.   "Concert Hall: Vocal." *American Composers Alliance Bulletin* 10, no. 3 (September 1962): 33. Report of performances P87g-j.

WB87d.   "100 Metronomes Charm 650 into Wild 'Bravo!'" *Buffalo Courier-Express*, 5 March 1965. "Allen Sapp's song cycle, 'The Lady and the Lute,' is a refined and appealing setting of the 17th century poetry extolling the virtues and beauty of womanhood."

WB87e.   Dwyer, John. "Creative Associates Balance Lyric Art with Musical Antics." *Buffalo Evening News*, 5 March 1965. "Sapp's settings were to Robert Herrick's lovely odes to ladies and love, and the soloist was soprano Carol Plantamura, with harpsichordist George Crumb. Radical as it may seem in our day, you could have learned the poems from the performance. By syllable and phrase, the music evoked the word, and the near-tonal play of line and meter seemed almost soluble in the stylized Herrick tone of voice and cameo-imagery."

WB87f.   Strongin, Theodore. "Music: Foss's 3d Evening." *New York Times*, 10 March 1965. "Mr. Sapp's cycle would have benefitted from a more agile and less fat-sounding voice than Miss Plantamura's. Without subtlety and lightness, the work's points are lost and the words and music seem in different universes."

WB87g.   "Courante." *American Composers Alliance Bulletin* 13, no. 1 (1965): 13. Report of performance P87l.

W88.   Seven Songs of Carew

Title on holograph: *7 Songs to Texts of Thomas Carew*
Earlier title for songs I and II: *Two Lyrics*
Medium: High voice and piano.
Composition date and location: 14-30 November 1961, at Buffalo (movements I and II); and June 1982, at Cincinnati (movements III-VII).
Dedication: "To David Adams"
Publisher: New York: American Composers Alliance, 1995.
Location of holograph: The composer.
Duration: 13 min.
Score: [14] p.
Vocal range: c - a′ (tenor) or c′ - a′′ (soprano)
Movements: I. "Give me more love or more disdain" (Slowly) -- II. "Ask me no more whither doth haste the nightengale when May is past" (Quickly) -- III. "Ask me no more where Jove bestows when June is past the fading rose" (Andante) -- IV. "Ask me no more whither doth stray the golden atoms of the day" (Quickly) -- V. "Ask me no more where those stars' light that downward fall in dead of night" (Moderately) -- VI. "Ask me no more if East or West the Phoenix builds her nest" (Animated) -- VII. "Give me a storme if it be love like Danae" (Agitated)
Notes: Text by Thomas Carew. Songs I and II (dated 30 November 1961 and 14 November 1961, respectively) were issued earlier by the composer under the title *Two Lyrics*.

First performance of *Two Lyrics* (1961 version):

P88a.   2 March 1982, David Adams, tenor, Sylvia Plyler, piano, at Patricia Corbett Theatre, University of Cincinnati College-Conservatory of Music.

First performance of *Seven Songs of Carew* (expanded 1982 version):

P88b.   24 April 1985, David Adams, tenor, Norma Bertolami Sapp, piano, at Patricia Corbett Theatre, University of Cincinnati College-Conservatory of Music.

Other known performances of *Seven Songs of Carew* (expanded 1982 version):

P88c.   9 October 1985, David Adams, tenor, Kenneth Griffiths, piano, at Corbett Auditorium, University of Cincinnati College-Conservatory of Music.

P88d.   6 May 1986, David Adams, tenor, Kenneth Griffiths, piano, at Patricia Corbett Theatre, University of Cincinnati College-Conservatory of Music.

W89.   *Moral Maxims (30 Songs for Thirty Years)*

Medium: High voice and piano.
Composition date and location: June-9 July 1982, in Cincinnati.
Dedication: "For my son Christopher"
Publisher: New York: American Composers Alliance, 1995.
Location of holograph: The composer.
Duration: 25 min.
Score: 33 p.
Vocal range: c - b♭′ (tenor) or c′ - b♭″ (soprano)
Movements: I. "Nature makes merit, but fortune sets it to work" (Very slowly) -- II. "We have not enough strength to follow all our reason" (Moderately fast) -- III. "Strength and weakness of mind are misnamed" (Slowly) -- IV. "There is real love just as there are real ghosts" (Rather quickly) -- V. "In growing old we become more foolish and more wise" (Cavatina) -- VI. "It is great folly to wish only to be wise" (Lightly) -- VII. "Youth is a continual intoxication" (Moving gracefully) -- VIII. "Sometimes we meet a fool with wit, never one with discretion" (Moving comfortably) -- IX. "Little minds are too much wounded by little things" (Lively) -- X. "We deceive ourselves if we believe that there are violent passions" (Languidly) -- XI. "Magnanimity despises all to win all" (Very slowly) -- XII. "It is far easier to be wise for others than to be so for oneself" (Moderately fast) -- XIII. "We often go from love to ambition" (Sadly) -- XIV. ""Wit sometimes enables us to act rudely with impunity" (Quickly) -- XV. "We forgive those who bore us" (Moving gracefully) -- XVI. "However we distrust" (Very slowly) -- XVII. "There is a great ability in knowing how to conceal one's ability" (Moderately fast) -- XVIII. "When we do not find piece of mind in ourselves" (Not too slowly) -- XIX. "We pardon in the degree that we love" (Nostalgically) -- XX. "They only are despicable who fear to be despised" (Moderately fast) -- XXI. "Absence extinguishes small passions" (Moving gracefully) -- XXII. "More persons exist without self-love than without envy" (Quickly) -- XXIII. "However rare true love is, true friendship is rarer" (Agreeably) -- XXIV. "In the human heart" (Not too fast) -- XXV. "It is difficult to define love" (Sinuously) -- XXVI. "What grace is to the body, good sense is to the mind" (Slowly) -- XXVII. "He is really wise who is nettled at nothing" (Crisply) -- XXVIII. "As it is the mark of great minds" (Smoothly) -- XXIX. "The extreme delight we take in talking of ourselves" (Not so quickly!) -- XXX. "In all professions we affect a part and an appearance to seem what we wish to be; thus the world is merely composed of actors" (Moving gracefully)
Notes: Text by François, duc de la Rochefoucauld, translated by G. H. Powell.

First performance:

P89a.   5 May 1987, David Adams, tenor, Kenneth Griffiths, piano, at Patricia Corbett Theatre, University of Cincinnati College-Conservatory of Music.

Other known performances:

P89b.   11 January 1988, David Adams, tenor, Kenneth Griffiths, piano, at Corbett Auditorium, University of Cincinnati College-Conservatory of Music.

P89c. 26 April 1993, David Adams, tenor, Kenneth Griffiths, piano, at a concert in honor of the composer upon his retirement from the University of Cincinnati College-Conservatory of Music, at Patricia Corbett Theatre, University of Cincinnati College-Conservatory of Music.

W90. Illusions and Affirmations

Medium: Bass voice and string orchestra, accompaniment arranged for piano by the composer (i.e., not yet orchestrated).
Arrangement date and location: 10-25 August 1982, in Cincinnati.
Dedication: "For my son Anthony"
Location of holograph: The composer.
Duration: 15 min.
Score: 25 p.
Vocal range: D - e′
Movements: I. "Deem not because you see me in the press of this world's children" (Quarter note = 72) -- II. "Tell me no more how fair she is" (Petulantly, with wit and irony) -- III. "If poysonous mineralls, and if that tree, whose fruit threw death on else immortal us" (Solemn, serious and agonized) -- IV. "Long time a child and still a child, when years had painted manhood on my cheek" (Flowing, with occasional bitterness) -- V. "Though night hath climb'd her peak of highest noon" (Brutal, rough and savage)
Notes: From title page: "Settings by authors of repute on themes of Hope, Regret, and Resignation." Texts by George Santayana, Henry King, John Donne, Hartley Coleridge, and Alfred, Lord Tennyson. A complete full score of this work has not been executed by the composer as of November 1995. The accompaniment is to be scored for string orchestra. No performances.

W91. Affliction

Medium: Mezzo soprano and piano.
Composition date and location: 29 June 1983, in Cincinnati.
Location of holograph: The composer.
Duration: 16 min.
Score: 18 p.
Vocal range: g - a′′
Movements: I. "When first thou didst entice to thee my heart" (Quarter note = 80) -- II. "I looked on thy furniture so fine" (Quarter note = 120) -- III. "What pleasures could I want" (Sensuously) -- IV. "At first thou gavist me milk and sweetnesses" (Circumspectly) -- V. "My flesh began unto my soul in pain" (Brilliantly) -- VI. "When I got health, thou took'st away my life and more" (Molto rubato, quasi un recitativo) -- VII. "Whereas my birth and spirit" (Boisterously!) -- VIII. "Yet for I threatened oft the siege to raise" (Smoothly and flowing) -- IX. "Yet lest perchance I should too happie be in my unhappinesse" (Very quickly) -- X. "Now I am here" (Seriously,

profoundly) -- XI. "Yet though thou troublest me, I must be meek" (With sadness and reverence)
Notes: Text by George Herbert. No performances.

W92.   *A Set of 12 Canons*

Medium: 2 sopranos, tenor, piano, basso continuo, 4 winds, and 6 strings (see specific instrumentation notes below).
Composition date and location: 10 December 1987, in Cincinnati.
Dedication: "Composed for and dedicated To My Dear Colleagues of the Division of History, Theory, Composition and Literature of The College-Conservatory of Music on the occasion of my 65th birthday"
Location of holograph: The composer.
Duration: 10 min.
Score: 9 p.
Vocal ranges: soprano I: d' - ab''; soprano II: db' - ab''; tenor: d - c'
Movements: I. For Sam (Moderato) [Vn., Va.] -- II. For Darrell (Vivace) [2 Ob.] -- III. For Jonathan (Presto) [Piano] -- IV. For Don (Gracefully) [Fl., Vc.] -- V. For Arthur (Not too slowly) [2 Vn., Vc.] -- VI. For Karin (Bright and happy) [Sop., Ten.] -- VII. For Bob (Fast) [2 Vn.] -- VIII. For Fred (Playfully) [Piano] -- IX. For Phil (Romanze) [2 Sop., B. C.] -- X. For Joel (Presto) [Piano] -- XI. For Seamas (Largo) [2 Cb.] -- XII. For Allen (Languidly) [Va., Bsn.]
Notes: Full names of Sapp's faculty colleagues for which these canons were composed (in order): Samuel Pogue, Darrell Handel, Jonathan Kramer, Donald Foster, Arthur Komar, Karin Pendle, Robert Zierolf, Frederick Bianchi, Phillip Crabtree, Joel Hoffman, James Riley (Seamas O'Reilly), and the composer. Text by the composer. No performances.

W93.   *Anoia*

Medium: Flute, clarinet, violin, violoncello, and soprano.
Composition date and location: January 1988, in Cincinnati.
Commissioned by: Cincinnati Composers' Guild.
Dedication: "For Cincinnati Composers Guild"
Location of holograph: The composer.
Duration: 2 min.
Score: 12 p.
Vocal range: eb'' (only one note used)
1 movement: Quarter note = 100
Notes: The text consists of one word, in the final measure of the work: "Death!"

First performance:

P93a.   13 February 1988, Kathy Stewart, flute, Stephen Gulasy, clarinet, Debbie Falco, violin, Eric Dochinger, violoncello, and Carol Oswalt, soprano, conducted by Janna Hymes, at a Cincinnati Composers' Guild concert at the Contemporary Arts Center, Cincinnati.

W94. Two Songs

Medium: Mezzo soprano and piano.
Composition date and location: Fall 1988, in Cincinnati.
Dedication: "For Sharon Radionoff"
Location of holograph: The composer.
Duration: 10 min.
Score: 24 p.
Vocal range: a - a''
Movements: I. Anonymous Eponymous -- II. Riley Set Wryly (Boisterously!)
Notes: No performances. The text of song II is "The Raggedy Man" by James Whitcomb Riley; the text to song I is anonymous ("I know a funny little man as quiet as a mouse").

W95. Dix chansons sphériques

Medium: Soprano and piano.
Composition date and location: February-March 1989, in Cincinnati.
Dedication: "For the wedding of Jennifer Nelson"
Publisher: New York: American Composers Alliance, 1995.
Location of holograph: The composer.
Duration: 16 min.
Score: [15] p.
Vocal range: c' - d'''
Movements: I. "Assez plus long qu'un siècle platonique me fut le mois que sans toi suis été" (Animé) -- II. "Bouche du corail précieux" (Modéré) -- III. "La harmonie, en doux concens nourrie des sept accords" (Lent) -- IV. "Bonjour mon coeur, bonjour ma douce vie" (Animé et capricieux) -- V. "Dame dont les beautés me possedent si fort" (Langoureux) -- VI. "Qu'est devenu ce front poli" (Vite) -- VII. "Quand je vois dans un jardin" (Mouvementé) -- VIII. "Quand j'entends la douce voix" (Agité) -- IX. "Mais quelle riche mer le corail receloit de cette belle lèvre" (Modéré) -- X. "Qui se pourrait d'elle lasser?" (Animé)
Notes: Texts by Maurice Scève (I), Clément Marot (II), Pontus de Tyard (III), Pierre de Ronsard (IV, VII, VIII), Jacques Davy du Perron (V), François Villon (VI), Jacques Tahureau (IX), and Charles d'Orléans (X).

First performance:

P95a.   28 October 1989, Jennifer Nelson, soprano, Karol Sue Reddington, piano, at a Cincinnati Composers' Guild concert at the Contemporary Arts Center, Cincinnati.

Other known performance:

P95b.   30 October 1989, Jennifer Nelson, soprano, Karol Sue Reddington, piano, at Patricia Corbett Theatre, University of Cincinnati College-Conservatory of Music.

W96.   Four Lyrics of Absence and Loss

Medium: Contralto, alto flute, violin, celesta, and marimba.
Composition date and location: June-July 1983 (movements I and II), and June 1990 (movements III-IV), at Cincinnati.
Location of holograph: The composer.
Duration: 15 min.
Score: 28 p.
Vocal range: e♭ - d♯''
Movements: I. Lament of Hsi/Chün (Nostalgically) -- II. The Other Side of the Valley (Rapidly) -- III. I Was Brought Up under the Stone Castle (Very quickly) -- IV. Song of Snow White Heads (Moderately, with sadness)
Notes: Texts to the first three songs are anonymous; text of song IV is by Cho Wēn Chün. There have been no performances of the entire work as of November 1995.

First partial performance:

P96a.   5 March 1991, Penelope Schenk, contralto, Karen Kutzke, violin, Keith Wright, alto flute, Carol Walker, celeste, Stan Ginn, marimba, at a Cincinnati Composers' Guild concert at the Contemporary Arts Center, Cincinnati (movements I and II).

CHORAL

W97.   Easter Day

Medium: Chorus (SATB) with piano accompaniment.
Composition date and location: 12 May 1941; no location given in holograph, but the composer was living in Cambridge, Mass. during this period.
Dedication: "To Suzanne King"
Location of holograph: The composer.
Duration: 3 min.
Score: 6 p.
Vocal ranges: soprano: d' - a''; alto: g♯ - d''; tenor: d - e'; bass: E - c'
1 movement: "On Easter Day as I was going through the woods, the winds were blowing" (Moderato)
Notes: Text by John Erwin. No performances.

W98.   A Song of Marriage

Alternate title: *The Marriage Song*[10]
Medium: Chorus (SATB) and chamber orchestra.
Composition date and location: 1948; no location given in holograph, but the composer was living in Cambridge, Mass. during this period.
Dedication: "To Phantis" [familial nickname for the composer's sister, Nancy]

Location of holograph: The composer.
Duration: 30 min.
Score: 161 p.
Vocal ranges: soprano: c′ - g♯′′; alto: g - d′′; tenor: c - g′; bass: E♭ - d♯′
Instrumentation: 1 Fl., 1 Ob., 1 Cl. in B♭, 1 Bn., 1 Hn., Strings.
Movements: I. The Time of the Marriage -- II. Equality of Persons -- III. Raising of the Bridegroom -- IV. Raising of the Bride -- V. Her Apparelling -- VI. Going to the Chappelle -- VII. The Wedding -- VIII. The Benediction -- IX. Feasts and Revells -- X. The Bride's Going to Bed -- XI. The Bridegroome's Coming -- XII. The Good Night
Notes: Text by John Donne. The entire work has not been performed as of April 1994. Accompaniment arranged for piano or organ by the composer, 1948; holograph (71 p.) held by the American Composers Alliance (New York, N.Y.), and published by them in 1952. First performance of arrangement for piano or organ with chorus: 2 October 1948, Ernest Willoughby, organ, and the choir of the Church of the Redeemer, Bryn Mawr, Pa. (partial performance).

First partial performance:

P98a.   1 May 1950, The Harvard and Radcliffe Music Club Singers, accompanied by Norma Bertolami Sapp, organ, W. C. Cummings and Peter S. Ødegaard, violins, Vernon Head, viola, Joan Brockway, violoncello, conducted by Peter G. Swing, at Appleton Chapel, Harvard University (movements I, III, and VIII).

W99.   In Grato Jubilo

Medium: Chorus (SSA) and chamber ensemble.
Composition date and location: 1949; no location given in holograph, but the composer was living in Cambridge, Mass. during this period.
Dedication: "For Serge Koussevitzky"
Location of holograph: Unknown.
Score: 87 p.
Instrumentation: Chorus (SSA), 1 Fl., 1 Ob., 1 Cl., 1 Bn., 1 Hn., 3 Tpt. in C, 2 Tbn., 1 Cb., Timp.
1 movement by Allen Sapp: IV. Andantino (p. 53-63, 3 min., instrumental interlude).
Notes: From title page: "A musical offering from the Boston Chapter of the Tanglewood Alumni Association, composed for Dr. Koussevitzky and performed for the first time at a testimonial dinner in his honor upon the completion of his twenty-fifth season as Conductor of the Boston Symphony Orchestra, Symphony Hall - May 2, 1949." Movements composed by other composers: I - Irving Fine; II - Daniel Pinkham; III - Gardner Read; V - Herbert Fromm; VI - Lukas Foss. Text by David McCord adapted from the Bible, Revelation 5: 9, 10.

First performance:

P99a.   2 May 1949, performed by former Tanglewood alumni (including vocal soloists Phyllis Curtin, soprano, and Eunice Roberts, contralto), conducted by Lukas Foss, at Symphony Hall, Boston.

Other known performance:

P99b.   16 November 1950, Boston University Orchestra and Chorus, conducted by Gardner Read, at Recital Hall, Boston University College of Music.

Bibliography:

WB99a.   Durgin, Cyrus. "Boston Pays Farewell Tribute to Koussevitzky." *Boston Globe*, 3 May 1949. While Durgin did not provide an evaluation of the composition or performance, he did quote the remarks of Koussevitzky: "I am deeply moved by your tribute. I am grateful . . . for the pleasure we all received from the musical offering of my young friends." This composition was the only music performed that evening. The event was attended by about 1000 dinner guests seated at tables on the ground floor; "Following dinner came the ceremonials. . . . For these, the public was admitted to the balconies, which were quickly filled."

W100.   Five Landscapes

Alternate Title: *Five Pieces to Texts of T.S. Eliot*
Medium: Chorus a cappella (SSATB)
Composition date and location: 1950, in Cambridge, Mass.
Dedication: "To A. T. Davison"
Location of holograph: The composer.
Duration: 11 min.
Score: 16 p.
Vocal range: soprano I: c' - ab''; soprano II: bb - gb''; alto: g - d''; tenor: c - ab'; bass: Gb - d'
Movements: I. New Hampshire -- II. Virginia (Not too slowly, flowing; thoughtfully) -- III. Usk (Quickly, with sudden changes of tempo) -- IV. Rannoch by Glencoe -- V. Cape Anne (Quickly)
Notes: Texts by T. S. Eliot.
Recordings: See D6a-b (recording of P100a); D7 (recording of P100d).

First performance:

P100a.   11 February 1951, Harvard-Radcliffe Music Clubs Chorus, conducted by Howard M. Brown, at a concert of the Harvard-Radcliffe Musical Clubs, Paine Hall, Harvard University.

Other known performances:

P100b.   4 March 1951, Harvard-Radcliffe Music Clubs Chorus, conducted by James Bolle, at a concert of the Harvard-Radcliffe Musical Clubs, Worcester Art Museum, Worcester, Mass.

P100c.   21 November 1954, Bach Society Chorus, conducted by Howard M. Brown, Paine Hall, Harvard University, under the program title *Five Pieces to Texts of T.S. Eliot*.[11]

P100d.   23 February 1968, University of Buffalo Composers' Choral Group, conducted by Dowell Multer, at Baird Recital Hall, State University of New York at Buffalo (movements I, IV, and III only).

P100e.   25 February 1988, ,Copiah-Lincoln Junior College Concert Choir, conducted by Sharon L. Radionoff, at "Festae Sappiana," Ewing Fine Arts Auditorium, Copiah-Lincoln Junior College, Wesson, Mississippi (movements I, II, and V only).

P100f.   30 May 1992, Cincinnati Choral Society, conducted by Peter Morabito, at a concert of the music of Allen Sapp produced by the Cincinnati Composers' Guild, at the Contemporary Arts Center, Cincinnati.

Bibliography:

WB100a.   Simon, Robert M. "Bach Society Chorus at Paine Hall." *Harvard Crimson*, 23 November 1954. "Mr. Sapp is blessed with a poetic sense to match his extraordinary musical gifts. Taking five poems of T. S. Eliot, he has not merely assigned each syllable a note and made the work a straight declamation. Rather, he has readily displaced certain lines to enhance the lyrical effect." Simon provides several examples of dramatic text displacement in this work.

W101.   American Fantasies

Alternate title: *God Enters the Boston Public Library*[12]
Medium: Chorus (TTBB) and 2 pianos.
Composition date and location: Ca. 1952 (date not given in holograph, estimated by the composer); no location given in holograph, but the composer was living in Cambridge, Mass. during this period.
Location of holograph: The composer (pencil sketch).
Duration: 10 min.
Score: 20 p.
Vocal ranges: tenor I: c - g♯´; tenor II: B♭ - f´; bass I: G - d♯´ ; bass II: F♯ - c♯´
1 movement: "It was a polished night of stars when God rode into the Boston Public Library" (Allegro)
Notes: Text by James Schevill. No performances. The title page of the only known holograph contains the indication "First draft," twice underlined, and is obviously not a fair copy.

Four Motets (1953): See W143; See also W107.

W102.   *The Little Boy Lost*

Medium: Chorus (SATB) and unspecified instrumental ensemble.
Composition date and location: 1 July 1953, in Lincoln and Cambridge, Mass.
Commissioned by: Berkshire Music Center, Department V.
Location of holograph: Missing.
Duration: 30 min.
Score: 58 p.
Vocal range: soprano: b - g''; alto: b - e''; tenor: A - g'; bass: A - eb'
Movements: I. Overture (Broadly - Lively - Broadly) -- II. First Invention (Vigorously) -- III. Laughing Song (Not too quickly, mostly joyfully) -- IV. Second Invention (Moderately and expressively) -- V. First Canzona (Gaily) -- VI. Third Invention (Bright, optimistic, rough!) -- VII. The Little Boy Lost (Quietly and intensely) -- VIII. The Shepherd (Pastoral waltz-time) -- IX. Fourth Invention (In moving quarters) -- X. Fifth Invention (Bright and cheerful) -- XI. Spring (Lively and light) -- XII. The Lilly (Calmly and whitely) -- XIII. Sixth Invention (Fast and busy) -- XIV. Second Canzona (Not too fast, solid and rich) -- XV. Epilog: The Rose Tree (Broadly)
Notes: Text by William Blake. The composer was awarded the Samuel Wechsler Award from the Berkshire Music Center for this work. The instrumental accompaniment consists of three parts marked A, B, and C, at times employed canonically, with no specific instrumentation indicated. The work is designed for performance by musicians at the intermediate level.

First performance:

P102a.   13 August 1953, musicians of Departments IV and V, Berkshire Music Center, conducted by Ingolf Dahl, in the Theatre-Concert Hall at Tanglewood (near Lenox, Mass.).

Other known performance:

P102b.   16 May 1954, musicians of the Harvard and Radcliffe Music Clubs, conducted by Michael Greenebaum, at Kirkland House Junior Common Room, Harvard University.

Bibliography:

WB102a.   Taubman, Howard. "Tanglewood Gives a Gala 'On Parade.' *New York Times*, 14 August 1953. "Mr. Sapp's cantata is a practical piece designed for instrumentalists and singers not too far advanced; at the same time, it has a maturity and sweetness of feeling."

WB102b.   Casler, Lawrence R. "The Music of Allen Sapp." *Harvard Crimson*, 18 May 1954. "Many of [Sapp's] compositions are experiments in form, style, and sonority that indicate a bold, creative musical mind searching for adequate means of expression. *The Little Boy Lost* cantata is such an experiment." Casler is rather critical of this work, but places part of the blame on inadequate rehearsal of the musicians.

W103.   A Birthday Piece for A. T. D.

Medium: Chorus a cappella (SSA).
Composition date and location: September 1953; no location given in holograph, but the composer was living in Cambridge, Mass. during this period.
Commissioned by: Harvard Glee Club.
Dedication: "For A. T. D." [Archibald T. Davison]
Location of holograph: The composer.
Duration: 2 min.
Score: 4 p.
Vocal ranges: soprano I: d′ - f″; soprano II: c′ - c″; alto: g - b♭′
1 movement: "Happy the man, and happy he alone, he who can call today his own" (Rather quickly at first, becoming gradually slower)
Notes: Text by Horace from *Odes* 3.29.41-48, translated by John Dryden.

First performance:

P103a.   4 December 1953, Radcliffe Choral Society, conducted by G. Wallace Woodworth, at Sanders Theatre, Harvard University.

Other known performances:

P103b.   11 December 1953, Radcliffe Choral Society, conducted by G. Wallace Woodworth, at Town Hall, New York, N.Y.

P103c.   30-31 March 1954, Radcliffe Choral Society, conducted by G. Wallace Woodworth, at Sanders Theatre, Harvard University.

Bibliography:

WB103a.   Casler, Lawrence R. "The Music Box: The Davison Concert at Sanders Theatre." *Harvard Crimson*, 31 March 1954. "Some rather academic music by Allen Sapp and Randall Thompson, and Henry Leland Clarke's complicated, episodic treatment of *Happy Is the Man* (Proverbs 3:13) at least proved how very diverse Davison's influence has been."

W104.   A Prayer for Commencement

Medium: Chorus a cappella (SATB)
Composition date and location: May 1954, in Cambridge, Mass.
Commissioned by: North Shore Country Day School, Winnetka, Illinois.
Dedication: "To Perry Dunlap Smith"
Publisher: New York: American Composers Alliance, 1995.
Location of holograph: Missing.
Duration: 2 min.
Score: 7 p.
Vocal range: soprano: d′ - f″; alto: a - c″; tenor: g - g′; bass: G - c′

1 movement: "Rejoice, O young man, in thy youth" (Moderately and very expressively)
Notes: Biblical text (Ecclesiastes 11.9).

First performance:

P104a.   Unknown. The composer recalls that it was composed for Perry Dunlap Smith in honor of his retirement as headmaster of the North Shore Country Day School in Winnetka, Illinois, and that it was obviously connected with a commencement ceremony, ca. May 1954.

W105.   *A Maiden's Complaint in Springtime*

Medium: Chorus (SSA), winds, and strings.
Composition date and location: Summer 1959-60, in Wellesley, Mass.
Commissioned by: Wellesley College, for the opening of the Jewett Arts Center.
Dedication: "Written in honor of the opening of the Jewett Arts Center of Wellesley College."
Location of holograph: The composer.
Duration: 15 min.
Score: 68 p.
Vocal ranges: soprano I: cb' - ab''; soprano II: a - ab''; alto: f - d''
Instrumentation: 1 Fl., 1 Ob., 1 E. H., 1 Bn., 2 Vn., 1 Va., 1 Vc., 1 Cb., Chorus (SSA).
Movements: I. "Softly the West Wind blows" (Eighth note = 150-160) -- II. "Goes forth the scarlet spring" (Quarter note = 104) -- III. "Dens for four-footed things" (Quarter note = 104) -- IV. "I see it with my eyes" (Quarter note = 132) -- V. "Alone with thought I sit" (Quarter note = 70) -- VI. "Do thou, O spring most fair" (Eighth note = 150-160)
Notes: Text from an anonymous Latin poem, "Levis exsurgit Zephyrus" (eleventh century), translated by Helen Waddell. Accompaniment arranged for piano by the composer, 1959-60; holograph (30 p.) held by the composer.
Recording: See D14a-b (recording of P115a).

First performance:

P105a.   17 April 1960, Wellesley College Madrigal Group, conducted by Howard M. Brown, at the Jewett Arts Center, Wellesley College, Wellesley, Mass.

W106.   *How True Love is Likened to Summer*

Medium: Chorus (SATB), 3 trumpets, and 3 trombones.
Composition date and location: September-October 1960, in Wellesley, Mass.
Commissioned by: Belmont Community Chorus, Belmont, Mass.
Dedication: "For the Belmont Chorus"

Publisher: New York: American Composers Alliance, 1995.
Location of holograph: The composer.
Duration: 14 min.
Score: 18 p.
Vocal range: soprano: c' - a''; alto: a - d''; tenor: c - g'; bass: G - e'
Movements: I. "And thus it passed on from Candlemas" (Maestoso) -- II. "For it giveth unto all lovers courage" (With spirit and verve) -- III. [Instrumental interlude] (Bright and lively) -- IV. "For like as winter" (Expressively and temperately) -- V. [Instrumental interlude] (Spiteful, mean, sharp) -- VI. "Therefore like as May month flowereth and flourisheth in many gardens" (Tenderly) -- VII. "But nowadays men cannot love" (Simple, expressive) -- VIII. "Wherefore I liken love nowadays unto summer and winter" (Maestoso)
Notes: Text by Sir Thomas Malory, from *Le morte d'Arthur* 18.25.

First performance:

P106a.   16 May 1961, Belmont Community Chorus, conducted by John A. Bavicchi, at Town Hall, Belmont, Mass.

W107.   *Canticum Novum Pro Pace*

Medium: Chorus (TTBB) and wind quintet.
Composition date and location: December 1962, in Buffalo.
Commissioned by: The Guido Chorus, Buffalo.
Location of holograph: The composer.
Duration: 21 min.
Score: 41 p.
Vocal ranges: tenor I: B♭ - g♯'; tenor II: c - g'; baritone: G - e♭'; bass: D - d'
Instrumentation: chorus (TTBB), 1 Fl., 1 Ob., 1 Cl., 1 Bn., 1 Hn.
Movements: I. Ritornello A -- II. Pacem relinquo vobis [Communion, Missa pro pace] -- III. Interlude A -- IV. Da pacem, Domine [introit, XVIII Sunday after Pentecost] -- V. Interlude B -- VI. Deus, auctor pacis [postcommunion, Missa pro pace] -- VII. Interlude C -- VIII. Da pacem, Domine [introit, XVIII Sunday after Pentecost] -- IX. Interlude D -- X. Hodie nobis de caelo [responsory, Nativity of Our Lord, lesson II] -- XI. Ritornello B
Notes: The vocal movements (II, IV, VI, VIII, and X) are apparently derived from his *Four Motets* (1953) for a cappella male chorus (see W143);[13] movements IV and VIII both contain music from one of the motets, "Da pacem, Domine," in variant settings. The only known holograph contains no text underlay.

First performance:

P107a.   31 March 1963, The Guido Chorus, conducted by Clyde King, with the University of Buffalo Wind Quintet (Robert Mols, flute, Ronald Richards, oboe, Allen Sigel, clarinet, Nelson Dayton, bassoon, Lowell ·Shaw, French horn), at the Mary Seaton Room, Kleinhans Music Hall, Buffalo.

W108.   Prayer

Medium: Chorus (SATB), and 2 treble voices.
Composition date and location: 4 January 1964, in Buffalo.
Commissioned by: Three Choir Hymn Festival, Buffalo, 1964.
Location of holograph: The composer.
Duration: 2 min.
Score: 5 p.
Vocal ranges: treble I: d′ - f′′; treble II: d′ - f′′; soprano: d′ - e′′; alto: b - g′;
tenor: e - d′; bass: G♯ - b
1 movement: "O Lord, open thou our lips"
Notes: Text by William S. Hudson, based on Psalm 51.15.

First performance:

P108a.   9 February 1964, combined choirs of Holy Trinity Lutheran Church,
                  Westminster Presbyterian Church, and Trinity Episcopal Church, at the
                  tenth annual Three Choir Hymn Festival, Trinity Episcopal Church,
                  Buffalo.

Bibliography:

WB108a.   "Hymn Festival Has Age-Old Appeal for All Concerned." *Buffalo*
                  Evening News. 10 February 1964. "An anthem *Prayer* by composer
                  Allen D. Sapp . . . to verses of the Rev. William S. Hudson, assistant
                  rector of the host church, was a stiff test of intonation and rhythmic
                  equilibrium. Solid tone structures in the work split away into double
                  and triple complexes, in several harmonic and rhythmic levels at the
                  same time, a rather daring use of voice movement, but hinting rather
                  strikingly at a medieval line, quite effective in offertory performance."

W109.   Motet, "Er, der Herrlichste von Allen..."

Medium: Soprano, alto, and tenor.
Composition date and location: Ca. 1986, in Cincinnati.
Dedication: "For Arthur K. [Komar] on the occasion of his 50th birthday"
Location of holograph: The composer.
Duration: 2 min.
Score: 2 p.
Vocal ranges: soprano: f′ - c′′; alto: g - d′′; tenor: f - g′
Notes: This work is a three voice textless motet, which incorporates elements of
Robert Schumann's "Er, der Herrlichste von allen" from *Frauenliebe und Leben*, op.
42, no. 2, and the tune "Happy Birthday." No performances. Ellipsis points are part
of the composer's title; no words have been omitted from the title transcription.

ORCHESTRAL

W110.   Andante for Orchestra

Composition date and location: 1941, in Cambridge, Mass.
Location of holograph: The composer.
Duration: 7 min.
Score: 18 p.
Instrumentation: 3 Fl., 3 Ob., 1 E. H., 3 Cl. in B♭, 1 B. Cl., 2 Bn., 1 C. Bn., 4 Hn., 3 Tpt. in C, 3 Tbn., 1 Tuba, Timp., Strings.
1 movement: Andante.
Notes: This work was awarded second prize in a national young composers' competition sponsored by the New York Philharmonic. It is an orchestration of the first movement of *Piano Sonata I* (W1), expanded from 93 to 136 measures.
Recording: See D1a-b (recording of P110a).

First performance:

P110a.   18 April 1942, New York Philharmonic, conducted by Rudolph Ganz, at Carnegie Hall, New York, N.Y.

Bibliography:

WB110a.   Lawrence, Robert. "Philharmonic Ends Series for Young People." *New York Herald-Tribune*, 19 April 1942. "His prize-winning work revealed definite talent, in a somewhat abstract direction. The scoring for orchestra proved sinewy and effective, while the musical content itself varied in interest."

Passacaglia on a Theme by Piston (July 1942): **See W111.**

W111.   Concertino for Piano and Chamber Orchestra

Title on holograph: *Concertino, no. 1*
Composition date and location: August 1942, in Bryn Mawr, Pa.
Commissioned by: Town Hall, Inc.
Dedication: "To Walter Piston"
Location of holograph: The composer.
Duration: 15 min.
Score: 88 p.
Instrumentation: 1 Fl., 1 Ob., 1 Cl. in B♭, 1 Bn., 2 Hn., 1 Tpt. in C, Piano solo, Strings.
Movements: I. Allegro -- II. Passacaglia on a Theme by Piston (Largo) -- III. Allegro

Notes: Arrangement for two pianos by the composer, October 1950; holograph (35 p.) held by American Composers Alliance (New York, N.Y.), and published by them in 1952. First performance of arrangement for two pianos: 17 October 1950, the composer and Norma Bertolami Sapp, at Adams House Lower Common Room, Harvard University. Additional performances of arrangement for two pianos: 22 April 1951, the composer and Norma Bertolami Sapp, at Kirkland House Junior Common Room, Harvard University; 4 May 1954, the composer and Norma Bertolami Sapp, at Kirkland House Junior Common Room, Harvard University, on a discussion-concert entitled "The New Cambridge Lyricism" (see B10) in the series "New Trends in Contemporary Music" (concert broadcast on WGBH-FM).

Recording: A recording of P111b was made by Radiodiffusion Française (see D42; see also discussion on p. 13), and is held by the Archives de la phonothèque de l'Institut national de l'audiovisuel, Maison de Radio-France.[14]

First performance of July 1942 version of movement II:

P111a.   Between 14 July and 13 August 1942,[15] Norma Bertolami, piano, a Tanglewood student orchestra under the direction of Walter Hendl, Berkshire Music Center, Lenox. Mass.

First complete performance of final version:

P111b.   19 April 1945, Monique Haas, piano, with the Orchestre de la Radiodiffusion Française, under the direction of André Girard [radio broadcast, Paris].

Bibliography:

WB111a.   case, lower [pseud.]. "The Music Box: Mr. and Mrs. Sapp." *The Harvard Crimson*, 24 April 1951. "Mr. Sapp . . . uses a jazzy, dissonant idiom which hints at times of Milhaud and Hindemith, but is distinctly his own. Nobody will be whistling any of the tunes, but the work holds together well and indicates real ability."

Symphony in D Minor (1943-44): See W42; See also p. 11.

W112.   Suite for Orchestra, no. 1

Title on holograph: *Suite for Orchestra*.
Composition date and location: 1949; no location given in holograph, but the composer was living in Cambridge, Mass. during this period.
Dedication: "To Hans Rosbaud"
Publisher: New York: American Composers Alliance, 1952
Location of holograph: American Composers Alliance, 170 West 74th Street, New York, NY 10023.

Duration: 17 min.
Score: 122 p.
Instrumentation: 2 Fl., 2 Ob., 1 E. H., 2 Cl. in B♭, 2 Bn., 4 Hn., 3 Tpt. in C, 2 Tbn., 1 B.Tbn., 1 Tuba, 1 Piano, 1 Hp., Strings.
Movements: I. Fanfare (Allegro) -- II. Ode -- III. Scherzo -- IV. Elegy -- V. Finale
Notes: Orchestral version has not been performed. Arrangement for two pianos by the composer, 1949; holograph (39 p.) held by the composer. First performance of arrangement for two pianos: 17 May 1953, the composer and Norma Bertolami Sapp, at Kirkland House, Harvard University (broadcast on WGBH-FM on 18 May 1953).

W113.   Suite for Orchestra, no. 2

Title on holograph: *Second Suite for Orchestra.*
Composition date and location: 1952-56, in Lincoln and Cambridge, Mass., and Rome.
Publisher: New York: American Composers Alliance, 1957.
Location of holograph: The composer.
Duration: 26 min.
Score: 95 p.
Instrumentation: 1 Picc., 2 Fl., 2 Ob., 1 E. H., 2 Cl. in B♭, 1 B.Cl., 2 Bn., 1 C.Bn., 4 Hn., 3 Tpt. in C, 2 Tbn., 1 B.Tbn., 1 Tuba, 1 Piano, 1 Hp., Strings.
Movements: I. Andante mesto -- II. Allegro giocoso -- III. Adagietto -- IV. Allegro molto
Notes: From verso of title page: "This work was written down first in 1952 in Lincoln and Cambridge, Massachusetts. It underwent minor revision, largely alterations in the scoring, in 1956 in Rome."
Recording: See D23 (recording of P113a).

First performances:

P113a.   8 and 10 December 1968, Buffalo Philharmonic Orchestra, conducted by Lukas Foss, at Kleinhans Music Hall, Buffalo.

Other performances:

P113b.   17 February 1993, Buffalo Philharmonic Orchestra, conducted by Charles Peltz, at Slee Hall, State University of New York at Buffalo.

P113c.   13 April 1995, Cincinnati Philharmonia Orchestra, conducted by Gerhard Samuel, at Corbett Auditorium, University of Cincinnati College-Conservatory of Music.

Bibliography:

WB113a.   Sapp, Allen. "Program Notes: Second Suite (1952)." *Overture* [Buffalo Philharmonic Orchestra program] (24 November-10 December 1968):

23-27. "My Second Suite was composer in 1952 during a summer at Lincoln, Massachusetts, amidst lovely country. I had decided to write a companion work for my First Suite of 1949 but to give it greater breadth. Lukas Foss, for whom I had played my First Suite in Boston, had given me encouragement to proceed with a second, while helping to arrange an audition of both works with Charles Munch of the Boston Symphony. . . . It contains two moods—tenderness and irony; the two slow movements (particularly the third) are expressive and lyrical while the fast movements are brisk, peppy pieces, aggressively irreverent. The orchestration favors solo instruments and purposely omits percussion effects. Technical characteristics of the style of all my music written since about 1950 appear in the use of tonal and serial schemes. The second Suite is in E flat, with each movement a 'different sort of E flat'—but there are equally strong serial elements. Another composer making use of such ingredients in recent years is Aaron Copland. In Rome (1957) the Second Suite was re-orchestrated and edited. No structural changes were made, a few notes here and there cleaned up. In common with the fundamentally romantic character of the Second Suite there are many clean thematic fragments, tunes if you will, and a prevailing optimistic tone. The composer is of the persuasion which inclines to the idiosyncratic and personal work rather than to the modish."

WB113b. Dwyer, John. "The Gift of Music is Neatly Packaged by Foss, Levine, Sapp." *Buffalo Evening News*, 9 December 1968. "The impulse is romantic in its songful parts, the rhythmic episodes have a breezy loose-jointed accuracy which we hear instantly and instinctively as American Urban. . . . It speaks of a young man's America 1952, certainly the music-theater world of Copland, de Mille, Gershwin, Robbins, right down to the torch song and syncopated dance. . . . For all the baroque and serial craft, it comes on as a popular piece, I think, and someone ought to look it over for modern ballet possibilities. The audience understood it right away, naturally, as of their world, and there were appreciative curtain calls."

WB113c. Putnam, Thomas. "Sapp's Suite Performed." *Buffalo Courier Express*, 9 December 1968. "The Second Suite is a solid and immediately pleasing work, clearly written and full of rich musical statement. The orchestra played it with assurance and personal identification."

WB113d. Trotter, Herman. "Composer Sapp Basks in Orchestra Salute." *Buffalo News*, 18 February 1993. "It is a well crafted work which expresses many different emotions or moods effectively. Probing drama and gesture dominate the first movement, jocularity and rhythmic impetus the second, reflectiveness turns rather acrid in the slow movement, and in the finale an assertive demeanor prevails, with hollow strings answered by brass chirps and a strong coda capping the work."

W114.   The Double Image

Composition date and location: April 1957, in Rome.
Publisher: New York: American Composers Alliance, 1995.
Location of holograph: The composer.
Duration: 12 min.
Score: 59 p.
Instrumentation: 1 Picc., 2 Fl., 2 Ob., 1 E. H., 2 Cl. in B♭, 1 B. Cl., 2 Bn., 1 C. Bn., 4 Hn., 3 Tpt. in C, 2 Tbn., 1 B. Tbn., 1 Tuba, Timp., Strings.
Movements: I. Andante -- II. Allegro -- III. Tempo I°
Recording: See D5 (recording of P114a).

First performance:

P114a.   28 May 1967, Buffalo Philharmonic Orchestra, conducted by Lukas Foss, at a special concert "honoring Martin Meyerson on his inauguration as President of the State University of New York at Buffalo," Kleinhans Music Hall, Buffalo.

Bibliography:

WB114a.   Trotter, Herman E. "Program Notes: The Double Image (1957), Allen Sapp." *Overture* [Buffalo Philharmonic Orchestra program], 28 May 1967. Provides a biographical sketch, but little information about the composition except the following: "Because of the relatively complex structure of the work, the composer feels that the audience should accept it at first hearing as a pure listening experience and not spend too much time looking for clues or allusions to support its title."

WB114b.   Dwyer, John. "New Foss Concerto, Noted Cellist Spark Musical Excitement." *Buffalo Evening News*, 29 May 1967. "It has a lovely transparent orchestration, most effective in the lower registers. . . . This has, in a debtless way, the disembodied quality, the mirrored lake feeling of 'The Swan of Tuonela,' so beautiful a work that there is a general scholarly view there is something low-grade about it."

WB114c.   Putnam, Thomas. "Philharmonic, Fredonia, Present Final Concert." *Buffalo Courier Express*, 29 May 1967. "It is a handsome work, with some surprises (the odd ending, with its repeated phrases). Why was it not performed before this? The opening for trombone, with other instruments joining at selected pitches and thus coloring the line, was effective."

See also: WB19b.

W115.   Overture, "The Women of Trachis"

Medium: Chamber orchestra.
Composition date and location: November 1960, in Wellesley, Mass.
Publisher: New York: American Composers Alliance, 1995.
Location of holograph: The composer (multilith master).
Duration: 13 min.
Score: 50 p.
Instrumentation: 2 Ob., 2 Hn., 8 Vn., 3 Va., 3 Vc., 1 Cb.
1 movement: Quarter note = 72
Notes: This overture was composed originally for a performance of Sophocles' play at Wellesley College, May 5-6, 1961.
Recordings: see D15a-b (recording of P115a); introduction to "Discography/Webography" (p. 139).

First performance:

P115a.   27 November 1960, Boston Fine Arts Chamber Orchestra, conducted by Eleftherios Eleftherakis, at Lecture Hall in the Museum of Fine Arts, Boston.

Other known performances:

P115b.   14 and 16 April 1963, Buffalo Philharmonic Orchestra, conducted by Josef Krips, at Kleinhans Music Hall, Buffalo.

P115c.   15 May 1988, Ohio University Chamber Orchestra, conducted by Markand Thakar, at Recital Hall, Ohio University, Athens, Ohio.

Bibliography:

WB115a.   Chapin, Louis. "Music from Two Centuries Played by Fine Arts Group." *Christian Science Monitor*, 28 November 1960. "Allen Sapp, in his expressive overture . . . began with tightly separated groups of three staccato chords. Before long a smooth line appeared, to carry the ear from one chord group to the next. This relationship pervaded much of Mr. Sapp's piece, based on Sophocles' story, and became in a sense its unity, leaving the listener aware of breadth and power combined, though the ending needed more strength."

WB115b.   Wolffers, Jules. "Fine Arts Chamber Orchestra Superb." *Boston Herald*, 28 November 1960. "Allen Sapp's Overture to 'The Women of Trachis' is a paragon of unity with its thematic structure showing economy, variety and contrast."

WB115c.   Sapp, Allen. "Program Notes: Overture: "The Women of Trachis." *Overture* [Buffalo Philharmonic Orchestra program] (14-16 April 1963): 10-12. "Composition of the *Overture* was under the double stimulus of the orchestral commission [from the Boston Fine Arts Chamber Orchestra] and a commission to compose incidental music to the play [to be performed at Wellesley College]. . . . The music attempts to synthesize this story and to evoke the general spirit and feeling of Greek tragedy." The composer also provides a synopsis of Sophocles' play.

WB115d.   Gill, Kenneth. "Local Composers, Stern, Share Concert Spotlight." *Buffalo Courier-Express*, 15 April 1963. "Its dark and somber brooding was laid in complimentary fashion by Sunday's reading." The work was "well enough received to prompt Krips to a second playing of the work."

W116.   June

Medium: Wind quintet and string orchestra.
Composition date and location: 8 June 1961, in Wellesley, Mass.
Commissioned by: Boston Arts Festival, 1961.
Location of holograph: The composer.
Duration: 13 min.
Score: 110 p.
Instrumentation: 1 Fl., 1 Ob., 1 Cl. in B♭, 1 Bn., 1 Hn., Strings.
Movements: I. Allegro molto -- II. Poco scherzando -- III. Andantino -- IV. Adagio -- V. Poco scherzando -- VI. Allegro molto
Notes: Based on the poem by William Cullen Bryant.

First performance:

P116a.   14 June 1961, Fine Arts Woodwind Quintet (Vincent Cavalli, flute, Richard Summers, oboe, Felix Viscuglia, clarinet, Frank Nizarri, Bassoon, Ralph Pottle, French horn), with the Fine Arts Chamber Orchestra, conducted by Eleftherios Eleftherakis, at Small Stage, Boston Arts Festival.

Other known performances:

P116b.   10 July 1964, Robert Mols, flute, Allen Sigel, clarinet, Lowell Shaw, horn, Rodney Pierce, oboe, and Nelson Dayton, bassoon, with the Buffalo Symphonette, conducted by Fred Ressel, at Baird Recital Hall, State University of New York at Buffalo.

P116c.   25 September 1966, Robert Mols, flute, Allen Sigel, clarinet, Lowell Shaw, horn, Rodney Pierce, oboe, and Nelson Dayton, bassoon, with the Buffalo Symphonette, conducted by Fred Ressel, at Mary Seaton Room, Kleinhans Music Hall.

Bibliography:

WB116a.   Dwyer, John. "Suite by UB Composer Well Done in Premiere." *Buffalo Evening News*, 11 July 1964. "It poses a Bach chorale [*Wir müssen alle sterben*] line against the sounds and swift-changing moods of summer, reflecting the perverse and human inclination to rejoice in

nature and mourn its passing, at the same time. . . . [There was] a
graceful, airborne quality in some episodes, and a fair comprehension
of the sweet-sad idea. The composer was called for well-applauded
bows."

WB116b.   Gill, Ken. "Symphonette Is Featured at Festival." *Buffalo Courier-
Express,* 11 July 1964. "A well-conceived work in six short segments.
. . . In substance the music had a turn, of pleasant effect, from
academic form to stringent harmonizing and good ensemble projection."

W117.   Colloquies I

Title on holograph: *Colloquies*
Medium: Piano and string orchestra.
Composition date and location: June-September 1963, in Buffalo.
Dedication: "For Blanche and Clarence Obletz"
Location of holograph: The composer.
Duration: 16 min.
Score: 47 p.
Movements: I. Larghetto -- II. Allegro molto -- III. Larghetto -- IV. Allegro molto
Notes: From preliminary text: "This work was composed at the suggestion of David
Diamond who was to have directed its first performance on November 23, 1963."
The performance was postponed in respect to U. S. President John F. Kennedy, who
was assassinated the previous day.

First performance:

P117a.   23 February 1964, Norma Bertolami Sapp, piano soloist, with the
Buffalo Philharmonic Orchestra, conducted by the composer, at
Kleinhans Music Hall, Buffalo.

Other known performance:

P117b.   31 July 1980, Norma Bertolami Sapp, piano soloist, with the Congress
of Strings, conducted by Phillip Spurgeon, at Corbett Auditorium,
University of Cincinnati College-Conservatory of Music.

Bibliography:

WB117a.   Sapp, Allen. "Program Notes: Colloquies." *Overture* [Buffalo
Philharmonic Orchestra program] (23 February-3 March 1964): 12.
"*Colloquies* is a series of four conversations in which the element of
dialogue, interchange of ideas, and varied discourse all play a part. Not
a concertino or concerto grosso or a concertante piece, the work is best
thought of as an amiable, at times serious and tender and at other
times capricious and arch, encounter between persons who know each
other very well. If there are meanings, they lie in the nuances of
differing combinations of strings and solo instrument. In structure
there are symmetries between first and third, and second and fourth

sections—somewhat like the XVIIth century Church suite. There are no special technical features other than the composer's customary blended use of unifying principles of tonality and serial processes. Written in the main as a work for Norma Bertolami, *Colloquies* recalls the composer's *Concertino* No. 1 of 1942 and reflects twenty years of life together."

WB117b. Dwyer, John. "New Composition by Dr. Sapp Applauded on Foss Program." *Buffalo Evening News,* 24 February 1964. "*Colloquies* is an intimate discourse for two voices. . . . Sapp's string orchestra voiced the motifs and developments quite well. . . . His pianist was right up to the line in the casual asides, dreamy turns of phrase and swift interjections. Composer and soloist acknowledged cordial rounds of applause."

WB117c. Gill, Kenneth. "Response is Varied at Concert." *Buffalo Courier-Express*, 24 February 1964. "*Colloquies* was mildly received and closely inspected for program values. Written . . . as a solo frame for his wife's playing, the sequence spoke as a dialogue between the solo and accompaniment with dissonance continuing in its harmonic outline and a contrast of instrumental chatter and lyric impressionism alternating throughout. Bertolami was a dominant figure at the piano, and Sapp's control of the string solos and choirs effected good ensemble."

W118. *Imaginary Creatures: A Bestiary for the Credulous*

Title on holograph: *Imaginary Creatures.*
Medium: Harpsichord and chamber orchestra.
Composition date and location: June 1981, in Cincinnati.
Commissioned by: Cincinnati Chamber Orchestra.
Dedication: "for Eiji Hashimoto"
Publisher: New York: American Composers Alliance, 1995.
Location of holograph: The composer.
Duration: 17 min.
Score: 70 p.
Instrumentation: 2 Fl., 2 Ob., 2 Cl. in B♭, 2 Bn., 2 Hn., 11 Vn., 4 Va., 3 Vc., 2 Cb., Hpscd. solo.
Movements: I. Halcyons (Swiftly) -- II. Basilisk -- III. Unicorn -- IV. Phoenix -- V. Centaurs
Notes: The program for the first performance listed the full title; this is the composer's preferred form of the title.
Recordings: see D39 (excerpt); introduction to "Discography/Webography" (p. 139).

First performance:

P118a. 21 March 1982, Eiji Hashimoto, harpsichord, with the Cincinnati Chamber Orchestra, conducted by Paul Nadler, at Emery Theatre, Cincinnati.

Bibliography:

WB118a. Chute, James. "Skill, Enjoyment Fill CCO Performance." *Cincinnati Post*, 22 March 1982. "With the exception of the unconvincing second movement, "Basilisk," in which solo harpsichord, flute, violin and cello simultaneously play seemingly independent, drawn-out melodic lines, the piece is vivid, colorful, and holds a listener's interest."

WB118b. Palmer, Bob. "CCO Fetes Bach and the Beasts." *Cincinnati Enquirer*, 23 March 1982. "All five of the movements feature the harpsichord—as part of the texture, or in dialogue with other instruments. And several of the movements project landscapes of richly imaginative texture. The "Unicorn" created an especially attractive scene, with its wispy veil of sustained high strings and its innocently wandering oboe. . . . The piece was most gratifyingly balanced in its final movement, where orchestra and soloist react in concerto fashion."

W119. Crennelations

Medium: Tenor and orchestra.
Composition date and location: April-October 1982, in Cincinnati.
Dedication: "For James Riley"
Publisher: New York: American Composers Alliance, 1995.
Location of holograph: The composer.
Duration: 22 min.
Score: 135 p.
Vocal range: A♯ - b′
Instrumentation: 2 Fl., 2 Ob., 2 Cl. in B♭, 2 Bn., 4 Hn., 2 Tpt. in C, 1 Tpt. in B♭, 3 Tbn., 1 Tuba, T. Dr., Solo Vn. (obbligato), Strings, Tenor.
1 movement: "A poor clerk I, 'Arnaut the less' they call me" (Eighth note=126-132)
Notes: This work is a setting of Ezra Pound's "Marvoil," from *Personæ*. *Crennelations* is misspelled as *Crewellations* in the tenth edition of *International Who's Who in Music and Musicians' Directory*. Arrangement for two pianos by the composer, 1982; holograph (48 p.) held by the composer.

First performance:

P119a. 26 February 1983, David Adams, tenor, Anna Choi, violin obbligato, with the Concert Orchestra of the University of Cincinnati College-Conservatory of Music, conducted by Teri Murai, at Corbett Auditorium, University of Cincinnati College-Conservatory of Music.

W120. Serenade for Flute and Strings after Lyrics of Simonides at Ceos

Medium: Flute and string orchestra.
Composition dates: 5 March 1983-27 June 1984.

Dedication: "To George Hambrecht"
Location of holograph: The composer.
Duration: 19 min.
Score: 97 p.
Instrumentation: 8 Vn., 5 Va., 6 Vc., 3 Cb., Fl solo. The score calls for the strings to be arranged in five small groups around the stage, with the flute at center stage.
Movements: I. Allegretto charmante (Ritornello) -- II. Larghetto doloroso -- III. Presto brillante
Notes: No performances.

W121.   Xenón Ciborium

Composition date and location: 15 June 1982-26 October 1985, in Cincinnati.
Commissioned by: Philharmonia Orchestra of the University of Cincinnati College-Conservatory of Music.
Dedication: "Composed as a work to honor a great musician, a splendid teacher and a dear friend, Gerhard Samuel"
Publisher: New York: American Composers Alliance, 1995.
Location of holograph: The composer.
Duration: 11 min.
Score: 19 p.
Instrumentation: 3 Fl., 1 Alto Fl., 3 Ob., 1 E. H., 1 Cl. in E♭, 3 Cl. in B♭, 1 B. Cl., 1 Cb. Cl., 3 Bn., 1 C. Bn., 6 Hn., 1 Tpt. in E♭, 2 Tpt. in C, 2 Tpt. in B♭, 3 Tbn., 1 B. Tbn., 2 Tubas, 1 Hp., 1 Cel., 1 Mar., 1 Vib., Strings.
1 movement: Eighth note = 60
Recording: See D33 (recording of P121a); D37 (excerpt).

First performance:

P121a.   11 October 1986, Philharmonia Orchestra of the University of Cincinnati College-Conservatory of Music, conducted by Gerhard Samuel, at Corbett Auditorium, University of Cincinnati College-Conservatory of Music.

W122.   A Concerto for Chamber Orchestra, "The Four Reasons"

Composition date and location: February-December 1993, in Cincinnati.
Dedication: Cincinnati Chamber Orchestra
Publisher: New York: American Composers Alliance, 1996.
Location of holograph: The composer.
Duration: 21 min.
Score: 109 p.
Instrumentation: 2 Fl., 2 Ob., 2 Cl. in B♭, 2 Bn., 2 Hn., 2 Tpt. in C, 1 Piano, Strings.
Movements: I. A Classical Sonata-Allegro (Allegro Molto) -- II. A Theme and Variations (Fluently) -- III. A Fugue (Larghetto) -- IV. A Rondo (Vivace)
Notes: The work is an orchestration of four movements from other works by Sapp. The first movement of the *Concerto* is the first movement of *Piano Sonata III*; the

second movement of the *Concerto* is the third movement of *Piano Sonata IV*; the third movement of the *Concerto* is the first movement of *Piano Sonata II*; the fourth movement of the *Concerto* is the fifth movement of *Polyhedra*. The key centers of the movements form the composer's initials: I = A, II = D, III = E♭ ("Es" in German, a homophone for "S"), returning to A for movement IV.
Recording: See introduction to "Discography/Webography" (p. 139).

First performance:

P122a.   20 March 1994, Cincinnati Chamber Orchestra, conducted by Keith Lockhart, at Memorial Hall, Cincinnati.

Bibliography:

WB122a.   Gelfand, Janelle.   "Chamber Orchestra Has 'Four Reasons' to Celebrate 20th." *Cincinnati Enquirer*, 20 March 1994. In this interview, serving as a preview to the concert, Sapp discusses the character of the work, his service as a member of the board of directors for the Cincinnati Chamber Orchestra, and briefly comments upon his period of private study with Aaron Copland.

WB122b.   Pratt, Holly.   "Allen Sapp: *The Four Reasons*."   Program notes, Cincinnati Chamber Orchestra, 20 March 1994. Although Sapp has never commented directly about the meaning of the title *The Four Reasons* (or on the obvious reference to Vivaldi), he probably had in mind four significant events occurring in 1993 which caused him to reflect upon his earlier music. Pratt writes, "The concerto is consciously retrospective, written in a year marked by milestones for the composer . . . 1993 was the year of Sapp's official retirement from university teaching; of his Harvard class's 50-year reunion; and of his 50th wedding anniversary.   Most importantly for this new piece, the production of a 20-volume complete edition[16] of his music put Sapp in touch with his earlier compositions again.   'The vitality, the personality, and the strong Romantic qualities of the earlier music didn't shock me, they pleased me. . . . The years between the earliest and the most recent music do not form an impassable gulf.'"

WB122c.   Gelfand, Janelle.   "Anniversary Celebrated in Style: Concert Review." *Cincinnati Enquirer*, 21 March 1994. "Each of its four movements had a distinctive, imaginative character, specifically tailored for its performers. . . . The lively first movement was a study in crisp playing, illuminating the work's themes and motives as they bounced between the instruments. . . . The second movement took its cue from 1920s Paris, offering a kaleidoscope of color changes and witty conversation. The most poignant lyricism came in the third movement, suffused with a post-romantic hue and ending on an atmospheric note.   The sheer brio of the performance was contagious in the finale, a buoyant summary of familiar motives."

ORCHESTRAL, UNFINISHED

W123.   Concerto for Piano and Orchestra

Composition date and location: 1940; no location given in holograph, but the composer was living in Cambridge, Mass. during this period.
Dedication: "To Elsie Louise Jones"
Location of holograph: The composer.
Score: 43, [28], [5] p.
Instrumentation: 2 Fl., 2 Ob., 2 Cl. in B♭, 2 Bn., 4 Hn., 3 Tpt. in C, 2 Tbn., Strings, Piano solo.
Movements: I. Allegro molto -- II. Andante con expressione -- III. Presto
Notes: Incomplete work: only the first movement appears to be finished; orchestration may also be unfinished in this movement. The second movement is largely finished, but stops just before the cadenza. Only the first 43 measures of the third movement are sketched out, consisting mostly of the piano part.

W124.   Concerto for Piano in One Movement

Composition date and location: 1942; no location given in holograph, but the composer was living in Cambridge, Mass. during this period.
Dedication: "To Norma Bertolami"
Location of holograph: The composer.
Score: [16] p.
Instrumentation: 3 Fl., 3 Ob., 3 Cl. in B♭, 3 Bn., 4 Hn., 3 Tpt. in C, 3 Tbn., 1 Tuba, B. Dr., Timp., Strings, Piano solo.
Movements: I. Introduction (Lento) II. Allegro
Notes: This appears to be an incomplete work, since the last page of the score contains only the piano part, and does not end in a double bar.

W125.   Introduction and Allegro for Violin and Orchestra

Composition date and location: 1942; no location given in holograph, but the composer was living in Cambridge, Mass. during this period.
Dedication: "To Viviane Bertolami"
Location of holograph: The composer.
Score: [14], [5] p.
Instrumentation: 2 Fl., 2 Ob., 3 Cl. in B♭, 2 Bn., 4 Hn., 3 Tpt. in C, 3 Tbn., 1 Piano, Vn. solo.
Movements: I. Introduction (Lento) II. Allegro
Notes: Incomplete work: only the first movement appears to be finished. The second movement is unfinished, with only the first 31 measures sketched out.

W126.   *Intermezzo for Orchestra*

Composition date and location: 1950, in Cambridge, Mass.
Location of holograph: The composer (pencil sketches).
Duration: 7 min.
Score: 7 p. of fair copy piano arrangement; 11 p. of draft piano sketches
Instrumentation: Not indicated in fair copy piano arrangement; draft piano sketch score contains occasional indications of orchestration, essentially calling for standard orchestra.
1 movement: Allegro
Notes: Piano arrangement has not been performed.

W127.   *The Heptagon*

Alternate Title: *The Septagon*
Composition dates and location: Begun 29 June 1957, in Rome; continued in Cambridge and Wellesley, 1959.
Location of holograph: The composer (pencil sketches).
Score: [30] p. of draft piano sketches.
Instrumentation: Draft piano sketch score contains occasional indications of orchestration, essentially calling for standard orchestra.
Movements: None of the movements bear verbal or metronomic tempo indications. An outline for the work contained in the same folder as the sketches gives the following labels to the movements: I. The Seven Ideas -- II. 7/8 -- III. 7 + 7 + 7 + 7 + 7 + 7 + 7 -- IV. Septuplets -- V. Septet *concertino* -- VI. 7 layers, i.e., 7 mensurations -- VII. The Seven Ideas Again.
Notes: The title *The Septagon* appears on the title page of the holograph, but *The Septagon* appears on the caption of the first page of music and on the headers of many subsequent pages.   Movements I through V appear to be complete.   The sketches for movement VI consist only of 48 blank measures in mixed meter, with full orchestration indicated in the left margin.   Since the sketches for movements I through V are all in piano score form, it is possible that a sixth movement piano score existed at one time and is now lost.   The title of movement VII from the outline perhaps indicates that the first movement was to be repeated to conclude the work.

WIND ENSEMBLE

W128.   *Colloquies III*

Medium: Piano and 10 winds.
Composition date and location: June 1981, in Cincinnati.
Location of holograph: Missing. Sold at auction during a fund-raising campaign for WGUC-FM, Cincinnati, ca. 1985.   Records of the sale could not be located at WGUC-FM.
Duration: 17 min.

Score: 22 p.
Instrumentation: 1 Fl., 1 Ob., 1 Cl. in B♭, 1 Bn., 2 Hn., 2 Tpt. in B♭, 1 Tbn., 1 Tuba, Piano.
1 movement: Quarter note = 60

First performance:

P128a.   25 April 1982, C.C.M. Contemporary Music Ensemble, conducted by Piotr Gajewski, at Patricia Corbett Theatre, University of Cincinnati College-Conservatory of Music.

Other known performance:

P128b.   9 April 1988, ensemble conducted by Craft Beck (Kathie Stewart, flute, Marcia Jaeger, oboe, Eugene Marquis, clarinet, Billy Harden, bassoon, Bill Cochran and Kathy Widlar, horns, Drew Cremisio and Bill Tipkemper, trumpets, Colleen MacDonald, trombone, David Aabot, tuba, Michael Chertock, piano), at a concert of the Cincinnati Composers' Guild, Fine Arts Building, Northern Kentucky University, Highland Heights, Kentucky.

W129.   Fanfare for WGUC

Medium: Brass ensemble.
Composition date and location: January 1982, in Cincinnati.
Commissioned by: WGUC-FM, Cincinnati.
Location of holograph: The composer.
Duration: 20 sec.
Score: 1 p.
Instrumentation: 4 Tpt., 4 Hn., 3 Tbn., 1 Tuba.
1 movement: Quarter note = 88

First performance:

P129a.   10:10 A.M., 2 June 1982, the Brass Ensemble of the College-Conservatory of Music, University of Cincinnati College-Conservatory of Music, conducted by Betty Glover, performed and broadcast from the studio of WGUC-FM, Cincinnati.

W130.   The Cheektowaga and Tonawanda Divisions

Medium: Wind ensemble.
Composition date and location: 6 September 1983, in Cincinnati.
Dedication: "for Frank Cipolla"
Location of holograph: The composer.
Duration: 18 min.
Score: 126 p.

Instrumentation: 1 Picc., 2 Fl., 2 Ob., 1 Cl. in E♭, 6 Cl. in B♭, 1 B. Cl., 1 Cb. Cl., 2 Bn., 1 Sop. Sax., 1 Alto Sax., 1 Ten. Sax., 1 Bar. Sax., 4 Hn., 4 Tpt. in B♭, 3 Tbn., 1 B. Tbn., 1 Euph., 2 Tubas, 2 Mar., 1 Glock., 1 Set of Bells, 1 Vib., 1 Xyl., 1 Cel.
1 movement: Half note = 66

First performance:

P130a.   11 December 1983, U.B. Wind Ensemble, conducted by Frank Cipolla, at Slee Hall, State University of New York at Buffalo.

Other known performance:

P130b.   7 March 1984, Cincinnati Wind Ensemble, conducted by R. Robert Hornyak, at Corbett Auditorium, University of Cincinnati College-Conservatory of Music.

W131.   The Four Winds

Medium: Wind ensemble.
Composition date and location: [summer] 1984, in Cincinnati. The date "July 30 1984" appears on p. 75 of the holograph.
Dedication: "To Robert Hornyak"
Publisher: New York: American Composers Alliance, 1995.
Location of holograph: The composer.
Duration: 16 min.
Score: 105 p.
Instrumentation: 1 Picc., 2 Fl., 2 Ob., 1 Cl. in E♭, 6 Cl. in B♭, 1 B. Cl., 1 Cb. Cl., 2 Bn., 1 Sop. Sax., 1 Alto Sax., 1 Ten. Sax., 1 Bar. Sax., 4 Hn., 4 Tpt. in B♭, 4 Tbn., 1 Euph., 2 Tubas, 1 Mar., Timp., Tom Tom, S. D., B. D.
Movements: I. Notos (the South Wind) -- II. Boreas (the North Wind) -- III. Zephyros (the West Wind) -- IV. Euros (the East Wind)
Recording: See D11 (recording of P131b).

First performance:

P131a.   1 February 1985, Cincinnati Wind Ensemble, conducted by R. Robert Hornyak, at Corbett Auditorium, University of Cincinnati College-Conservatory of Music.

P131b.   27 February 1985, Cincinnati Wind Ensemble, conducted by R. Robert Hornyak, at the College Band Directors National Association Conference, Boulder, Colorado.

W132.   Cincinnati Morality and Consolation

Medium: Wind ensemble.
Composition date and location: Summer 1985, in Cincinnati.

Location of holograph: The composer.
Duration: 10 min.
Score: 68 p.
Instrumentation: 1 Picc., 2 Fl., 1 Alto Fl., 4 Ob., 1 Cl. in E♭, 6 Cl. in B♭, 1 B. Cl., 1 Cb. Cl., 3 Bn., 1 C. Bn., 2 Alto Sax., 1 Ten. Sax., 1 Bar. Sax., 4 Hn., 6 Tpt. in B♭, 4 Tbn., 1 B. Tbn., 1 Euph., 4 Tubas.
1 movement: Quarter note = 120

First performance:

P132a.   21 May 1986, Cincinnati Wind Ensemble, conducted by R. Robert Hornyak, at Corbett Auditorium, University of Cincinnati College-Conservatory of Music.

DRAMATIC

W133.   The Ascent of F-6

Medium: Incidental music for two pianos, intended to supplement the incidental music of Benjamin Britten.[17]
Composition date and location: Ca. spring 1940, in Cambridge, Mass.
Location of holograph: Not located.[18]
Notes: Play by Christopher Isherwood and W. H. Auden.

First performances:

P133a.   2-4 May 1940, Harold Shapero and Allen Sapp, pianists, at Sanders Theatre, Harvard University.

W134.   The Family Reunion

Medium: Incidental music for piano solo.
Composition date and location: Ca. autumn 1940, in Cambridge, Mass.
Location of holograph: Not located.[19]
Notes: Play by T. S. Eliot. Apparently only the prelude was precisely notated. The composer recalls that he "wrote incidental music: preludes, interludes, all kinds of things. I played on the piano, there being no money for anything else. . . . The music for *Family Reunion*, I wrote out the prelude, which was a rather dark and gloomy tone poem really. Several pages of rather dark atonal kind of music. It was a really emotional kind of thing. I sketched and had notes for the other interludes. There were about eight interludes. . . . Harry and Agathe [the principal characters] go into periods when they are obviously disjuncted from the current reality, going into a kind of dream stance, or inner psychological state. I wrote interludes which corresponded to that. I worked out those [scenes] with notes and a kind of sketch of where I wanted to go and texture and so on, but without writing notes, because I didn't want to get into the business of the actors following the timing, you see, of my piece. I

was interested in the idea that from rehearsal to rehearsal, from dress rehearsal and performance . . . there were fluctuations. Unlike movie music, where you get something which is frozen and you can time it. I didn't know [how long the scenes would last], and that was one of the advantages of my being there, to add a little bit, to shorten a little bit. That's why it was a kind of approach which is very interesting really."[20]

First performances:

P134a. 8-9 November 1940, Harvard Dramatic Club, directed by S. Roger Sheppard and A. George Rock; incidental music for piano performed by Allen Sapp.

Bibliography:

WB134a. R. C. H. "The Playgoer: 'The Family Reunion' at Sanders Theatre." *Harvard Crimson*, 8 November 1940. "'The Family Reunion' is student-produced in its entirety. It is directed, staged and acted entirely by students. Even the overture and chorus-accompaniment were originally composed and are played with heightening effect by Allen Sapp '43."

WB134b. "The Stage in Review: Sanders Theatre, 'The Family Reunion.'" *Boston Globe*, 9 November 1940. "The Harvard Dramatic Club prepared 'The Family Reunion' with great earnestness, and for that they deserve credit. So does Allen Sapp, for the original piano music he performs during the play."

WB134c. A. W. W. "The Theater: Harvard Dramatic Club 'The Family Reunion.'" *Boston Herald*, 9 November 1940. "The music, however good in itself, distracts one alarmingly from the poetic choruses. The whole subject of incidental music to plays is one that can not, of course, be discussed at the end of a review!"

W135.   Alice in Wonderland

Medium: Vocal and incidental music for two pianos by Irving Fine and Allen Sapp.
Composition date and location: Ca. spring 1942, in Cambridge, Mass.
Location of holograph: Not located.[21]
Notes: Text adapted for the stage by Eva LeGallienne and Florida Friebus from Lewis Carroll's *Alice in Wonderland* and *Through the Looking-Glass*.

First performances:

P135a. 22-23 May 1942, students of the Erskine School, directed by Phyllis Stohl; incidental music and vocal accompaniment for two pianos performed by Irving Fine and Allen Sapp, at John Hancock Hall, Boston.

Bibliography:

WB135a.   Pollack, Howard. *Harvard Composers: Walter Piston and His Students from Elliott Carter to Frederic Rzewski.* Metuchen, N.J.; London: Scarecrow Press, 1992, p. 135. "During the war, Fine also wrote some music for . . . Eva LeGallienne's adaptation of Carroll's *Alice in Wonderland.* . . . Fine needed to write many more songs as well as incidental music for the *Alice* production, and to meet the deadline, he called on the help of a young Harvard student, Allen Sapp. The show was a local success."

W136.   *The Trojan Women*

Medium: Incidental music for chorus, two female voices, flute, and harp or harpsichord.[22]
Composition date and location: Ca. winter 1960, in Wellesley, Mass.
Location of holograph: Not located.[23]
Notes: Play by Euripides.

First performances:

P136a.   25 March 1960, Greek Department of Wellesley College, directed by Patricia Graham, Mary Lefkowitz, and Barbara McCarthy, at Jewett Auditorium, Wellesley College, Wellesley, Mass.; incidental music performed by Howard Brown, flute, Allen Sapp, harpsichord, and student chorus and soloists. Performance repeated by the same personnel on 8 May 1960 at the Hay Outdoor Theatre, Wellesley College.

W137.   *The Way of the World*

Medium: Presumably a single composition for solo female voice, perhaps with piano accompaniment; it was simply entitled "Song" in the program.
Composition date and location: Ca. spring 1960, in Wellesley, Mass.
Location of holograph: Not located.[24]
Notes: Play by William Congreve.

First performances:

P137a.   22-23 April 1960, Vera Clifford, vocalist, at Jewett Arts Center, Wellesley College, Wellesley, Mass.

W138.   *The Frogs*

Medium: Tape recording of incidental music for piano, violin, flute, and violoncello, occasionally manipulated electronically.

Composition date and location: Ca. winter 1961, in Wellesley, Mass.
Location of original tape recording: The composer.
Duration of tape: 30 min.
Notes: Play by Aristophanes. No holograph score exists for the music on the tape. The composer combined various tape recordings of music composed by various baroque, classical, and romantic composers with his own original music for piano solo, resulting in a *music concrète* incidental music tape. This composition is one of only two works Sapp would compose for tape performance, the other being incidental music for *The Women of Trachis*. Writing for tape was necessary in this case since the play was to be performed in the college's swimming pool!

First performance:

P138a.   13 February 1961, accompanying a cast of the Greek Department of Wellesley College, directed by Barbara McCarthy, at Wellesley College Natatorium, Wellesley, Mass.

W139.   *The Women of Trachis*

Medium: Tape recording of incidental music for percussion and flute.
Composition date and location: Ca. spring 1961, in Wellesley, Mass.
Location of original tape recording: The composer.
Duration of tape: 14 min.
Notes: Play by Sophocles. No holograph score exists for the music on the tape.

First performance:

P139a.   5 May 1961, Barnswallows Dramatic Association (Wellesley College), directed by Paul R. Barstow, at Hay Outdoor Theatre, Wellesley College, Wellesley, Mass.

WORKS WRITTEN UNDER A PSEUDONYM

Several Sapp holographs bear pseudonyms. The earliest example is probably his *Sonata Movement for String Trio* (W50, written under the pseudonym "Spēs"), an undated holograph most likely written and submitted to the George Arthur Knight Prize Competition in 1941. Sapp's authorship of this work is confirmed through an additional title page found with the holograph. The second known example is his *Cello Sonata I* (W51, written under the pseudonym "Hezekiah Fundless") which was the recipient of the 1942 Bohemians Prize at Harvard University. His authorship of this work was confirmed through documentation at the Harvard University Archives where the holograph is located. The third known example is *And the Bombers Went Home* (W53, written under the pseudonym "S. M. Sebbél"), which was apparently submitted for the 1944 George Arthur Knight Prize at Harvard University, according to an inscription on the holograph title page. His authorship of this work was confirmed by the existence of a second fair copy holograph which was sent to his fiancée, Norma Bertolami, in January 1943. Two other works by Sapp are likely to have once had title pages bearing pseudonyms since they were submitted for composition contests at Harvard, but these title pages are now missing; these works are: *Violin Sonata II* (W54; awarded 1949 George Arthur Knight Prize); and *Viola Sonata* (W55; awarded 1950 Bohemians Prize).

The following three brief compositions (W140-142) appear as examples of musical encryption within Sapp's text *Censorship Cryptanalysis* (B2), all bearing pseudonyms. This text was prepared for use in training his staff in the Civil Censorship Division of the United States Forces (European Theater), where Sapp served as Chief Cryptanalyst. Most of the 143 examples of coded messages in this text are handwritten or typed letters; a few are graphic documents (e.g., chess diagrams, artistic sketches, and children's drawings). The three musical compositions are all in Sapp's hand, but no acknowledgement to his authorship of the works was made within the text. Sapp confirmed his authorship of these works in a telephone conversation with the author on 19 August 1995: "It was a long summer of working on this book, so I couldn't resist taking a few musical diversions."

W140.   *Aria fuer Klavier*

Pseudonym: Karl Meyer
Medium: Piano solo.
Composition date and location (from colophon): 18 July 1946, in Frankfurt am Main, Germany.
Location of holograph: missing.
Duration: 2 min.
Score: 4 p.
Location in *Censorship Cryptanalysis*: Volume I, example BM-1.
1 movement: Nicht langsam
Notes: No performances. From the explanatory notes in Volume II: "Only the music appearing in the treble clef, i.e., the melody, is to be considered in the recovery of the secret text. Each different note is substituted for a Morse value. Dotted half notes, quarters, and sixteenth notes are used for dots; half notes, eighth notes and dotted quarters are used for dashes. The end of each measure is a break. To recover the secret text take out in order all the notes in the melody, marking off each group of notes at the end of every measure. Then substitute the proper More [*sic*] symbol and convert to plain text. MESSAGE: AMI [American] OFFIZIERE IN PASSAU VON EINHEIT WILLI BERTA AQT [acht] ERSQOSSEN [erschossen]."

W141.   *Rhapsodie pour les courageux*

Pseudonym: Jacques Troisaent
Medium: Violoncello and piano.
Composition date and location: [July or August] 1946; no location given in score, but the composer was stationed in Frankfurt am Main, Germany during this period.
Location of holograph: missing.
Duration: 2 min.
Score: 2 p.

Location in *Censorship Cryptanalysis*: Volume I, example BM-2.
1 movement: Tres lent
Notes: No performances. From the explanatory notes in Volume II: "The secret text is inserted in the cello part only. The remainder of the music can be ignored as far as the secret text goes. To recover the secret text take out each note as it occurs in the cello part and substitute the values given in the "Cipher" section below [in text] for each note. The length of notes, and the rhythm, etc. have no bearing on the system. . . . MESSAGE: DREI HUNDERT LITER AMI [American] BENZIN VERKAUFT. AQT [acht] TAUSEND GRAM FETT UND ZWEI HUNDERT LITER FISCHOEL IN LAGER. (SPSP)"

W142.   *Basse de M. Laurent*

Pseudonym: François Gédalge
Medium: Four unmarked, untexted voices (two treble clef, two bass clef).
Composition date and location: 5 August 1946; no location given in score, but the composer was stationed in Frankfurt am Main, Germany during this period.
Location of holograph: missing.
Duration: 1 min.
Score: 3 p.
Location in *Censorship Cryptanalysis*: Volume I, example BM-3.
1 movement: No tempo indication; cut time meter indicated.
Notes: No performances. From the explanatory notes in Volume II: "It would be almost impossible for anyone but a professional musician to solve this problem because a knowledge of harmony is essential. The whole exercise must first be analyzed according to the normal "Functional Harmony" apparatus of the XIX century. There are normally throughout the exercise two changes of harmony per measure, but this is not strictly adhered to. The various voices and melodies have no bearing on the secret message except insofar as they are part of the main harmonic stream. To recover the secret text first analyze the whole piece. Then treat each new change of harmony as a cipher unit and solve as a monoalphabetic system. . . . MESSAGE: AUTOBAHNBRUECKE AQT [acht] KM NOERDLICH ROSENHEIM WIRD MORGEN GESPRENGT WERDEN."

MISSING WORK

W143.   *Four Motets*

Medium: Male chorus a cappella (TTBB).
Composition date and location: 1953, Cambridge, Mass.?
Location of holograph: Missing.
Duration: approx. 15 min.
Movements: I. Pacem relinquo vobis [Communion, Missa pro pace] -- II. Da pacem, Domine [introit, XVIII Sunday after Pentecost] -- III. Deus, auctor pacis [postcommunion, Missa pro pace] -- IV. Hodie nobis de caelo [responsory, Nativity of Our Lord, lesson II]

Notes: No performances. No copy of the score could be located. The work is cited in the list of Sapp's compositions in *Baker's Biographical Dictionary of Musicians*, 5th ed. (B56) and *The International Cyclopedia of Music and Musicians*, 9th ed. (B64), presumably reported by the composer to the editors of those publications. Sapp apparently used these four motets as the basis for the choral movements in *Canticum novum pro pace* (W107).[25]

III. DISCOGRAPHY/WEBOGRAPHY

THIS DISCOGRAPHY IS ARRANGED ALPHABETICALLY by title, with multiple recordings of a work listed chronologically by recording date. This list contains all commercially produced sound recordings (both in-print and deleted), as well as all known non-commercial recordings located in libraries, archives, or available on the world-wide web. Each recording is assigned a "D" number; when a non-commercial recording exists in multiple formats, these entries share the same "D" number differentiated by a lowercase letter (D1a, D1b, etc., with the master or "best copy" assigned "a").

Several more recordings of Sapp compositions will become available over the next several years through new recording and sound file mounting projects. Keith Lockhart plans to record three works conducting the Cincinnati Chamber Orchestra in autumn 1996, to be released on the Composers Recordings (CRI) label; these works are *Overture, "The Women of Trachis"* (W115), *Imaginary Creatures* (W118, featuring Eiji Hashimoto as harpsichord soloist), and *A Concerto for Chamber Orchestra: "The Four Reasons"* (W122). The *Allen Sapp Home Page* (B149), mounted by the author on the world-wide web server at the Ohio State University Music & Dance Library, currently contains seven complete sound file copies of private recital recordings (see D16b, D18b, D19b, D20b, D22b, D24b, and D32c). Additional sound files of Sapp compositions will be added to the *Allen Sapp Home Page* as clearance is obtained from performers to mount broadcast-quality recordings. The *Allen Sapp Home Page* may be found at the following URL address:

http://muslib.lib.ohio-state.edu/sapp/index.htm

This site also contains sound files corresponding to all musical examples in this book (see pages following p. 50). Citations for these excerpts are included at the end of this list in example order (D34-41), with see references included in the alphabetical list.

Andante for Orchestra (W110)

D1a. New York Philharmonic, conducted by Rudolph Ganz (recording of P110a). New York: Carnegie Hall Recording Co. Recorded 18 April 1942. Non-commercial instantaneous acetate recording (two 12-inch discs, 78 r.p.m.). Ohio State University Music & Dance Library.

D1b. Analog reel tape preservation copy and analog cassette public use copy of D1a, Ohio State University Music & Dance Library, 12 November 1995.

And the Bombers Went Home (W53)

D2. Martin Gelland, violin, Lennart Wallin, piano. On *Lyrische Aspekte unseres Jahrhunderts*. Vienna; Wilmington, Del.: Vienna Modern Masters, VMM 2017. Recorded 24 August 1995, Tonhallen, Sundavall, Sweden; released December 1995. Compact disc.

Colloquies IV: "The Lament for Adonis" (W74)

D3. Lee Fiser, violoncello, Kenneth Griffiths, piano. Non-commercial analog reel tape recording, 30 October 1988 (recording of P74e). Ohio State University Music & Dance Library.

Colloquies VI: "Socrates and Phaedrus Speak of Love by the Banks of the Illisus" (W81)

D4. Bloom, Sara Lambert, oboe (with Elizabeth Pridonoff, piano). On *Premiere Chamber Works*. Baton Rouge, La.: Centaur, CRC 2217. Recorded June 1993, Watson Hall, University of Cincinnati College-Conservatory of Music; released 1995. Compact disc. See also: WB81a (review).

Concertino for Piano and Chamber Orchestra (W111): See D42.

The Double Image (W114)

D5. Buffalo Philharmonic Orchestra, conducted by Lukas Foss. Non-commercial analog reel tape recording, 28 May 1967 (recording of P114a). Ohio State University Music & Dance Library.

Five Landscapes (W100)

D6a. Harvard-Radcliffe Music Clubs Chorus, conducted by Howard M. Brown (recording of P100a). Boston: Trans Radio Productions. Recorded 11 February 1951. Non-commercial acetate recording (12-inch disc, 33 1/3 r.p.m., transferred from a wire master recording now missing). Ohio State University Music & Dance Library.

D6b. Analog reel tape preservation copy and analog cassette public use copy of D6a, Ohio State University Music & Dance Library, 15 November 1995.

D7. University of Buffalo Composers' Choral Group, conducted by Dowell Multer. Non-commercial analog reel tape recording, 23 February 1968 (recording of P100d). Tape Archives, Music Department, State University of New York at Buffalo. (Movements I, IV, and III only.)

Four Hand Piano Sonata I (W42)

D8a. Title on label: *Four Hand Sonata (1944)*. Norma Bertolami Sapp and Allen Sapp (recording of P42d). Philadelphia: Reco-Art Sound Recording Co.; recorded 11 April 1950. Non-commercial acetate recording (10-inch disc, 33 1/3 r.p.m., transferred from an analog reel tape master in the composer's collection). Ohio State University Music & Dance Library.

D8b. Analog reel tape preservation copy and analog cassette public use copy of D8a, Ohio State University Music & Dance Library, 14 November 1995.

Four Hand Piano Sonata II (W44)

D9. Frina Arschanska Boldt and Kenwyn Boldt. Non-commercial analog reel tape recording, 10 December 1982 (recording of P44a). Tape Archives, Music Department, State University of New York at Buffalo. See also: D38.

Four Impromptus for Piano (W17)

D10. Norma Bertolami Sapp. Non-commercial analog reel tape recording, 8 May 1970 (recording of P17a). Tape Archives, Music Department, State University of New York at Buffalo.

The Four Winds (W131)

D11. Cincinnati Wind Ensemble, conducted by R. Robert Hornyak (recording of P131b). On *1985 CBDNA National Conference, Boulder, Colorado*, volume 5. [Madison, Wis.]: College Band Directors National Association, CBDNA 85-5. Recorded 27 February 1985; released 1985; no longer available. Analog cassette tape.

Imaginary Creatures (W118): See D39.

The Lady and the Lute (W87)

D12a. Title on label: *Eight Songs of Robert Herrick.* Jean Lunn, soprano, Norma Bertolami Sapp, piano (recording of P87a). Boston: Trans Radio Productions. Recorded ca. late summer 1952. Non-commercial instantaneous acetate recording (12-inch disc, 33 1/3 r.p.m.). Ohio State University Music & Dance Library.

D12b. Analog reel tape preservation copy and analog cassette public use copy of D12a, Ohio State University Music & Dance Library, 14 November 1995.

D13. Carol Plantamura, soprano, George Crumb, harpsichord. Non-commercial analog audiocassette tape recording, 4 March 1965 (recording of P87k). Cassette 19, "Evenings for New Music" Sound Recording Collection, Archive of the Center of the Creative and Performing Arts, Music Library, State University of New York at Buffalo.

A Maiden's Complaint in Springtime (W105)

D14a. Title on label: *Maiden's Complaint.* Wellesley College Madrigal Group, conducted by Howard M. Brown (recording of P105a). Boston: Trans Radio Productions. Recorded 17 April 1960. Non-commercial instantaneous acetate recording (10-inch disc, 33 1/3 r.p.m.). Ohio State University Music & Dance Library.

D14b. Analog reel tape preservation copy and analog cassette public use copy of D14a, Ohio State University Music & Dance Library, 12 November 1995.

Overture, "The Women of Trachis" (W115)

D15a. Title on label: *The Woman of Trachis (overture)*. Boston Fine Arts Chamber Orchestra, conducted by Eleftherios Eleftherakis (recording of P115a). Boston: Trans Radio Productions. Recorded 27 November 1960. Non-commercial instantaneous acetate recording (10-inch disc, 33 1/3 r.p.m.). Ohio State University Music & Dance Library.

D15b. Analog reel tape preservation copy and analog cassette public use copy of D15a, Ohio State University Music & Dance Library, 12 November 1995.

Piano Sonata II (W16)

D16a. Norma Bertolami Sapp. Non-commercial digital Sony Beta tape sound recording, 3 November 1988 (recording of P16e). Ohio State University Music & Dance Library.

D16b. Digital sound file copy of D16a. Available from the *Allen Sapp Home Page*: http://muslib.lib.ohio-state.edu/sapp/index.htm

Piano Sonata III (W19)

D17. The composer. Non-commercial analog reel tape recording, 23 April 1965 (recording of P19i). Tape Archives, Music Department, State University of New York at Buffalo.

D18a. Norma Bertolami Sapp. Non-commercial analog cassette tape, 14 May 1984 (recording of P19n, transferred from an analog reel tape master in the composer's collection). Ohio State University Music & Dance Library. See also: D35.

D18b. Digital sound file copy of D18a. Available from the *Allen Sapp Home Page*: http://muslib.lib.ohio-state.edu/sapp/index.htm

Piano Sonata IV (W20)

D19a. Norma Bertolami Sapp. Non-commercial analog reel tape recording, 4 November 1986 (recording of P20g). Ohio State University Music & Dance Library

D19b. Digital sound file copy of D19a. Available from the *Allen Sapp Home Page*: http://muslib.lib.ohio-state.edu/sapp/index.htm

Piano Sonata V (W23)

D20a. Norma Bertolami Sapp. Non-commercial analog reel tape recording, 2 November 1982 (recording of P23a). Ohio State University Music & Dance Library

D20b. Digital sound file copy of D20a. Available from the *Allen Sapp Home Page*: http://muslib.lib.ohio-state.edu/sapp/index.htm

D21. Norma Bertolami Sapp. Non-commercial analog reel tape recording, 10 December 1982 (recording of P23c). Tape Archives, Music Department, State University of New York at Buffalo.

Piano Sonata VI (W24)

D22a. Norma Bertolami Sapp. Non-commercial analog reel tape recording, 14 January 1982 (recording of P24a). Ohio State University Music & Dance Library

D22b. Digital sound file copy of D22a. Available from the *Allen Sapp Home Page*: http://muslib.lib.ohio-state.edu/sapp/index.htm

Suite for Orchestra, no. 2 (W113)

D23. Buffalo Philharmonic Orchestra, conducted by Lukas Foss. Analog reel tape recording, "Limited edition; recorded and distributed by the Recording Guarantee Project, American International Music Fund, Koussevitzky Music Foundation."[1] Recorded 8 and 10 December 1968 (recording of P113a); release date unknown; no longer available. Copy owned by the Rodgers & Hammerstein Archives of Recorded Sound of The New York Public Library for the Performing Arts (call number: *LT-7 2233).

Suite for Piano (W14)

D24a. Norma Bertolami Sapp. Non-commercial analog reel tape recording, 12 November 1985 (recording of P14g). Ohio State University Music & Dance Library. See also: D34.

D24b. Digital sound file copy of D24a. Available from the *Allen Sapp Home Page*: http://muslib.lib.ohio-state.edu/sapp/index.htm

Taylor's Nine (W67)

D25. University at Buffalo Percussion Ensemble, conducted by Jan Williams. Non-commercial analog reel tape recording, 10 December 1982 (recording of P67b). Tape Archives, Music Department, State University of New York at Buffalo. See also: D40-41.

Viola Sonata (W55)

D26. Boris Kroyt, viola, Norma Bertolami Sapp, piano. Non-commercial analog reel tape recording, 19 April 1965 (recording of P55c). Tape Archives, Music Department, State University of New York at Buffalo.

D27. Boris Kroyt, viola, Arthur Balsam, piano. Non-commercial analog reel tape recording, 4 March 1966 (recording of P55d). Coolidge Auditorium tape collection, Library of Congress (call number: LWO 4782).

D28. Boris Kroyt, viola, Murray Perahia, piano. Non-commercial analog reel tape recording, 29 March 1967 (recording of P55e). Tape Archives, Music Department, State University of New York at Buffalo.

D29. Pamela Ryan, viola, Robert Spano, piano. Non-commercial analog cassette tape recording, 29 March 1989 (recording of P55i). Music Listening Center, Jerome Library, Bowling Green State University, Bowling Green, Ohio.

Violin Sonata I (W52)

D30a. Viviane Bertolami, violin, Norma Bertolami Sapp, piano (recording of P52a). New York: Carnegie Hall Recording Co. Recorded 21 January 1945. Non-commercial instantaneous acetate recording (two 12-inch discs, 78 r.p.m.). Ohio State University Music & Dance Library.

D30b. Analog reel tape preservation copy and analog cassette public use copy of D30a, Ohio State University Music & Dance Library, 16 November 1995.

Violin Sonata II (W54)

D31. Charles Haupt, violin, August Martin, piano. Non-commercial analog reel tape recording, 18 April 1968 (recording of P54d). Tape Archives, Music Department, State University of New York at Buffalo.

Violin Sonata IV (W68)

D32a. Thomas Halpin, violin, Norma Bertolami Sapp, piano. Non-commercial analog reel tape recording, 10 December 1982 (recording of P68a). Tape Archives, Music Department, State University of New York at Buffalo. See also: D36.

D32b. Analog cassette tape copy of D32a, Ohio State University Music & Dance Library, 21 November 1995.

D32c. Digital sound file copy of D32a. Available from the *Allen Sapp Home Page*: http://muslib.lib.ohio-state.edu/sapp/index.htm

"The Women of Trachis" Overture
See *Overture, "The Women of Trachis"*

Xenón Ciborium (W121)

D33. Philharmonia Orchestra of the University of Cincinnati College-Conservatory of Music, conducted by Gerhard Samuel. Non-commercial analog reel tape recording, 11 October 1986 (recording of P121a). Ohio State University Music & Dance Library. See also: D37.

MUSICAL EXAMPLES

Items D34-41 are digital sound files of excerpts used as musical examples in this book (see pages following p. 50), available via the world-wide web from the *Allen Sapp Home Page* (B149) at the following URL address:

http://muslib.lib.ohio-state.edu/sapp/index.htm

D34. Example 3.1, *Suite for Piano* (W14), fourth movement, measures 1-33. Digital sound file excerpt of D24a (recording of P14g).

D35. Example 3.2, *Piano Sonata III* (W19), first movement, measures 1-18. Digital sound file excerpt of D18a (recording of P19n).

D36. Example 8.1, *Violin Sonata IV* (W68), second movement, measures 164-196. Digital sound file excerpt of D32a (recording of P68a).

D37. Example 8.2, *Xenón Ciborium* (W121), measures 0-6. Digital sound file excerpt of D33 (recording of P121a).

D38.   Example 8.3, *Four Hand Piano Sonata II* (W44), third movement, measures 1-32. Digital sound file excerpt of D9 (recording of P44a).

D39.   Example 8.4, *Imaginary Creatures* (W118), third movement ("Unicorn"), measures 1-12. Eiji Hashimoto, harpsichord, with the Cincinnati Chamber Orchestra, conducted by Paul Nadler. Digital sound file excerpt, originally recorded 21 March 1982 (recording of P118a, transferred from an analog reel tape master in the composer's collection).

D40.   Example 8.5, *Taylor's Nine* (W67), measures 1-27. Digital sound file excerpt of D25 (recording of P67b).

D41.   Example 8.6, *Taylor's Nine* (W67), measures 252-257. Digital sound file excerpt of D25 (recording of P67b).

ADDENDUM

The following recordings were reported to the author just a few days prior to the publication deadline for this book:

Concertino for Piano and Chamber Orchestra (W111)

D42a. Monique Haas, piano, with the Orchestre de la Radiodiffusion Française, conducted by André Girard (recording of P111b). Paris: Disque Ph. Miller, recorded 19 April 1945.   Non-commercial instantaneous acetate recording. Archives de la phonothèque de l'Institut national de l'audiovisuel, Maison de Radio-France, Paris.

D42b. Analog reel tape preservation copy of D42a, Archives de la phonothèque de l'Institut national de l'audiovisuel, Maison de Radio-France, Paris.

IV. WRITINGS BY SAPP

LISTED BELOW ARE ALL OF THE KNOWN published writings and the extant major unpublished writings of Allen Sapp. Unless otherwise noted, all items listed below as "unpublished" were located among Sapp's personal papers at his home in Cincinnati.

B1. "An Introduction to Orchestral Analysis as Applied to Seven Works of Igor Stravinsky." A. B. honors thesis, Harvard University, 1942.

A detailed orchestration analysis of seven works by Stravinsky. The study is organized into separate sections illustrating the five "types" of orchestra for which he composed music between 1917 and 1938; listed below are chapter titles, followed by the studied works in parentheses: "The Standard Orchestra" (*Jeu de cartes*); "The String Orchestra" (*Apollon Musagète*); "The Chamber Orchestra" (*Suite No. 1*, *Suite No. 2*, and *Concerto in E-flat: "Dumbarton Oaks"*); "The Accompaniment Orchestra" (*Violin Concerto*); and "An Experimental Wind Orchestra" (*Symphony of Psalms*). As the title implies, this study works toward a broader scope of suggesting a new approach toward instruction and analysis in the technique of orchestration: rather than studying each instrument or family of instruments in succession, this study follows close examination of several works with description of specific textures in each work, essentially cataloging certain types of frequently employed orchestration "effects." Also examined is Stravinsky's use of "tone color conservation" for several works in order to illustrate his use of texture as a tool to accentuate formal design.

B2. *Censorship Cryptanalysis*. N.l., Civil Censorship Division, United States Forces, European Theater, 1946.

This text was written while Sapp was serving as Chief Cryptanalyst of the Civil Censorship Division, United States Forces, European Theater. It is a two-volume text which was used to train his staff in detecting coded messages in a variety of documents, including hand-written and typed letters, graphic documents, and even musical compositions. The first volume, entitled *One Hundred and Forty Three Sample Communications*, contains the document facsimiles which are interpreted in the second volume, *Explanatory Notes*. The three musical compositions were composed by Sapp, and appear under different pseudonyms in the text (see W140, W141, and W142).

B3.   "Schoenberg's Quintet: Integration in E♭." Paper presented to the Seminar in Music History at Harvard University, autumn 1949. Unpublished.

An extensive analysis of Arnold Schoenberg's *Wind Quintet*, op. 26. Sapp focuses on the "organizing principles in the twelve tone technique which correspond to if not actually duplicate methods of tonal movement" (p. 15). The analysis is accompanied by a complete hand transcription of the work in four-color ink representing the serial row forms (black for prime, purple for inversion, red for retrograde, green for retrograde inversion). The study includes an introductory section on the historical context and the nearly universal negative reception of the work. In spite of its lack of appeal to audiences, the work stands as "a miraculous treatise" (p. 35) on the serial method of composing.

B4.   "The Vital Balance." Paper presented at the fifth annual meeting of the College Music Association, Sarah Lawrence College, 1951. Unpublished.

Institutions should take care to maintain a balance between required musical courses and general liberal arts training for undergraduate music scholars. Specific recommendations for efficient yet thorough undergraduate musical training are made for courses in music theory and analysis, counterpoint, orchestration and music history. In all areas of study it is recommended to thoroughly examine a smaller number of great works rather than to take a cursory look at the entire spectrum of music literature.

B5.   "Music of the Baroque." A series of 52 lectures originally broadcast on Boston radio stations WGBH-FM and WMEX-AM (under the series title "The Music's the Thing") between 29 August 1951 and 1 September 1952 (dates of original broadcast given in parentheses following the program titles below). Program produced through the Lowell Institute in association with several Boston area universities and artistic institutions, and distributed nationally to stations affiliated with the National Association of Educational Broadcasters. Scripts unpublished. See also: B55.

1.   "Claudio Monteverdi" (29 August 1951)
2.   "Giralomo Frescobaldi" (5 September 1951)
3.   "Heinrich Schütz" (12 September 1951)
4.   "Dietrich Buxtehude" (19 September 1951)
5.   "Henry Purcell" (26 September 1951)
6.   "Arcangelo Corelli" (3 October 1951)
7.   "Antonio Vivaldi" (10 October 1951)
8.   "Alessandro Scarlatti" (17 October 1951)
9.   "The Chorale Prelude, I" (24 October 1951)
10. "The Chorale Prelude, II" (31 October 1951)
11. "The Keyboard Sonata, I" (7 November 1951)
12. "The Keyboard Sonata, II" (14 November 1951)
13. "Jean-Baptiste Lully" (21 November 1951)
14. "The Sinfonia" (28 November 1951)

15.   "The Concerto Grosso, I" (5 December 1951)
16.   "The Concerto Grosso, II" (12 December 1951)
17.   "Schütz: *The Christmas Oratorio*" (19 December 1951)
18.   "Marc-Antoine Charpentier" (26 December 1951)
19.   "The Chorales" (2 January 1952)
20.   "Jean-Phillipe Rameau" (9 January 1952)
21.   "François Couperin" (16 January 1952)
22.   "The Keyboard Suite, I" (23 January 1952)
23.   "The Keyboard Suite, II" (4 February 1952)
24.   "The Fugue, I" (11 February 1952)
25.   "The Fugue, II" (18 February 1952)
26.   "Georg Philipp Telemann" (25 February 1952)
27.   "Bach's *Musical Offering*" (3 March 1952)
28.   "French Clavecin Music" (10 March 1952)
29.   "The Solo Sonata" (17 March 1952)
30.   "The Art of the Fugue" (24 March 1952)
31.   "The Arias of Handel" (31 March 1952)
32.   "Handel's Choruses" (14 April 1952)
33.   "Handel's Orchestral Style" (21 April 1952)
34.   "French Instrumental Music" (28 April 1952)
35.   "The Solo Cantata" (5 May 1952)
36.   "French Orchestral Music" (12 May 1952)
37.   "John Blow: *Venus and Adonis*" (19 May 1952)
38.   "The German Passion" (26 May 1952)
39.   "Carissimi" (2 June 1952)
40.   "French Organ Music" (9 June 1952)
41.   "The Keyboard Variation, I" (16 June 1952)
42.   "The Keyboard Variation, II" (23 June 1952)
43.   "Italian Sacred Music: Stile Concertato, I" (30 June 1952)
44.   "Italian Sacred Music: Stile Concertato, II" (7 July 1952)
45.   "The Beggar's Opera" (14 July 1952)
46.   "Popular Music of the Restoration: The Catch and the Glee" (21 July
        1952)
47.   "Bach Sacred Cantatas, I" (28 July 1952)
48.   "Bach Sacred Cantatas, II" (4 August 1952)
49.   "Bach Secular Cantatas" (11 August 1952)
50.   "The Sound Ideal of the Baroque" (18 August 1952)
51.   "Forms of the Baroque" (25 August 1952)
52.   "The Richness of Baroque Music: Summary and Conclusion"
        (1 September 1952)

B6.   "This Week's Symphony." Radio preview program for the Boston Symphony
Orchestra on WGBH-FM (Boston). Occasional appearances as a substitute
for the regular host, G. Wallace Woodworth. Broadcast dates of known
programs are given below. Scripts unpublished.

3 April 1952
4 December 1953 [script missing]
2 October 1958 [script missing]
9 October 1958

16 October 1958 [script missing]
22 October 1958 [script missing]
30 October 1958 [script missing]
6 November 1958 [script missing]
13 November 1958 [script missing]
20 November 1958 [script missing]
27 November 1958 [script missing]
4 December 1958 [script missing]
11 December 1958 [script missing]
18 December 1958 [script missing]
25 December 1958 [script missing]

B7.   "Music of Our Time." A series of 52 lectures originally broadcast on WGBH-FM (Boston) and WMEX-AM (Boston) between 18 October 1952 and 25 October 1953 (dates of original broadcast given in parentheses following the program titles below). Program produced through the Lowell Institute in association with several Boston area universities and artistic institutions, and distributed nationally to stations affiliated with the National Association of Educational Broadcasters. Scripts unpublished.

1.   "The Crisis in Tonality, I" (19 October 1952) [with guest Leonard Burkat]
2.   "The Crisis in Tonality, II" (26 October 1952)
3.   "Aspects of Experimentalism, I" (2 November 1952) [with guest Leonard Burkat; script missing]
4.   "Aspects of Experimentalism, II" (9 November 1952) [with guest Leonard Burkat; script missing]
5.   "Serge Prokofiev" (16 November 1952)
6.   "Contemporary Use of Folk Music, I" (23 November 1952)
7.   "Contemporary Use of Folk Music, II" (30 November 1952)
8.   "The Crisis in Tonality, III" (7 December 1952)
9.   "Arthur Honegger" (14 December 1952)
10.   "White Music of the 20th Century, I" (21 December 1952)
11.   "White Music of the 20th Century, II" (28 December 1952)
12.   "Sacred Music of the 20th Century, I" (4 January 1953)
13.   "Sacred Music of the 20th Century, II" (11 January 1953)
14.   "Arnold Schoenberg" (18 January 1953) [with guest F. Judd Cooke script missing]
15.   "The Crisis in Tonality, IV" (25 January 1953)
16.   "The Crisis in Tonality, V" (1 February 1953)
17.   "Rhythmic Features of 20th Century Music, I" (8 February 1953)
18.   "Rhythmic Features of 20th Century Music, II" (15 February 1953)
19.   "Roger Sessions" (22 February 1953)
20.   "Music for Solo Voice" (1 March 1953)
21.   "Berlin, 1925" (15 March 1953)
22.   "Boston, 1930" (22 March 1953)
23.   "New York, 1935" (29 March 1953)
24.   "Easter in Music" (5 April 1953) [script missing]
25.   "Roy Harris" (12 April 1953)
26.   "Alban Berg" (19 April 1953) [script missing]

27.   "Igor Stravinsky" (26 April 1953) [with guest Claudio Spies; script missing]
28.   "New Currents in Opera, I" (3 May 1953)
29.   "New Currents in Opera, II" (10 May 1953)
30.   "New Currents in Opera, III" (17 May 1953)
31.   "Incidental Music for the Theatre" (24 May 1953)
32.   "Music of the Films" (31 May 1953)
33.   "Les Six, I" (7 June 1953)
34.   "Les Six, II" (14 June 1953)
35.   "Darius Milhaud" (21 June 1953)
36.   "Walter Piston" (28 June 1953)
37.   "Neo-Classicism, I" (broadcast date unknown) [script missing]
38.   "Neo-Classicism, II" (20 July 1953)
39.   "Bela Bartok" (broadcast date unknown) [script missing]
40.   "Neo-Romanticism, I" (2 August 1953)
41.   "Paul Hindemith" (9 August 1953)
42.   "Solo Keyboard Music" (broadcast date unknown) [script missing]
43.   "New Ideas from Popular Music, I" (24 August 1953)
44.   "New Ideas from Popular Music, II" (30 August 1953)
45.   "The Colossal" (5 September 1953)
46.   "The Miniature" (12 September 1953)
47.   "Neo-Romanticism, II" (20 September 1953)
48.   "Old Books, Old Friends: *Music and Imagination*, Aaron Copland" (27 September 1953)
49.   "How Wide is the Gap between Producer and Consumer of Modern Music?" (4 October 1953) [script missing]
50.   "The Business of Being a Composer" (11 October 1953)
51.   "Design and Structure in Contemporary Music" (18 October 1953)
52.   "The Sound Ideal of Our Time" (25 October 1953)

B8.   "The Gurre-Lieder Poem." In *The Gurre-Lieder* [recording booklet], 16-23. Accompanies the recording *Gurre-Lieder* by Arnold Schoenberg. Chorus and orchestra of the New Symphony Society of Paris, conducted by René Leibowitz. Boston: The Haydn Society, 1953 (HSL 100). Reissues: New York: Vox, 1962 (VBX 204); New York: Berkshire, n.d. (BH-1012; 2 analog tape reels).

An essay on the historical facts and later fictional variations in the Danish legend of Waldemar and Tove; analysis and background on Jens Peter Jacobsen's adaptation of the legend in his poem; and Schoenberg's setting of the German translation of Jacobsen's poem by Robert Franz Arnold, including an overview of textual variations between the text employed by Schoenberg and that published by R. F. Arnold in 1899.

B9.   Review of a recording of *Pelléas et Mélisande*, by Claude Debussy. L'Orchestre de la Suisse Romande. Ernest Ansermet. London LLA 11. *Musical Quarterly* 39 (April 1953): 310-14.

A lengthy review focusing primarily on the opera's characteristics rather than the performance (Sapp praises the performance and engineering of the recording, but not until the final brief paragraph). Four major aspects of the opera are discussed: its position and importance in operatic history; a review of some facts concerning its earliest performances; discussion of the characters' role qualities; and significant attention to Debussy's compositional style. While Sapp mildly criticizes a few specific passages "where the harmonic style falters," he otherwise lavishes praise upon the work. "In its flawless prosody, particular attention to rhythmic matters, and exquisite taste, *Pelléas* epitomizes the purest ideals of French dramatic music. Not a word is missed, no thought obscured, no accent misplaced. Every musical phrase is rooted in the necessity for conveying not only the meaning of the text but also its rhythmic shape as a prose form." See also: B70.

B10.   "The New Cambridge Lyricism." Paper delivered by Allen Sapp at a lecture-recital given by him and his wife, Norma Bertolami Sapp, on 4 May 1954 at Kirkland House Junior Common Room, Harvard University in the series "New Trends in Contemporary Music." Broadcast live on WGBH-FM. Unpublished.

Sapp defines a school of composers "with the common denominator of the lyric impulse and traditional training. The union of a sense of the past and a vital stimulus along melodic and direct lines. . . . The general orientation of this group is French rather than German, international rather than nationalistic, traditional rather than experimental, 'white' [diatonic] rather than 'black' [chromatic], and in general extremely romantic in outlook." Sapp lists the "chief members" of the group as Walter Piston ("dean and leader"), Harold Shapero, Robert Middleton, Irving Fine, Paul Des Marais, and himself. Sapp presents his critical opinion on each composer and on the unifying and differentiating stylistic elements of the group.

Sapp's *Concertino for Piano and Chamber Orchestra* was performed at this event in an arrangement for two pianos (see "Notes" under W111).

B11.   Reviews of *String Quartet No. 2* (New York: Peer International, 1954) by Charles Ives; *Musik zum Gedächtnis der Einsamen, für Streichquartett* (Mainz: B. Schott, 1953) by Philipp Jarnach; *String Quartet No. 1* (New York: Boosey & Hawkes, 1954) by Benjamin Lees; *String Quartet No. 2* (London & New York: Oxford University Press, 1954) by Alan Rawsthorne; and *String Quartet No. 2* (New York: Boosey & Hawkes, 1954) by William Denny. *Notes* 12, no. 3 (June 1955): 489-92.

Sapp gives mixed reviews to the first four works, but praises William Denny's *String Quartet No. 2*. "This quartet has the stature of the Piston quartets, and it is even more dedicated to long phrases, slow evolution, and lucid texture. . . . In Denny, who has been growing slowly and unspectacularly, it is plain that we have a composer of high rank."

B12.   "The Search for Language in American Music." Six lectures sponsored by the Charles R. Walgreen Foundation for the Study of American Institutions at the University of Chicago on 17, 19, 21, 24, 26, and 28 October 1955. Unpublished.

Several "schools" of composers and specific musical works from different periods of American history are discussed from the viewpoint of their distinct relationships to American culture. The lectures proceed largely in chronological order from the colonial era through the 1950s. Lecture I, "Praising God in English," focuses on religious music from 1640 to 1800, with emphasis on New England psalmody, the Moravian music of Pennsylvania, and the composers of Spanish masses and motets in the Franciscan missions of California.   Lecture II, "Symphonies and Operas in German and Italian," examines the progression of the American musician and composer from amateur to professional during the nineteenth century, and the extent to which composers looked toward—or away from—the established musical influences of Europe. Lecture III, "New England Lyricism," provides a close examination of the work of Edward MacDowell and Charles Ives, the latter being described as "the first American composer of serious music who can stand in the mainstream" (p. [4]). Lecture IV, "A French Accent," examines the strong connection to this musical culture in the work of American composers from Gottschalk through Copland and Piston.   Lecture V, "The American Language: Crisis in Vocabulary and Diction," discusses the "obsessive importance" American composers placed on the ability "to speak without an accent, to shape ideas and insights in a language free from the inflections of different cultures" (p. [1]). Lecture VI, "American Music: The Lingua Franca," presents an overview of the musical state of America in the 1950s.

B13.   "The Record Review: Content and Purpose." In *Essays on Music in Honor of Archibald Thompson Davison by his Associates.* Cambridge: Department of Music, Harvard University, 1957.

A survey of the many aspects of a recording which should (and should not) be considered when writing a record review. This essay is perhaps most interesting in its observations about the status of the sound recording in the mid-1950s, noting the rapid expansion of available repertoire, recording and editing problems, and the less-than-enthusiastic acceptance of "facsimile sound" among some members of the musical community.

B14.   "The School of Schoenberg: Expressionism and the Cycle of Notes and Time." Paper delivered prior to a concert of works by Schoenberg, Berg and Webern at Harvard University, 25 April 1958. Unpublished.

A basic introduction to the music of the three composers is presented, as well as specific commentary on the works to be performed: Schoenberg's *Das Buch der Hangenden Gärten*, Berg's *Piano Sonata*, and Webern's *Variations*, op. 28. Brief commentary is presented on then-current trends in German music influenced by the "Second Viennese School," Paul Hindemith, and Carl Orff; the latter's *Carmina Burana* is cited as an "approach which starts over from the beginning with a kind of primeval delight in rhythm and percussion . . . easily dismissed by most musicians as trashy, it may in fact be much more the sign of a way out of what appears to be a serious impasse" [with the later developments of serial technique].

B15.   "Ethnographie Musicale: États-Unis." In *Encyclopédie de la Musique*, ed. François Michel, v. 3, 944-48. Paris: Fasquelle, 1958-61.

Sapp presents an overview of American music history from 1607 to 1960, covering essentially the same areas studied in his Walgreen Lectures (see B12). Especially noteworthy is the final section covering the period from 1920 to 1960, where the works of about 45 American composers are discussed in relation to developments in national and international style.

B16.   Reviews of *String Quartet No. 1* (New York: Southern Music, 1958) by Harold
Shapero; *String Quartet No. 2* (New York: Southern Music, 1958) by David
Diamond; *String Quartet Nr. 1* (Wien: Universal Edition, 1958) by Gunther
Schuller; *Fantasia for String Trio* (New York: Mills Music, 1959) by Irving Fine;
Concerto da Camera: String Quartet No. 7 (New York: Southern Music, 1958)
by Bohuslav Martinů; and *Streichquartett Nr. 4* (Mainz: B. Schott, 1958) by
Kurt Hessenberg. *Notes* 16 (September 1959): 625-26.

Each of the six quartets is described in character and craft, with
largely positive comments for each work.   Perhaps the most interesting
description is given to "Schuller's arrestingly personal *Quartet*, [which] exudes
the *Krypton* of Stockhausen, Boulez, and Nono *but*: first it has beginnings,
middles, and ends; second, it permits the performer to improvise within the
strict serial technique; third, it avoids any 'total organization' of time, making
possible a drama above the density flux and registration scatter which accounts
for much of the post-Webern music."

B17a.   "The Personal Gesture."   Frederic Slee Lecture Series, "Three Modes of
Musical Communication," 19 October 1961, Butler Auditorium, Capen Hall,
University of Buffalo. Unpublished, manuscripts missing, not taped.

According to a review of this lecture-recital by John Dwyer (see
WB16b), Sapp focused on the concept of the composer as "a magician, a
genius of white magic. The possessor of secret knowledge, he gives illusions
to the disillusioned world." In the surviving tape of the third lecture in this
series, (see B17c), Sapp summarizes the first lecture as examining the mode
of musical communication which "is a channel from physical gesture to musical
information. . . . We enjoy, we understand, we are receptive to music in a
measure as we are attuned to the implicit physical substrata transformed from
reality by a composer."

The composer performed his *Piano Sonata III* (see W19, P19h) at the
event, and his wife Norma Bertolami Sapp performed the other two Roman
sonatas, *Piano Sonata II* (see W16, P16c) and *Piano Sonata IV* (see W20,
P20d).

B17b.   "The Lyric Impulse."   Frederic Slee Lecture Series, "Three Modes of
Musical Communication," 30 November 1961, Butler Auditorium, Capen Hall,
University of Buffalo. Unpublished, manuscripts missing, not taped.

According to the summary of this second Slee lecture offered in the
surviving tape of the third lecture in the series (see B17c), Sapp discussed the
lyrical mode of musical communication, described as a "double channel [which]
relates to language on one track, and dramatic expression on another. . . . The
communication of a song which was most significant took place because of
some especial matched, almost symbiotic relationship between words and
music. One might fail to understand the words, and be totally baffled by the
musical style, and yet grasp deeply, or at least be deeply affected by the
composition. . . . A composer tries to discover a music which will render a
whole impression, and he may do so by selecting the symbol in the text, or by
carefully underscoring the words, adding a second dimension, so to speak, to
the first one."

Mezzo-soprano Jennie Tourel assisted Sapp with performances at this
lecture, but no Sapp compositions were featured.

B17c. "The Corporate Experience." Frederic Slee Lecture Series, "Three Modes of Musical Communication," 5 February 1962, Butler Auditorium, Capen Hall, University of Buffalo. Unpublished, manuscripts missing. Incomplete tape recording (22 min.) held by the Tape Archives, State University of New York at Buffalo Music Department.

In the final lecture of the Slee series, Sapp addresses three types of communal musical experiences. "The first instance . . . is an effort to get at the kinds of feelings which musicians playing together, playing chamber music in particular, experience. In the second instance we shall explore the kinds of feelings groups of listeners have, when suddenly in the midst of a rich unfolding, there is a corporate rather than an individual sensation. In the third instance, this corporate experience is the making physically coherent of a combination of symbols and signs and ideas, in fact it is the reverse translation of the process we discussed in 'The Physical Gesture' [i.e., the first lecture, 'The Personal Gesture']. . . . What really interests me is the writing of music, and that secondarily what excites me is the quest for understanding in its communication. I find in the incredible meshing of a fine quartet, or the breathing together of a singer and her accompanist, or the potent command of a strong solo performer, in these I find a mystery and a revitalization."

The Bel Arte Trio (Joseph Silverstein, violin, Joseph de Pasquale, viola, and Samuel Mayes, violoncello) performed Sapp's *String Trio* (see W60, P60b) at the lecture. See also: WB60a.

B18. Review of *Tonal Harmony in Concept and Practice* (New York: Holt, Rinehart and Winston, 1962) by Allen Forte. *College Music Symposium* 2 (Fall 1962): 72-75.

Sapp praises Forte for his "textbook which is an excellent introduction to college music study. . . . It invigorates rather than revolutionizes; it restores dignity and excitement to what can so easily become lugubrious and infertile effort."

B19. "Contemporary Music in Secondary Music Education." *College Music Symposium* 3 (1963): 21-22.

An appendix to a report (ibid., p. 13-19) of the College Music Society Committee on Music in the Elementary and Secondary Schools from the meeting in Columbus on 29 December 1962. Sapp observes three reasons to focus on new music in secondary schools: exposure to a new repertory, extension of personal and ensemble performing skills, and as a tool to raise "awareness of the function of art without the historical or traditional biases associated with the *proper* or the canonical. In other words there is not yet the stamp of official approval, textbook indorsement, or accumulated authority to interfere with the student's shock in finding out why music can be the stethoscope to life."

▶ "Program Notes: Overture: "The Women of Trachis." *Overture* [Buffalo Philharmonic Orchestra program] (14-16 April 1963): 10-12. See: WB115c.

B20. Review of *String Quartet* (New York: Boosey & Hawkes, 1961) by Herbert Fromm. *Notes* 21 (Winter-Spring 1963-64): 255-56.

A highly favorable review, commending Fromm's work for its "fresh orthodoxy. . . . His music is never sensational, never shocking, rarely aggressive, usually ingenious, and invariably polished. . . . The work speaks first to the musically cultivated, weary of sham and posture. It is perhaps more daring in its uprightness than the *effluvia* of Darmstadt with all its gimmickry."

B21. "Broadening the Musical Repertory." In *Music in Our Schools: A Search for Improvement; Report of the Yale Seminar on Music Education.* Edited by Claude V. Palisca. Washington: U. S. Department of Health, Education, and Welfare; Office of Education, 1964.

Sapp served as "reporter" for a subgroup of seminar participants concerned with improving and broadening the repertoire used in elementary and secondary music education in the school systems of the United States. In particular, recommendations are made for use of authentic (as opposed to arranged) music, and for such music to be published in new school music collections. "Much of the passion for arranging among education editors is born, not from a dearth of authentic music suited to the voices and instruments available, but from a wish to cater to the taste for the familiar" (p. 12). Other recommendations include increasing foundation commissions to experienced composers to write classroom and school ensemble music; preparing a series of films on musical cultures of the world; and the preparation and distribution of library reference materials for schools. [Sapp's original typescript of this report, containing more description of the group's comments not included in the published report, is held at the University Archives, State University of New York at Buffalo (16/5A/482: box 5, folder 2)]. See also: B136.

▶   "Program Notes: Colloquies." *Overture* [Buffalo Philharmonic Orchestra program] (23 February-3 March 1964): 12. See: WB117a.

B22. "Notes for a Concert of New Music." *Overture* [Buffalo Philharmonic Orchestra program] (23 Feb.-2 March 1965): 21-24.

These notes serve as a preface to the 1965 Buffalo Festival of the Arts Today, and particularly for the Buffalo Philharmonic Orchestra concerts on 28 February and 2 March. These are not remarks on the specific pieces to be performed (those are found elsewhere in the program booklet); rather, it is an essay on some of the major trends, or "tendencies," of new music since 1910. His inventory includes: 1) "the search for new sonorities;" 2) "the replacement of the idea of music as 'mirror of man' by music as a rationalization of time, space, and color;" 3) "humor as a source of delight, of amusement, of satire, of elegant wit and vulgar punning;" and 4) "violence, deliberate and massive blows on a shoddy and empty and exhausted matrix of social values."

B23. "Music and Language." Lecture under the auspices of the Frederic Slee Chair at the University of Buffalo on 11 October 1965. Unpublished, manuscripts missing. Tape recording held by the Tape Archives, State University of New York at Buffalo Music Department.

Sapp describes a crisis in contemporary language. It is being pulled in three different directions: the increasing level of encoding of discipline-specific scholarly language; the severely limited vocabulary of modern popular language; and the conscious political manipulation of language (and of people by extension) by the mass media. "We have sacrificed to specialists or to mediocrities or to manipulators the controls of our speech. We have virtually abandoned good conversation, swept away debate, eliminated grace of expression, in an effort to achieve—what? Clarity? Economy? Precision? Power? I don't believe that we can afford to surrender to the code experts. If we do, we shall be communicating by typewriters attached to telephones. Speech as we know it will have disappeared." Sapp then discusses his experiences with coded language as a cryptanalyst during and after World War II. The final section of his address turns to a description of some of the problems faced in contemporary musical culture, including the growing gulf between composer and audience at least partially caused by the highly "encoded" nature of most new music. Sapp suggests that perhaps a key to bridging this gap is the appearance of new theatrical and vocal works written by composers such as Kagel (in *Sur scène*) and Stockhausen (in *Momente*) who "turn back to the fructifying strength and sources of language." He predicts that "we are on the brink of a great age of music of the theater. . . . We are going to have something new, perhaps something involving cinematic techniques rather more than traditional theatrical or operatic techniques." See also: B69.

B24.   "Music 1965: The Advance Guard." *Arts and Society* 3 (winter 1965-66): 194-98.

A review of the major experimental trends in contemporary music is presented, including such areas as electronic music, indeterminacy, total organization, and "action-music." This is framed by observations on the rise of the composer-performer, the return to chamber ensembles, the technical demands made of the performer, and the influence of the *avant-garde*. Sapp observes that "one contribution of a vigorous *avant-garde* is its role as a point of reference. It is a kind of outer limit in the frame of expressive possibilities with coordinates in the axis of time. To composers of the middle and quite possibly far more significant range such as Elliot Carter, Leon Kirchner, and Andrew Imbrie, the functioning of this outer limit has uses, more or less personal. . . . There is always at least as much social effect as musical product in the affairs of the *avant-garde*. It is their very concern for society which gives them privilege.   They rasp at solemnities and ridicule pomposities; they generally do not have the masterwork syndrome."

B25.   "Inward Resources."   Position paper delivered to the Buffalo Model City Conference, 1967.   Manuscript missing.   Excerpts published in *Buffalo Alumnus* 6, no. 1 (March 1967): 29.

A paper outlining opportunities for Buffalo to take advantage of the Model Cities Program to enhance the cultural life of the city. Particularly, Sapp suggests investment in "decentralized cultural activities. It should be possible to establish nuclear theater units, small halls suitable for experimentation in jazz and in avant-garde chamber music. Rooms formerly lofts or warehouses could become dance centers. While great central facilities have an important role, it is clear that an equally important thrust must be to fragment art, to relieve art of its insulation and barriers, to make it accessible, natural, normal and vivid to everyone."

B26. "This Problem of the Relationship of the Arts and Humanities." Keynote address presented to the Performing Arts Convocation sponsored by the New York State Education Department and Lincoln Center, 27 June 1967. Published in *Encounter with the Performing Arts*. [Albany]: University of the State of New York, State Education Department, Division of the Humanities and the Arts, 1968.

In an essay focusing on the areas of interrelation and of distinction between the arts and humanities, Sapp relates his experiences of arguing against the separation of the arts faculty from the humanities faculty at the State University of New York at Buffalo. He also recalls a discussion with Michael Tilson Thomas on the role of anger within the creative process. Sapp also discusses the "magic" powers of artistic experience made possible through symbolic communication.

B27. *Matrices and Lattices: Federal Help for Music in the Last Quarter of the 20th Century*. Washington, D.C.: National Endowment for the Arts, 1968.

A primary goal for this report (apparently requested by William Schuman, according to the "Acknowledgements" page), was "to set up a few contexts to describe a few realms . . . so that applications when solicited or when reviewed as groups can be assigned priorities, can be weighted against each other in prospect and eventually can be evaluated in terms of some national objectives." The opening chapter, "The Current Music Scene and Some of Its Dilemmas," presents a sort of musical "State of the Union" essay, logically laying the groundwork for the studies and proposals in the later chapters: II) Institutions: Power and Responsibility; III) Composers of New and Not-So-New Music; IV) Arts Councils and Culture Architecture; V) Communications Media and the Commercial Music Business; VI) Listeners, Amateurs and Audiences; VII) · Research and Education; VIII) The Professionals of High and Middle Degree; IX) Regional Centers: A Case for Decentralization; X) Conservation—Innovation—Quality—and Adventure; XI) Musical Theater, Mixed Forms, Popular and Special Interest Music; XII) National Goals: Priorities and Some Programmatic Schemas.

▶ "Program Notes: Second Suite (1952)." *Overture* [Buffalo Philharmonic Orchestra program] (24 November-10 December 1968): 23-27. See: WB113a.

B28. "New Goals in Arts Education." Article (written ca. 1971) intended for publication in a *Festschrift* for retired SUNY Chancellor Samuel Gould (the *Festschrift* was never published). Unpublished.

Several problems associated with arts education are described in some detail. Three primary goals for improving educational efforts in the arts are suggested. "*First*—given an understanding that instruction in the arts can flourish no longer in a vacuum, we must devise ways of creating a climate which will be manifest of excellent performance, a promoter of taste and a developer of catholic interests. *Second*—we must devise ways of freeing instruction in the arts from too mechanical or too inhibiting testing, without sacrificing important goals. *Third*—we must attempt curricular reforms of increasingly radical nature, while preserving those elements which have been tested in the profession over the years."

B29.   "Community Arts: Community Survival." Closing address given to the conference, "Community Arts and Community Survival," sponsored by the American Council for the Arts in Education, the Los Angeles Community Arts Alliance, and the Department of Arts and Humanities, University Extension, University of California, Los Angeles, June 1972. Unpublished.

"A community without the arts is like a frozen body tucked away in some unthinkable mausoleum waiting for reawakening at some future time. Cold, immobile, and inert it rests collapsed and imploded into itself with all signs of despair, community torpor, individual frustration, and collective negativism. . . . And yet I am far from discouraged; this is not going to be forty minutes of wailing and lamentation. I hope to do a number of things: *One*—to recapitulate some of the nationally significant efforts bearing ultimately on our subject . . . ; *Two*—to examine a few specific situations where the community and the arts and education have worked out solutions of promise [including the Langston Hughes Center in Buffalo, the Hoosic Community Foundation project of Mary Ann Beinecke in North Adams, Mass., and Eddie Edwards' Art Shop and Gallery in San Diego] . . . ; *Three*—to search with you for some new definitions and vocabulary; *Four*—to make a few modest proposals, perhaps not so much those Utopian ones I tend to favor but, rather, realistic and pragmatic ones for accelerating our movement, clarifying it, aggregating its as yet splintered forces." These proposals include a training program for community arts specialists in the "special problems of developing and securing community arts projects and plans;" the establishment of "an escrow trust similar to the highway trust with a four mill tax obtained from all public spectator events (including sports), and placed in an account to be made available on some formula basis for community arts;" and to engage foundations (such as the Charles F. Kettering Foundation) in negotiations "to aid American metropolitan regions to recreate [through the arts] that sense of community without which cities already in trouble may perish."

B30.   "Five Questions for Which I Have Some Answers and One for Which I Don't." Address to the National Theatre Conference, New York City, 7 December 1972. Unpublished.

Sapp addresses the problems associated with public support for the arts. The five questions posed are: "What about the phony grant application which funds basic continuity by inventing make-work and make-shift projects? . . . When are we going to stop asking artists to subsidize the arts [through inadequate compensation for their work]? . . . How do we sustain the established, the libraries, museums, long existing performing organizations, whose claim to public support is being made increasingly as an index of increased services when in fact their value may be quite simply inherent, intrinsic, immeasurable? . . . Where does education fit into the scheme of public support to the arts? . . . How is public support to be divided between the community based neighborhood groups and the visible established and traditional groups?" As the title implies, Sapp offers suggestions and observations of model projects for each of these five problems. The paper closes with the sixth question (for which he does not supply an answer): "How can we live with ourselves as artists in a time in which public support for the arts is so miserable, so grudging, so inadequate, so pitiful?" See also: B92.

B31.   "Preface." In *Arts and the People: A Survey of Public Attitudes and Participation in the Arts and Culture in New York State*. New York: National Research Center for the Arts; American Council for the Arts in Education, 1973.

A summary of the goals of the American Council for the Arts in Education (ACAE), the primary of which was "bringing the arts to positions of parity in the formal educational structure with the sciences, literature, mathematics, and social studies." The four projects of the council are summarized, of which the survey was one; other included review and reformulation of existing state and federal data related to the arts; study of cultural planning for new towns; and the activities connected with the annual conference of the ACAE.

B32.   "Decentralization of the Arts." Address presented to an unknown conference, ca. summer 1973. Unpublished.

Sapp does not recall the name or location of the conference at which he gave this address. It focuses on the public need for community based art, "bringing all the arts to all the people." Sapp bemoans the post-war "lunatic construction of arts centers, conceived in vanity, executed in vulgar massiveness, and operating now as wards of the public benefice. . . . while program planning has been added on at the last minute, often as some Byzantine dedication ceremony seemed to be imminent." Sapp calls this a form of "cultural colonialism, . . . [bringing] great art . . . to the unknowing and unfeeling masses . . . [through building] shrines and temples to these great arts everywhere so that new converts can be brought to nearby places to worship. This process has all the high purposes of colonialism and most of its inherent problems as well." While certainly not arguing for abandonment of the great professional arts organizations, Sapp strongly urges better planning for inclusion of smaller, community based cultural organizations in public support and civic planning.

B33.   "United Funding Desirable for Arts." *Buffalo Evening News*, 3 August 1973.

Sapp responds to the editorial of 30 July 1973, "United Giving for the Arts?" supporting the idea of establishing a central organization in the Western New York region to raise and equitably dispense funds to arts institutions. Using the analogy of united community fund-raising for social welfare organizations, Sapp recommends that "overseeage is best managed by boards of people chosen for their experience and dedication rather than by institutional representatives." He also suggests that the change to unified fund-raising must be gradual; before the various arts institutions can be expected to give up their private fund-raining efforts, the new arts service organizations must "prove their worth, gain the respect and confidence of their clientele and develop the staff of high caliber."

B34.   "Program Notes." *Overture* [Buffalo Philharmonic Orchestra program] (1973-74, 1974-75, and 1975-76 seasons).

Program notes for works performed during these three seasons. Sapp is the only named program note author during this period. The first program bearing his name in this three year series is for the concert of 20 October 1973; the final Sapp program is dated 25-27 April 1976.

B35. "Education in a New Key." Paper presented at the general session, "Youth, Education and the Arts" at the 17th annual conference of the Association of College and University Concert Managers, New York City, 18 December 1973. Published in *ACUCM Bulletin*, Supplement no. 37 (March 1974): [1-3].

Sapp urges not only an increase in direct artistic activity in general education, but also making "the disciplines of science and the social sciences and of the humanities . . . richer, more real, more drawn in by intermixtures and interpolations from the arts. . . . Education in a new key is quite simply the arts pervasive, basic, elemental, and real in the entire structure from early years to final times. The rationale for this massive change is: the *hunger* for aesthetic experience visible all around us in young people; the *evident failure* of our general education system to give us the equipment by which to live and contribute and even to survive in these times; the *obligation to restore* the missing half of human development and capacity suppressed through the long push to a society preoccupied with materialism—but above all (and from a very personal point of view as a teacher of thirty years) the miracle of that sudden phase-shift in a young person as she becomes *at once herself* in the triangulation of an arts experience."

B36. "Cultural Complex for Columbia." Report presented at the Governor's Cultural Center Symposium, University of South Carolina, 25-27 March 1974. Published in *Viewpoints on a Cultural Complex*. [Columbia: University of South Carolina, 1974?]

Sapp presents his reactions to the prospectus for the cultural center planned for the city of Columbia, South Carolina and the University of South Carolina.

B37. "Government Support for the Arts." Address to the Thursday Club of Buffalo, 11 April 1974. Unpublished.

As American cultural organizations become increasingly reliant on government support, Sapp expresses several concerns about the effects of this shift of funding patterns. These include ever-increasing staff resources to comply with grant application requirements, and the avoidance of potentially controversial programming. "We do want to continue to perform the plays which strike us as lively and important, to put on our programs music which is both recognized and unrecognized, to continue in this city to purchase works of art reflecting the cutting teeth of our times, to publish poets if their poems are blue rather than mauve, to sponsor films which hurt our eyes with images too unbearable to stand, to develop dance companies whether in or out of bodyskins."

B38. "National Cultural Policy: A Time for Change." Report prepared at the request of Senator Richard Stone (Democrat, Florida), 12 September 1977. Unpublished.

A 23-point position paper and plan of action for reshaping United States national cultural policy and funding initiatives. The topics addressed range widely: from support for the individual creative artist to policy on preserving national landmarks; from film, television and mass communication policy to support for libraries and scholarly publication. On the latter point, Sapp observes that "There are serious gaps in the publication of primary materials of the American experience. We do not have anything resembling the *Monumenta* of the European nations. And for this reason we have an unclear and distorted perception of the value of our own accomplishments in Music, in Theater, in the Visual Arts, in the extraordinary Modern Dance movements so intimately associated with the American creative genius." His final point calls for the revival of the Office of Special Assistant to the President for Cultural Affairs, which "should be staffed by a toughminded person, experienced in political action but well credentialed as a leader in the Arts and Humanities." Among the 16 "controversial, unusual and well qualified persons" he suggests for this post are Leonard Bernstein, Kitty Carlisle, Kingman Brewster, and Barbara Walters.

B39. "Preface." In *Evenings for New Music: A Catalogue, 1964-77.* Buffalo: Department of Music, State University of New York at Buffalo, 1978.

A history of the genesis and development of the Center of the Creative and Performing Arts and the "Evenings for New Music" series at Buffalo's Albright-Knox Art Gallery and New York City's Carnegie Recital Hall.

B40. "A Look at the 1979 Congress of Strings at the University of Cincinnati Campus." *International Musician* 78 (October 1979): 4.

A review of activities during the tenth summer season of the Congress of Strings, a string orchestra education program primarily for college and advanced high school players, sponsored by the American Federation of Musicians.

B41. "Pavane and Galliard on Silence Preserved." In *A Rededication to Scholarship: Papers Presented at the Dedication of the New Central Library, University of Cincinnati, April 25-27, 1979,* edited by James K. Robinson, 10-22. Cincinnati: University of Cincinnati, 1980.

A wide ranging essay touching on many aspects of the contemporary state of the arts and of arts scholarship. Among the artistic topics discussed are the "romantic counter-revolution . . . the rediscovery of the theme in literature and music"; the problematic relationship of art with mass communication; the concept of authenticity and permanence in artistic creation versus replication and disposability; and the dangers of growing dependence upon governmental subsidy of the arts, leading "to a paralysis of invention and a sapping of courage." Issues addressed in contemporary arts scholarship include the shameful lack of scholarship (especially *monumenta*) on major American artistic figures; the scholar's role in choosing what is and is not to be preserved; the "many perils (and not a few pleasures) in completeness" of modern scholarly documentation practice; and the pressing need for "research into the literacy of the senses," the study of improving general education "to create a sense of the hunger and the excitement and the wonder of the arts which I know as a professional."

B42a. "Facts Amidst Appearances." Thomas James Kelly Lecture Series, "Obvious Questions, Impossible Answers," 28 January 1980, Patricia Corbett Theatre, University of Cincinnati College-Conservatory of Music.

Sapp speaks on the general theme of "scholarship in an age of images. . . . Emerson, in his great address to Phi Beta Kappa on August 25, 1837 ["The American Scholar"] said that 'The office of the scholar is to cheer, to raise, and to guide men by showing them facts midst appearances.' Never have these injunctions been more timely and more appropriate than right now. But the facts, so dear to the sage of Concord, and the appearances, so dear to the barons of communication, are blurred. . . . The role of scholarship is ever to decipher, to decode, to exercise the relentless quest for cryptographic unravellings. . . . But how increasingly difficult it is to know whether the decoded message is but decipherment of yet another message more elusive, more fundamental, more fortified in a thornier technical system."

Sapp's *Piano Sonata III* (see W19, P19k) was performed at the lecture by his wife, Norma Bertolami Sapp.

B42b. "In Time Take Time While Time Doth Last, For Time Is No Time When Time Is Past." Thomas James Kelly Lecture Series, "Obvious Questions, Impossible Answers," 30 January 1980, Patricia Corbett Theatre, University of Cincinnati College-Conservatory of Music.

Sapp provides an autobiographical sketch of the development of his compositional career in three distinct periods: childhood (through 1939); his Boston period (1939-61); and his post-Boston period (1961-1980). During a brief focus upon the series theme, "Obvious Questions, Impossible Answers," Sapp addresses (but does not really "answer") three of the most puzzling questions concerning his career: 1) "Why, if you want to use serial techniques, do you find it necessary to work in keys and forms which are clearly identified with other eras?" 2) "Why is it that you permit [works] which you obviously believe in, and for which you have obviously continued affection, to languish unpublished [and] unperformed?" 3) "Why aren't you writing more?" The latter "obvious question" is in reference to Sapp's nearly two decade long hiatus from productive composition. Surprisingly, Sapp predicts his own sudden dramatic outburst of compositional activity and depth of expression which would begin several months later: "The decade lying ahead is the one in which the marvelous experiences of building enterprises, of ensuring their continuity, of learning the joy of creating institutions and the bitterness of seeing them wither or collapse, can be folded into the musical technique and the expressive vocabulary, to make a series of works far more broad and far more strongly communicative than anything I've done in the past."

Sapp's *Violin Sonata III* (see W62, P62d) was performed at the lecture by Mimi Bryant, violin, and Pat Sinozich, piano.

B42c. "Silence More Musical Than Any Song." Thomas James Kelly Lecture Series, "Obvious Questions, Impossible Answers," 31 January 1980, Patricia Corbett Theatre, University of Cincinnati College-Conservatory of Music.

Sapp discusses many of the considerations made by composers in selecting and setting texts to music, including background on his selection of the Robert Herrick poems for his *The Lady and the Lute* (W87). In the second half of the lecture, Sapp addresses the role of silence in music: "Silence is infinitely more than the absence of sound. It is a presence of resonances and accumulated musics. It is an affirmation of human needs for rest. . . . Need I remind everyone that it is from interior silence that music comes in the first place. We composers have stimuli of every sort, but we must make ourselves silent before we start to compose. If we do not, we create a music somehow tainted, less pure, less ourselves, and probably less true."

Sapp's *The Lady and the Lute* (see W87) was supposed to be performed live at the lecture by soprano Nelga Lynn Dinerstein and pianist Norma Bertolami Sapp, but due to a sudden illness of the soprano a tape recording of a recent performance by these two performers (see P87m) was played instead. Following Sapp's address, Norma Bertolami Sapp performed his *Piano Sonata III* (see W19, P19l)

B43. "Congress of Strings Orchestra Concert Reviews." *International Musician* 80 (September 1981): 5, 38.

Sapp reviewed three concerts performed by the Congress of Strings student orchestra at the University of Cincinnati College-Conservatory of Music. The concerts were conducted by Gunther Schuller, Rafael Druian, and Morton Gould, and featured works by Gould, Britten, Dvořák, Elgar, Mozart, Tchaikovsky, David Diamond, David Koblitz, and Nicolai Miaskowski.

B44. "New Buildings: New Obligations." *UB Today* (March 1982): 13.

An address delivered at the dedication ceremonies in Slee Hall, the new concert hall at the State University of New York at Buffalo, 22 November 1981. Sapp presented seven obligations to the university: "First, you have an obligation to General Education. . . . Second, an obligation to Scholarship. . . . Third, the obligation to resume and intensify Buffalo's unique contribution to composers and to new music. . . . Fourth, the obligation to produce new breeds of performers . . . Buffalo's mission is to develop performers with minds, heads, hearts, brilliance and imagination of the most stunning sort. . . . Fifth, the obligation to leadership in the artistic community must be met by students and faculty as they work outside the academic world, lest the achievements of the new structure, the new cultural fabric of this country be lost in the stringent times ahead. . . . Sixth, the obligation to work within the fields of the arts and sciences with colleagues of equal stature and imagination to break down the traditional disciplinary barriers . . . Seventh—and finally—the obligation to the planners, builders and visionaries of this place and of this institution to whom we now all pay tribute. It is not possible that all of you can fail the dreams of Cameron Baird, and the forcefulness of Frederic Slee, and the grand architectural scale of Clifford Furnas, and the remarkable tenacity and courage of Robert Ketter."

B45. "Gielen's Challenge." *Cincinnati Enquirer*, 18 April 1982.

Sapp's letter to the editor urges the subscribers, the musicians, and board of directors of the Cincinnati Symphony Orchestra to give their full support to their conductor, Michael Gielen, following the board's decision to renew his contract for three years (his initial seasons had caused some discontent over his frequent programming of contemporary music).

B46. "Thea Musgrave: Perspective." Keynote address at a symposium of the same title at the University of Cincinnati College-Conservatory of Music, 16 January 1986. Unpublished.

An overview of the career and compositional style of Thea Musgrave. Sapp includes some personal reminiscences in the section concerning Musgrave's years of training with Nadia Boulanger, and a passage concerning Sapp's first occasion of hearing Musgrave's music in London in 1968-69.

B47. "Ruth Crawford-Seeger." Paper presented at a symposium, "Ruth Crawford-Seeger, Composer and Educator," at the University of Cincinnati College-Conservatory of Music, 9 April 1987. Unpublished.

This colorful introductory essay for the symposium opens with a presentation of numerous statistics and news facts of 1901, the year of Crawford-Seeger's birth, and continues this thematic element throughout the essay. The bulk of the essay provides a biographical sketch of the composer and some of the significant personalities and events that contributed to the development of her career.

V. WRITINGS ABOUT SAPP

THIS CHAPTER IS AN ANNOTATED BIBLIOGRAPHY of all known published items containing biographical information about Allen Sapp. The citations are presented in chronological order; author access is provided through the general index. Items which are primarily reviews of his compositions have been excluded from this section, and may be found with the entries for compositions in the "Works and Performances" section (given "WB" numbers).

B48. "Composer, Aged 12, Wins First Prize." *New York Times*, 3 February 1942.
Sapp's *Andante for Orchestra* (W110) shared second prize with Luise Vosgerchien's *Window Shopping* in the New York Philharmonic Young Composer's Contest of 1942. First prize was won by André Mathieu of Montreal, for his *Concertino for Piano and Orchestra*. Dika Newlin was awarded third prize for her *Piano Concerto*. Gunther Schuller (for "two movements of a symphony") and Mario di Bonaventura (for *Three Symphonic Sketches*) shared in a special fourth prize. Harry John Brown received honorable mention for his work *Arizona*.

B49. "Three Commissions." *New York Times*, 7 June 1942.
Allen Sapp, William Bergsma, and Norman Dello Joio were selected as recipients of the Town Hall Composition Award. "They were chosen by their respective schools [Harvard, Eastman, and Juilliard] as the outstanding students, whose work in composition was felt deserving of recognition by performance before the city's music public and critics." The three works for chamber orchestra were to be performed on a subscription concert by the Saidenberg Little Symphony (conducted by Daniel Saidenberg) on 17 February 1943; for some reason, this program was canceled in favor of a concert featuring works by Aaron Copland. Sapp completed his *Concertino for Piano and Orchestra* (W111) in fulfillment of the commission, but the work was never performed by the Saidenberg Little Symphony.

B50. Reis, Claire R. *Composers in America: Biographical Sketches of Contemporary Composers with a Record of Their Works.* Rev., enl. ed. New York: Macmillan, 1947.

A brief biographical sketch, with a selective list of compositions and reporting of recent performances. The sentence, "His works were performed in London, Paris, Belgium, Luxembourg and in Munich where he was stationed," should be clarified: while the performances in Paris (P111b), Belgium (P42a, in Namur), and Munich (P42b) were public concerts, Sapp recalls that the performances in London and Luxembourg were private "house" concerts featuring draft versions of his *Four Hand Piano Sonata I* then considered to be piano sketches for a symphony (telephone conversation with the author, 1 September 1995).

B51. "Music 51." In *The Harvard Crimson Confidential Guide to Freshman Courses, 1949.* Cambridge: The Harvard Crimson, September 1949.

In a review of instructors for the course "Music 51" (elementary harmony and analysis with "keyboard drill"), Sapp was rated as "very helpful and as interesting as possible under the circumstances."

B52. Parmenter, Ross. "The World of Music." *New York Times*, 24 August 1952.

Brief notice of Sapp being awarded the Samuel Wechsler Commission for *The Little Boy Lost* (W102), a work written for the Tanglewood Study Group.

B53. Westergaard, Peter. "Harmony in the Four String Quartets of Arnold Schönberg." B.A. honors thesis, Harvard University, 1953.

In his acknowledgements, the author cites his "debt to the aid and counsel of my tutor, Mr. Allen Sapp. Without his exhaustive knowledge of the music treated here, this essay could never have been written."

B54. Thomson, Virgil. "Music and Musicians: Choral Conference." *New York Herald Tribune*, 16 August 1953.

Thomson presents a summary of the conference entitled "The American Composer and Choral Music," held at Harvard University on 10 and 11 August 1953. The conference was organized by Sapp, and featured as speakers and panelists Archibald T. Davison, Perry Dunlap Smith, Robert Middleton, Irving Fine, Elliott Carter and Sapp; G. Wallace Woodworth and Virgil Thomson served as moderators. Discussions at the conference centered on why there seems to be a lack of interest among American composers in writing for chorus. Some of the reasons given were "the musical and textual limits of the choral medium, . . . its compromising associations with musical amateurism and its hopeless involvement with all that is most basic in American life." Commissioning programs were suggested as a means of luring American composers to write choral works. Finding money for commissioning works was seen as less of a problem than "how to choose the composers, how to inspire them and how to cooperate with them on the technical level." See also: B135.

B55. Gropius, Walter, and Mrs. [Ise Frank] Gropius. Letter to the editor of *Good Listening* 3, no. 9 (February 1955): 4.

Walter Gropius and his second wife nominated Sapp for *Good Listening*'s second annual Man of the Year in Music Award in appreciation for his nationally syndicated radio series, "Music of the Baroque" (see B5). They recognized him "for his sustained effort at giving us a carefully built-up demonstration of a particularly fascinating phase of musical development: the baroque. His scholarly and loving presentation and his exemplary style of delivery are a delight to the listener."

B56. "Sapp, Allen Dwight." In *Baker's Biographical Dictionary of Musicians*, revised by Nicolas Slonimsky. 5th ed. New York: G. Schirmer, 1958.

Brief biographical article and selective works list. The list includes *Four Motets* (W143), a work which is currently missing. See also: W107, B64, B103, B129, B141.

B57. "Sapp, Allen Dwight." In *Musikkens Hvem Hvad Hvor*, edited by Ludvig Ernst Bramsen. Copenhagen: Politikens Forlag, 1961.

Brief biography (in Danish) and a selective list of major compositions.

B58. "A. D. Sapp Is Named New Chairman of UB's Music Department." *Buffalo Evening News*, 10 March 1961.

A notice of Sapp's appointment as Chairman of the University of Buffalo's Music Department and a brief biographical sketch.

B59. "UB Music Section Head Is Appointed." *Buffalo Courier-Express*, 11 March 1961.

A notice of Sapp's appointment as Chairman of the University of Buffalo's Music Department and a brief biographical sketch.

B60. Hartnett, Jean D. "New UB Music Head Established Composer." *Buffalo Courier-Express*, 13 August 1961.

Basic biographical information is provided, along with some of Sapp's immediate plans for the young Music Department: "We are going to move rather quickly into an expanded area of graduate work to meet the new challenge we are facing here at the University as a whole." Sapp also provides a summary of his compositional style: "There are many functions, many platforms, many areas of communion in music. There is not only one kind of music, as there is not only one kind of person. Music has various purposes of refreshing the inner life, providing *divertisments*, entertaining, uplifting. . . My music ranges from extremely simple, pleasing pieces to extremely thorny, knotty ones. I think that's the way people are."

B61. Eaton, Erna P. "Live Concerts Still Best, Pianist Says." *Buffalo Courier-Express*, 19 October 1961.

An interview with Norma Bertolami Sapp prior to her performance of her husband's *Piano Sonatas II* and *IV* (see P16c and P20d) at his first 1961 Slee Lecture, "The Personal Gesture" (see B17a). Mrs. Sapp mentions that her husband's *Sonatas II* and *IV* were written in Rome, but "do not reflect any Roman influence. But during the time we spent in Rome, Allen experienced great inspiration for composing." The article also provides an overview of

Mrs. Sapp's career as a pianist and teacher, and discusses the musical studies of their sons Christopher and Anthony.

B62. Bergholtz, Berna. "Krips Returns." *Musical America* 82, no. 1 (January 1962): 126.

In an article describing musical activities in Buffalo (in the "National Report" section), mention is made of Sapp's appointment as Chairman of the University of Buffalo Music Department and of his Slee Lecture Series (see B17a-c).

B63. Ericson, Raymond. "Buffalo Takes a Flyer on Foss." *New York Times*, 24 November 1963.

In this interview with Lukas Foss, he mentions the concept which he developed with Sapp for a group of "25 musicians—12 instrumentalists, 1 conductor, 4 vocalists, 4 composers and 4 theoreticians—to take up residence in the community and develop a program of concentrated music-making." This idea eventually developed into the Center of the Creative and Performing Arts at the State University of New York at Buffalo, initially funded through the Rockefeller Foundation the following year.

B64. "Sapp, Allen Dwight." In *The International Cyclopedia of Music and Musicians*, edited by Robert Sabin. 9th ed. New York: Dodd, Mead & Co., 1964.

Brief biographical article and selective works list. The list includes *Four Motets* (W143), a work which is currently missing. See also: W107, B56.

B65. Salzman, Eric. "Far Out in Buffalo." *New York Herald Tribune Magazine* (10 May 1964): 31.

An announcement of the formation of the Center of the Creative and Performing Arts at the State University of New York at Buffalo. The center, founded by Sapp and Lukas Foss, was started through a grant from the Rockefeller Foundation, and will bring a group of composers and musicians interested in experimental new music together in a setting similar to a research center.

B66. Bugelski, Vicki. "Fine Memorial Concert Set for Baird Saturday Evening." *Spectrum* [State University of New York at Buffalo], 4 December 1964.

Presents details of the memorial concert organized by Sapp for Irving Fine, who died in 1962 before his prospective appointment as a visiting Slee Professor at the State University of New York at Buffalo. "Allen Sapp . . . was Fine's first tutorial student at Harvard. They became good friends."

B67. "Talk of the Town: Foss." *The New Yorker* (30 January 1965): 22-24.

An interview with Lukas Foss, which describes activities of the first year of the Center of the Creative and Performing Arts at SUNY-Buffalo. Sapp is mentioned as a collaborator in the establishment of the Center.

B68. "The Avant-Garde: New Faces in the Creative Arts." *Buffalo Alumnus* 4, no. 4 (fall 1965): 1-8.

The activities and personalities associated with the stunningly successful first year of the Center of the Creative and Performing Arts at the State

University of New York at Buffalo. "Given logistic and moral support by the University, the Center cooperates also with the Buffalo Philharmonic Orchestra, the Albright-Knox Art Gallery, and the Buffalo Foundation for the purpose of maintaining, in the words of Mr. Sapp, 'a community of artists working in series and in parallel—unique in American university and metropolitan life.'"

B69. Dwyer, John.   "Scholar Sees Threat to Language by Jargon, Computer." *Buffalo Evening News*, 12 October 1965.

A summary of Sapp's lecture "Music and Language" (see B23) given the previous evening under the auspices of the Frederic Slee Chair at the State University of New York at Buffalo.

B70. Austin, William W. *Music in the 20th Century, from Debussy through Stravinsky.* New York: W. W. Norton, 1966.

Sapp is listed as one of the "expert composers" who developed under the guidance of Walter Piston at Harvard University (p. 441). Elsewhere, in a discussion of the important influence of Debussy's music upon composers of the mid 20th century, Austin quotes Sapp's remark (p. 42) concerning *Pelléas et Mélisande*, which "presages our day, when we feel no longer the need for a tradition" (see B9).

B71. "UB a Cultural Hub for Area, New Faculty Members Told; Incoming Teachers Hear about the City of Good Neighbors, Advantages of Winter." *Buffalo Evening News*, 13 September 1966.

Sapp, speaking to an assembly of new faculty members at the State University of New York at Buffalo, describes the "remarkable climate" of Buffalo's artistic community, made possible in part by close interaction of the major cultural institutions: the university, Studio Arena Theater, Albright-Knox Art Gallery, and the Buffalo Philharmonic Orchestra.

B72. "$500,000 Pledged in 5 Months to Philharmonic Matching Fund." *Buffalo Evening News*, 9 December 1966.

Martin Meyerson, President of the State University of New York at Buffalo, announced the appointment of Sapp to the newly-created position of Director of Cultural Affairs at a fund-raising dinner for the Buffalo Philharmonic Orchestra. "Mr. Meyerson praised Prof. Sapp . . . for 'his exemplary taste and tact and entrepreneurial skill as well as academic proficiency . . . We will depend upon him to help formulate educational policy regarding the arts at our university and to help carry through an ever more broadening program in the arts.'"

B73. Dell, Virginia C. "Cultural Alliance Asked Here." *Buffalo Courier-Express*, 9 December 1966.

Another account of . President Meyerson's remarks at a Buffalo Philharmonic Orchestra fund-raising dinner, announcing the appointment of Sapp as Director of Cultural Affairs for the State University of New York at Buffalo.   Meyerson enumerated several possible projects that Sapp could develop to extend the mutually beneficial relations between the university and the orchestra, including "offering sabbatical or Nieman-type fellowships for professional enrichment of musicians; making special arrangements with the orchestra to perform new works; assisting in technical and financial arrangements for a series of recordings by the orchestra; commissioning new music in collaboration with the orchestra; and furthering scholarly foundation of music by offering study in related fields to composers and theorists."

B74. Schlaerth, J. Don. "CBS to Televise New Music at UB." *Buffalo Evening News*, 14 December 1966.

Notice of an upcoming feature segment on the Center of the Creative and Performing Arts on the CBS Evening News (exact broadcast date not supplied). The reporter, George Herman, planned to include interviews with Sapp and Foss as well as excerpts from performances of works by Maryanne Amacher and Cornelius Cardew.

B75. "Sapp's Busy Program Inhibits Composing." *Buffalo Courier-Express* 30 April 1967.

This interview took place at a time when Sapp held four concurrent positions at the State University of New York at Buffalo: Professor and Chair of the Department of Music; Co-Director of the Center of the Creative and Performing Arts; Head of the Division of Languages, Literature and the Arts; and Director of Cultural Affairs. "The only thing that bothers him is that his duties have left him without any time for composing. . . . He described his work as co-director of the center as 'the fun job. That's where the action is.'" The author also praises Sapp's accomplishments as a cultural ambassador for the city, and presents his views on the need for "interaction and respect" between the scholar, performer, and composer.

B76. Foss, Lukas. "Buffalo Is Not a Vacuum." *New York Times*, 28 May 1967.

Foss remarks that his radical programming of contemporary music with the Buffalo Philharmonic Orchestra met with considerable community opposition, especially after giving the American première of Stockhausen's *Momente* in 1964. "There are no champions of modern music on my Buffalo Philharmonic board, but there are men of wisdom willing to take a chance. They allowed me to continue; moreover, they decided to support me and Allen Sapp (a man for whom I have unlimited respect), in our bid for an entire festival of new music. Seymour Knox became interested and the result was Buffalo's Festival of the Arts Today." Foss also describes the first three years of new music concerts given by the Center of the Creative and Performing Arts at the State University of New York at Buffalo, describing Sapp and himself as the "harassed founding fathers" for the center.

B77. Tepas, Susan K. "Buffalo's Revolution in the Arts: January 1963 through June 1965." Master's thesis, University of Minnesota, September 1967.

An excellent chronicle of two and a half years of rapid development in the major arts institutions of Buffalo based largely on newspaper reports and interviews with several of Buffalo's leading artistic figures (including Sapp). A copy of this paper is held by the University Archives, State University of New York at Buffalo.

B78.   Dwyer, John F. "New Opera Era in Buffalo: Vision Hazy Yet Rosy." *Buffalo Evening News*, 14 October 1967.

Opera performances in Buffalo by visiting professional companies and the local opera program at the State University of New York at Buffalo were becoming more frequent, with an even brighter possible future.   Sapp discussed the necessity to cooperate with other local cultural institutions in order to bring about operatic performances of a high caliber.   This was evident from the three university productions planned for that season: Britten's *Rape of Lucretia* staged in the sculpture court of the Albright-Knox Art Gallery; Rossini's *Barber of Seville* in a fully staged version with the Buffalo Philharmonic Orchestra on their subscription series; and the première of Henri Pousseur's *Votre Faust* at the 1968 Buffalo Festival of the Arts Today (Albright-Knox Art Gallery) featuring musicians of the UB Center of the Creative and Performing Arts.

B79.   "Park School Names 3 Trustees." *Buffalo Evening News*, 21 October 1967.

Sapp is appointed as a trustee to Park School, a private grade school in Buffalo, along with Martin Meyerson, President of the State University of New York at Buffalo, and John Chandler, a former president of the National Association of Independent Schools.

B80.   Behrman, David.   Liner notes for Terry Riley, *In C*.   Terry Riley, with members of the Center of the Creative and Performing Arts in the State University of New York at Buffalo.   Columbia Masterworks MS 7178. [Released ca. 1968.]

Briefly mentions Sapp as co-director (with Lukas Foss) of the Center of the Creative and Performing Arts.

B81.   Brady, Karen. "UB to Start Six Colleges on Amherst Site in Fall; 4 Masters Chosen as University Takes 1st Step." *Buffalo Evening News*, 19 June 1968.

As the State University of New York at Buffalo embarked on establishing separate colleges within the university along the lines of those at Cambridge, Harvard and Yale, Sapp was appointed Master of "College B" (one concerned with the fine arts). The other founding college masters were poet Mac Hammond, physicist Lyle Borst, and engineer John Huddleston. Sapp remarked that "we are attempting to evolve in our own university some of the most successful features of the best institutions in England, Canada and the U.S. . . . Information is not the key in the college—but the quality of thought is. . . . It will be a place where descriptions will not be enough. We will try to make an effort to see what makes the geologist tick, or the artist the way he is. These are things you largely find out from peers. . . . The master will be close, but not so close that he will be suffocating . . . he will be close, but not so close that he will be suffocated."

B82.   "UB Picks Masters for New Colleges." *Buffalo Courier Express*, 19 June 1968.

A brief announcement of Sapp being named as one of the four founding masters of the collegiate system at the State University of New York at Buffalo. Each of the masters apparently committed to moving their families within the residence halls of the college once the new facilities were built on the new Amherst Campus.

B83.   "Allen Sapp of UB Urges Support for Philharmonic." *Buffalo Evening News*, 11 December 1969.
A summary of Sapp's letter written to Erie County (N.Y.) Executive B. John Tutuska, urging him to consider offering emergency financial support for the Buffalo Philharmonic Orchestra.

B84.   Putnam, Thomas. "Encounter to Offer Two Guest Artists." *Buffalo Courier-Express*, 14 June 1970.
A description of the planned one-week residencies of violinist Rafael Druian and composer Daniel Pinkham, sponsored by College B of the State University of New York at Buffalo. Sapp conceived these residencies as an experimental model for future artistic residencies within College B (with the project title "Encounter"): they were designed "to break some molds, set some new patterns." Instead of simply bringing in guest artists for a single concert, the week long residency would allow for greater interaction with students and faculty of the university, as well as members of the musical community (e.g., public master classes and informal discussion sessions). Each residency would also feature two public concerts: one at the university, and one outside the university. "We will be creating the kind of situation the artist wants and doesn't get. . . . We will be making it possible for him to be himself—to create his own occasion."

B85.   "10 Receive Awards for Linking Campus and Community." *Buffalo Evening News*, 6 February 1971.
Sapp received a "Town and Gown" award from the Women's Committee of the Buffalo Museum of Science for his contributions toward energizing the artistic life of Buffalo during the previous decade.

B86.   "UB Professor Takes Arts Post," *Buffalo Evening News*, 26 February 1971.
A brief article announcing Sapp's two-year leave of absence in order to accept the appointment as Director of Arts/Worth, a project of the American Council for the Arts in Education, supported by the National Endowment for the Humanities and the National Endowment for the Arts. "The aim of the program is to 'strengthen the roles of the arts in education' . . . bringing the arts 'into a more central place in the educational system of this country.'"

B87.   "Meeting to Stress Education in Arts." *Indianapolis Star*, 9 May 1971.
An announcement of Sapp's keynote address to be given on 15 May 1971 to the conference "Education through the Arts" at the Indianapolis Museum of Art, sponsored by the Indiana State Arts Commission. Sapp's address was entitled "Esthetic Sensitivity: What it Means in Our Children."

B88.   Gardner, Paul. "Conference to Study Urban Arts Centers as Links to Schools." *New York Times*, 19 June 1972.
A preview on the eve of the opening of the conference, "Community Arts and Community Survival," sponsored by the American Council for the Arts in Education, the Los Angeles Community Arts Alliance, and the Department of Arts and Humanities, University Extension, University of California, Los Angeles. Sapp remarked that one of the major activities would

be observing "how the art centers relate to public education by visiting several centers in Los Angeles. Our guests will see what's being done here and, hopefully, take some ideas back to their own cities."

B89. "Allen Sapp Named Head of Council." *Buffalo Courier-Express*, 25 June 1972.

A brief notice of Sapp's appointment as Executive Director of the American Council for the Arts in Education.

B90. "UB Educator Sapp Elected Council for Arts Director." *Buffalo Evening News*, 26 June 1972.

A brief notice of Sapp's appointment as Executive Director of the American Council for the Arts in Education.

B91. Foote, Ted. "The Arts Organize." *School Arts* 72 (October 1972): 10.

"Arts/Worth," a major project of the American Council for the Arts in Education (ACAE) under Sapp's direction, was described by ACAE president Edward L. Kamarck as having the mission of "dramatizing the merits and logic of incorporating the arts into the U.S. educational system from nursery school through graduate school and on into adult education."

B92. "Williams Gets Theater Award." *New York Times*, 8 December 1972.

A report of events at the opening meeting of the 1972 National Theater Conference in New York City. Sapp's remarks focus on the problems associated with public support for the arts. For a summary of his address, see B30.

B93. "Conference Offers Free Journey into World of Art." *Buffalo Evening News*, 2 May 1973.

Sapp served as a panelist during a three day conference in Buffalo entitled "The University, the Community and the Arts," sponsored by the State University of New York University-wide Committee on the Arts. This touring conference, which featured performances and exhibits by many Buffalo arts organizations at several venues, was modeled upon the June 1972 Los Angeles conference entitled "Community Arts and Community Survival," sponsored by the American Council for the Arts in Education (see B88).

B94. Putnam, Thomas. "Need is Cited for Regional Arts Council." *Buffalo Courier-Express*, 11 December 1973.

Sapp spoke at a workshop for community arts leaders sponsored by the new Buffalo regional arts council, Arts Development Services (ADS). Sapp's remarks were a balance of "elation and sobriety": elation over the long awaited and much needed "true launching" of ADS, and sobriety in reflection upon the many needs of local arts organizations for financial and organizational support.

B95. "Sapp Resigns College B Post, Stays in Music Department." *Buffalo Evening News*, 17 January 1974.

Sapp resigned as Master of College B at the State University of New York at Buffalo on 13 January 1974. A spokesperson for the university cited "the press of Dr. Sapp's other duties" as the main reason for his resignation from this post.

B96. "Sapp, Allen Dwight." In *Riemann Musik Lexikon*, edited by Carl Dahlhaus. 12th ed. Mainz: B. Schott's Söhne, 1975.

Brief biographical article and selective works list in German. The works list includes *"Fantasie für Vc.*, 1965" (*Fantasy for Violoncello*) a work which was commissioned by Mischa Schneider of the Budapest Quartet, but was never completed.

B97. "Symphony Women Told of City Cultural Boost." *Buffalo Evening News*, 16 April 1975.

In an address to the Women's Association for Symphony Orchestras held in Buffalo, Sapp said that civic morale in 1961 was extremely low. The major cultural institutions "seized leadership of the psyche," and their rapid development in the 1960s helped to restore community pride.

B98. "Allen Sapp Takes Post at Florida State." *Reporter* [State University of New York at Buffalo], 11 September 1975.

An announcement of Sapp's resignation from the State University of New York at Buffalo to accept the position of Provost, Division of Communication and the Arts, at Florida State University.

B99. "Prof. Sapp to Leave UB for Fla. State U. Post." *Buffalo Courier-Express*, 11 September 1975.

An announcement of Sapp's resignation from the State University of New York at Buffalo to accept the position of Provost, Division of Communication and the Arts, at Florida State University.

B100. "UB's Dr. Sapp Named Provost at Florida State." *Buffalo Evening News*, 11 September 1975.

An announcement of Sapp's resignation from the State University of New York at Buffalo to accept the position of Provost, Division of Communication and the Arts, at Florida State University.

B101. "Harvard Honoree." *Buffalo Evening News*, 12 November 1975.

Sapp was given the 1975 "Man of the Year" award by the Harvard-Radcliffe University Club of Buffalo.

B102. "Retiring Department Head Honored." *Buffalo Courier-Express*, 12 November 1975.

Another notice of Sapp's 1975 "Man of the Year" award from the Harvard-Radcliffe University Club of Buffalo.

B103. "Sapp, Allen Dwight." In *Baker's Biographical Dictionary of Musicians*, revised by Nicolas Slonimsky. 6th ed. New York: Schirmer Books, 1978.

Brief biographical article and selective works list. The biography contains one minor erroneous statement (also in 7th and 8th editions): "attended classes of Aaron Copland and Nadia Boulanger in Cambridge (1942-43)." Sapp actually attended Copland's composition class at the Berkshire Music Center (near Lenox, Mass.) in the summer of 1942, then studied privately with Copland in New York City during the following autumn and winter. His studies with Boulanger were also private, and were held each

week at the Peabody Conservatory of Music in Baltimore; he also
accompanied Boulanger on one segment (Philadelphia to Baltimore) of her
weekly commuter train between Boston and Baltimore for additional study.
See also: B56, B129, B141.

B104. "Sapp, Allen Dwight." In *Frank/Altmann Kurzgefaßtes Tonkünstler-Lexikon.*
15 ed. Wilhelmshaven: Heinrichshofens Verlag, 1978.
    Abbreviated biographical entry in German.   The compositions and
biographical information provided were out of date by two decades at the time
of publication, e.g., "Komp., lehrt seit 1949 an d. Harvard Univ." (Sapp left
Harvard in 1958).

B105. Thomson, William.   "Acknowledgements."   In *Evenings for New Music: A
Catalogue, 1964-77.* Buffalo: Department of Music, State University of New
York at Buffalo, 1978.
    Thomson pays tribute to Sapp, "whose genius for initiating worthy
human endeavors is widely acknowledged. He was the real source of the
Center, and we remain indebted to him for his vision."

B106. "UC Names Dean of Music College." *Cincinnati Post*, 23 June 1978.
    Brief notice of Sapp's appointment as Dean of the University of
Cincinnati College-Conservatory of Music. His predecessor, Eugene Bonelli,
left to accept the position of Dean of the Meadows School of the Arts in
Dallas.

B107. "Sapp is Appointed CCM Dean." *UC This Week*, 13 July 1978.
    In addition to giving basic biographical information, this brief article
on Sapp's appointment lists the members of the decanal search committee,
including conductor and composer Gerhard Samuel and musicologist James
Riley.

B108. "Appointments." *The Diapason* 69 (September 1978): 11.
    Brief notice of Sapp's appointment as Dean of the University of
Cincinnati College-Conservatory of Music.

B109. Chute, James. "CCM Has New Dean, Spirit." *Cincinnati Post*, 29 September
1978.
    Sapp outlines some of his plans for renewing the spirit and reputation
of the University of Cincinnati College-Conservatory of Music, including an
intensification of effort in recruiting and fund raising, expanding CCM's
commitment to the local region through community outreach efforts,
establishing associations or partnerships with other large music schools
(especially overseas), and emphasizing quality instruction and counseling of
students.

B110. McGuirk, Kevin. Sapp Excited with CCM." *The News Record* [University of
Cincinnati], 6 February 1979.
    This article, written by a student reporter, presents basic biographical
information about Sapp. When asked the odd question who would be his
"favorite composers to be stranded with on a desert island," Sapp responded

with "Josquin, Mozart, Rameau, and Arnold Schoenberg, whom he likes for the 'religious and moral quality' of his music. . . . His favorite piece of all time is Bach's *Art of the Fugue*."

B111. "Palombo and Sapp help coordinate AFM's 1979 Congress of Strings." *International Musician* 77 (March 1979): 4.

Sapp, then Dean of the University of Cincinnati College-Conservatory of Music, served as host for the 1979 Congress of Strings, a summer training orchestra program sponsored by the American Federation of Musicians. (A concurrent session was held on the West Coast at the University of Washington, coordinated by Paul Palombo.)   The article contains a biographical sketch of Sapp outlining his education and compositional career, but primarily emphasizing his administrative affiliations and achievements.

B112. Chute, James.   "UC's Music School Dean Feels 'Renewed Optimism.'" *Cincinnati Post*, 26 December 1979.

Upon his appointment as Dean of the University of Cincinnati College-Conservatory of Music in 1978, Sapp considered the most serious problem facing his office to be the low faculty and student morale, caused in part by the departure of several key faculty members, including pianist Raymond Dudley, vocalist Jon Spong, and former deans Jack Watson and Eugene Bonelli. Sapp set about building morale by several methods: making himself easily available to faculty and students by instituting an informal, open-door policy; attending as many "routine CCM functions" as possible, such as recitals and student productions; making improvements in methods of recruiting students; and making several new faculty appointments of distinguished teachers and performers, including violist Donald McInnes and pianist Bela Siki.

B113. Levine, Arthur. *Why Innovation Fails.* Albany: State University of New York Press, 1980.

Chapter 3 contains a history of the collegiate system developed under the leadership of President Martin Meyerson in the late 1960s. Mention is made of Sapp as one of the original six College Masters, but little detail of his leadership of College B is offered. Levine's account also contains a few minor errors: "Allen Sapp went on sabbatical during 1969-70" (p. 48; Sapp's administrative leave actually took place during the 1968-69 academic year); "Allan [*sic*] Sapp . . . was dean of the U. B. College of Arts and Letters" (p. 45; Sapp actually served as Head of the Division of Languages, Literature and the Arts from 1965 to 1967, and Master of College B, the newly created arts and philosophy college, from 1968 to 1974.)

B114. O'Connell, Doris. "National Music Council General Meeting." *National Music Council Bulletin* 39, no. 2 (1980): 6-7.

The article summarizes Sapp's report given at the meeting of the National Music Council at the John F. Kennedy Center for the Performing Arts, Washington D.C., 17 January 1980. Sapp reported on two meetings held by the International Committee of the National Music Council during the previous year (the other members of the committee included Barry Brook, Donald Leavitt, Merle Montgomery, and Gunther Schuller). The committee saw as their primary mission to develop plans and funding for enhancing the international reputation of "American 'serious' or 'symphonic' music—and to some extent, even 'serious jazz'" through various methods of international communication such as recordings and broadcasting.

B115. "Reports from Member Organizations: National Guild of Community Schools of the Arts." *National Music Council Bulletin* 39, no. 2 (1980): 36-37.

Sapp is announced as the newly-elected president of the National Guild. The article lists some of Sapp's early accomplishments in office, including the establishment of the National Guild's Governmental Relations and Development office in Washington, a long-range planning committee, and strengthening the student certification program.

B116. "Sapp, Allen Dwight." In *The New Grove Dictionary of Music and Musicians*, edited by Stanley Sadie. London: Macmillan, 1980.

Brief biographical article and selective list of compositions.

B117. Brown, Ellen. "CCM's Allen Sapp Calls It Quits." *Cincinnati Enquirer*, 7 November 1980.

A brief announcement of Allen Sapp offering his resignation as Dean of the University of Cincinnati College-Conservatory of Music on 5 November 1980. No details are offered of the circumstances surrounding his resignation.

B118. Chute, James. "Music Dean Resigns, May Stay as Teacher." *Cincinnati Post*, 7 November 1980.

John P. McCall, Senior Vice President and Provost of the University of Cincinnati, accepted Allen Sapp's resignation as Dean of the College-Conservatory of Music on 6 November 1980. According to McCall, "It was not a problem with Dean Sapp's role as an academic planner and as a leader, but with his role as a fiscal planner and manager." Sapp apparently had approved the appointment of too many part-time instructors at the beginning of the 1980-81 academic year, which left CCM's budget, according to McCall, "overdrawn or about to be overdrawn."

B119. Lee, Felicia. "CCM Dean Resigns after Budget Disclosures." *Cincinnati Enquirer*, 10 November 1980.

John P. McCall, Senior Vice President and Provost of the University of Cincinnati, denied that Allen Sapp's resignation as Dean of the College-Conservatory of Music had been requested by the administration; he apparently offered his resignation since "the problems were such it was very difficult to proceed." Sapp overspent his 1980-81 budget by $8,000, and apparently had additional requests for funds pending. "A high-ranking university official who asked not to be named said that had those proposals been met without investigation, CCM would have been $88,000 over its allotted budget. . . . 'What we're looking at is not a major difficulty for the college budget,' McCall said. 'I'm anticipating a good year for the college.'"

B120. "Regional News [Ohio]." *United Press International* (via *Lexis/Nexis*), 10 November 1980.

Announcement of Sapp's resignation as Dean of the University of Cincinnati College-Conservatory of Music.

B121. "Opinion and Comment: Keep Academic Integrity." *The News Record* [University of Cincinnati], 14 November 1980.

An article criticizing the administration of the University of Cincinnati for their handling of Allen Sapp's resignation. "We have to raise serious questions about supplanting excellent academicians in their field, such as Sapp, with those who are more adept at balancing the budget. . . . Sapp . . . was obviously chosen to be dean because of his musical excellence—not because of his ability to manage a balance sheet. . . . Does [the] necessary budgetary mission override the vital academic mission of this or any other university? We do not think so." The editorial calls for the appointment of qualified financial officers to be appointed at the college level to assist deans, who should not have to personally manage their institutional budgets.

B122. Jablonski, Edward. "Sapp, Allen Dwight." *The Encyclopedia of American Music.* Garden City, N.Y.: Doubleday, 1981.

Brief biographical article and selective works list.

B123. Walters, Teresa. "Nadia Boulanger, Musician and Teacher: Her Life, Concepts, and Influences." D.M.A. diss., Peabody Institute of Music, Johns Hopkins University, 1981.

Mentions Sapp in passing as a student of Boulanger; no other information on Sapp's interaction with Boulanger is provided.

B124. Anderson, E. Ruth. "Sapp, Allen Dwight." In *Contemporary American Composers: A Biographical Dictionary.* 2nd. ed. Boston: G. K. Hall, 1982.

Brief biographical entry and selective list of works (without dates). Erroneously states that he "was professor, State Univ. of New York at Buffalo, 1972-74" (his actual dates of service were from 1961 to 1975).

B125. "Around Town." *Cincinnati Enquirer,* 14 March 1982.

Brief notice of Sapp's appointment as Chair of the Board of the American Music Scholarship Association.

B126. Putnam, Thomas. "Sapp Returns to Play His Music." *Buffalo News,* 11 December 1982.

In addition to reviewing the works performed on this concert celebrating the composer's 60th birthday, Putnam summarized his views on Sapp based on his many years of reviewing his music. "All those years, Sapp's dedication was to the muse of others, for he was foremost a teacher and administrator with a vision. His music was heard here infrequently. . . . As a composer [he] is a talent of great warmth and intelligence. Sapp's music is remarkably congenial without being routine. He draws on the resources of this century knowingly, and with a wonderful craft he makes pieces that one appreciates hearing." See also: WB23a, WB44a, WB68a.

B127. "Sapp, Allen Dwight." In *Who's Who in American Music: Classical.* 1st ed. New York: R. R. Bowker, 1983.

Brief biographical entry in a highly abbreviated and telegraphic style and a small list of selected works written in the early 1980s. An identical article for Sapp appears in the second edition (1985).

B128. "World Premieres." *Symphony* 34 (June-July 1983): 145.

An announcement of the première performance of Sapp's *Crennelations* (W119) for tenor and orchestra (see P119a).

B129. "Sapp, Allen Dwight." In *Baker's Biographical Dictionary of Musicians*, revised by Nicolas Slonimsky. 7th ed. New York: Schirmer Books, 1984.

Brief biographical article and selective works list. The list includes "*Colloquies IV* for Orch. (1983)." This composition, which did not make much progress before being abandoned, was originally planned for very large orchestra. Sapp eventually gave this series title to a 1984 composition for cello and piano, *Colloquies IV: "The Lament for Adonis"* (W74). See also: B56, B103, B141.

B130. Copland, Aaron, and Vivian Perlis. *Copland, 1900 through 1942*. New York: St. Martin's, 1984.

Mentions Sapp only in passing as one of Copland's students at the Berkshire Music Center in the summer of 1942.

B131. "Sapp, Allen Dwight." In *International Who's Who in Music and Musicians' Directory*, edited by Ernest Kay. 10th ed. Cambridge, England: Melrose Press, 1984.

Brief biographical outline and selective list of compositions and writings. His work for tenor and orchestra, *Crennelations* (W119), is misspelled in this list as "*Crewellations*."

B132. Almquist, Sharon G. "A History of the State University of New York at Buffalo Music Department to 1968." Master's thesis, State University of New York at Buffalo, 1986.

The final two chapters, "Interregnum" and "The Sapp Years: The Growth of the Music Department," provide a detailed history of Sapp's recruitment to Buffalo and his radical restructuring and aggressive development of the Music Department, as well as the early history of the Center of the Creative and Performing Arts. See also: B144.

B133. "Sapp, Allen Dwight." In *The New Grove Dictionary of American Music*, edited by H. Wiley Hitchcock and Stanley Sadie. London: Macmillan, 1986.

Brief biographical article and selected works list. The latter contains an entry for a non-existent work: a second viola sonata, supposedly composed in 1981.

B134. "1986-87 Premieres and Season Highlights." *Symphony* 37 (October-November 1986): 24.

An announcement of the première performance of Sapp's *Xenón Ciborium* (W121) for orchestra (see P121a).

B135. Forbes, Elliot. *A History of Music at Harvard to 1972.* Cambridge: Department of Music, Harvard University, 1988.

In addition to providing a description of events and personalities within the Music Department during Sapp's years at Harvard University, Forbes also supplies specific years of Sapp's faculty appointments (Teaching Fellow, 1948-50; Instructor 1950-53; Assistant Professor 1953-58), and specific titles and terms of many courses taught by Sapp, including an "innovative" graduate course in 1957-58, "Studies in American Music." Forbes also describes the two summer school conferences organized by Sapp, "The American Composer and Choral Music" in 1953 (see B54), and "Music in the Church" in 1954.

B136. Steele, Daniel L. "An Investigation into the Background and Implications of the Yale Seminar on Music Education." Doctoral dissertation, University of Cincinnati College-Conservatory of Music, December 1988.

Steele interviewed Sapp about his participation in the 1963 Yale Seminar on Music Education (see B21). Sapp mentioned that conference participants were encouraged to be highly critical of the current state of music education in the U.S. The strong criticism contained in the published report of the seminar "'caused a violent reaction' among music educators which led to the Tanglewood Symposium [Music Educators National Conference (MENC), 23 July-4 August 1967]; and that the symposium became 'the main historical value' of the Yale Seminar" (p. 154). The aftermath of the Yale Seminar also helped to change "the intellectual tone of the MENC by upgrading the format of the *Music Educators Journal*" (p. 8).

B137. Cowan, Joanna. "Bowling Green Stages New Music and Art Festival." *Flute Talk* 8 (February 1989): 18-19.

In a review of performances given at this festival, the première of Sapp's *Colloquies II* (see W71, P71a) is noted, but not described in any detail. The author gives the incorrect dates of composition for this work, "1978; 1984" (actual dates are 1978, revised 1982). Mention is made of Sapp's work for alto flute and piano, *Colloquies V: The Cage of All Bright Knocks* (W79), even though it was not performed at the festival; however, the first and last words in the title were misspelled in the article: "*Colloquy V: The Cage of All Bright Knock*."

B138. Green, Alan A. "Catalog of the Works of Allen Dwight Sapp, Arranged According to *The Dickinson Classification*." Unpublished paper, State University of New York at Buffalo, April 1990.

The first version of the works catalog presented in this volume, prepared as a final assignment for the course "Music Librarianship I" at the State University of New York at Buffalo under the direction of Carol June Bradley. The catalog was arranged according to Bradley's revision (*The Dickinson Classification*, Carlisle, Pa.: Carlisle Books, 1968) of George Sherman Dickinson's *Classification of Musical Compositions* (Poughkeepsie, N.Y.: Vassar College, 1938).

B139. Perone, Karen. *Lukas Foss: A Bio-Bibliography.* New York; Westport, Conn.: Greenwood Press, 1991.

Sapp is briefly mentioned as co-founder and co-director of the Center of the Creative and Performing Arts at the State University of New York at Buffalo. Perone includes a discographical entry (D114 in Perone) for Foss's recording of Sapp's *Suite for Orchestra, no. 2* (see D113a in this volume); her entry lists the recording dates as "December 8 and 10, 1969"; the month and days are correct, but the correct year for this recording is 1968.

B140. "UC President Not Worried about No-Confidence Vote." *United Press International* (via *Lexis/Nexis*), 24 November 1991.

A brief article about the no-confidence vote taken by the faculty of the University of Cincinnati after President Joseph Steger announced severe budget-cutting measures including layoffs of 200 faculty and cancellation of academic leave. Sapp, at that time President of the UC Faculty Senate, was quoted as having said that "a no-confidence vote was threatened but never taken in 1976 against then-President Warren Bennis."

B141. "Sapp, Allen Dwight." In *Baker's Biographical Dictionary of Musicians*, revised by Nicolas Slonimsky. 8th ed. New York: Schirmer Books, 1992.

Brief biographical article and selective works list. The list includes *"Colloquies IV* for Orch. (1983)." This composition, which did not make much progress before being abandoned, was originally planned for very large orchestra. Sapp eventually gave this series title to a 1984 composition for cello and piano, *Colloquies IV: "The Lament for Adonis"* (W74). See also: B56, B103, B129.

B142. Foreman, B. J. *College-Conservatory of Music, 1867-1992: CCM 125.* Ed. by Jerri Roberts. Cincinnati: University of Cincinnati College-Conservatory of Music, 1992.

Briefly mentions Sapp's tenure as Dean of CCM, "whose incredible eye for talent brought pianist Bela Siki and violist Donald McGinnes onto the faculty. Sapp had visionary plans for CCM, abandoned when he returned to teaching and composing. Sapp, still on the faculty at CCM, recently was honored by being elected chairman of the UC Faculty Senate."

B143. Pollack, Howard. *Harvard Composers: Walter Piston and His Students from Elliott Carter to Frederic Rzewski.* Metuchen, N.J.: Scarecrow Press, 1992.

The first published study of significant length on Sapp's music; the primary body of remarks on Sapp, both biographical and analytical, falls on pages 219-230, but important commentary also appears many times in the later chapters of the book. Pollack sets an admirably wide scope in this work, offering insight into the musical and personal relationships among the many composers who studied with Piston, as well as their interaction with Piston himself. Pollack suggests that Sapp's careful study and adoption of serial technique in 1949, having "anticipated its vogue in America" (p. 226), may have had a very strong influence on other composers associated with Harvard who later incorporated the technique, including Irving Fine, Gordon Binkerd, Peter Westergaard, and even Aaron Copland. Sapp's idiosyncratic and "fairly inscrutable" (ibid.) use of the technique is discussed, including his frequent use of incomplete rows (or pitch series less than twelve), and the retention of tonal organization. Pollack makes a few general observations on works including *Piano Sonatas I* and *II, Taylor's Nine, The Lady and the Lute, A Maiden's Complaint in Springtime, Crennelations,* and *The Double Image,* but offers more substantive and technical commentary on *Piano Sonatas III* and *IV,* and the *Suite for Piano.*

Pollack groups Sapp in a chapter with his longtime friend Robert Middleton and observes the many similarities between their music and their careers, including the following: they both composed in relative obscurity with very few publications or recordings, perhaps primarily due to lack of self-promotion; their employment of serial technique within a framework of tonality; and how they both—along with others in the "third wave" (p. 426) of Piston students—turned to Nadia Boulanger for additional guidance as Piston's teaching style became more withdrawn during and after the Second World War.

A few minor errors in dates of performance and composition appear in the text. *The Double Image* was composed in 1957 (Pollack states 1956 on p. 223, but gives the correct date on p. 227). Commenting upon the long period of time it took to obtain a performance of *The Double Image,* he writes that "the work was not even performed until Lukas Foss played it with the Buffalo Philharmonic in 1963;" however, the actual date of the première occurred even later, in 1967. On p. 227 Pollack lists "*The Septagon* (1959)" (i.e., *The Heptagon,* W127) suggesting the work was completed in 1959, when actually the work remains unfinished. Finally, Pollack states on p. 228 that *Imaginary Creatures* was composed in 1980, but the correct date is 1981.

B144. Almquist, Sharon G. "Music at the University of Buffalo—The Baird Years." *American Music* 10, no. 1 (Spring 1992): 53-79.

Mentions Sapp in passing as the successor to Cameron Baird as Chair of the Music Department at the University of Buffalo (later, State University of New York at Buffalo). This is a revised version of the early chapters of Almquist's Master's thesis (see B132).

B145. *Buffalo Musicians.* Buffalo: Music Library, State University of New York at Buffalo, January 1993.

Provides official titles and years of tenure for Sapp within the Music Department of SUNY at Buffalo.

B146. "New Music's New Wave: In the Latest Incarnation of Classical Music, Listeners are Rediscovering Rhythm and Spirit." *Buffalo News,* 5 November 1993.

Sapp is mentioned along with Lukas Foss, Lejaren Hiller, Morton Feldman, Jan Williams and Yvar Mikhashoff as a person who helped to establish a strong "international presence" for Buffalo in the world of new music.

B147. Wolff, Christine. "Retirement Rule Too Late for Professor in Full Bloom." *Cincinnati Enquirer,* 1 January 1994.

Ohio outlawed the age 70 mandatory retirement rule, effective 1 January 1994; Allen Sapp turned age 71 on 10 December 1993, twenty-one days too soon to be exempted from the rule. Therefore, he was forced to retire on 1 September 1993. Sapp remained active as a part-time faculty member with emeritus status. "I hated to retire. I guess I'm feeling a little sorry for myself. I feel a certain amount of wistfulness about my situation. . . . I'm in full bloom, and I enjoy the teaching environment. I think the end of the [mandatory retirement rule] is good."

B148. Green, Alan A. "Allen Sapp: Composer, Teacher, and Administrator." Master's thesis, State University of New York at Buffalo, September 1994.

Strikingly similar to the present volume, but lacking the annotated bibliographies of writings by and about Sapp, the "Discography/Webography," and the general index. The present volume also contains many addenda and corrigenda for B148 in the "Works and Performances" section and updates the biography. One section not carried over from B148 to the present volume is the comprehensive "Works Consulted" section; it would have largely duplicated the annotated bibliography chapters in the present volume except for citations of unpublished documents in archives (many of which are cited in notes in this volume) and published literature not specifically about Sapp.

B149. Green, Alan A. *Allen Sapp Home Page.* World-wide web site, initiated 4 March 1995. http://muslib.lib.ohio-state.edu/sapp/index.htm

Provides basic biographical information, a collection of unpublished program notes written by the composer, and sound file copies of several broadcast-quality private recital recordings (see "Discography/Webography" section). This site also contains sound files corresponding to all musical examples in this book (D34-41; musical examples follow p. 50).

B150. Gelfand, Janelle. "Obituaries: Norma Sapp Taught at CCM, Pianist Once Worked for Leonard Bernstein." *Cincinnati Enquirer*, 6 June 1995.

Norma Bertolami Sapp died of complications from leukemia on 5 June 1995. In addition to her many accomplishments as a teacher, as a chamber music performer, and as a soloist with orchestras (including the Boston Pops under Arthur Fiedler), the article mentions her period as Leonard Bernstein's assistant while they were faculty members at Brandeis University in the early 1950s. Her final two performances were the 1993 première of her husband's *Fantasy III: "Homage to Mendelssohn"* (W41) in Buffalo (P41a), and a second performance of the same work in Cincinnati (P41b).

B151. Demaline, Jackie. "The Arts: Granted." *Cincinnati Enquirer*, 18 June 1995.

An announcement of Allen Sapp receiving an Individual Artist Fellowship Grant from the Ohio Arts Council. The grant is in support of a forthcoming CRI recording by Keith Lockhart and the Cincinnati Chamber Orchestra of Sapp's *Concerto for Chamber Orchestra: "The Four Reasons"* (W122), *Imaginary Creatures: A Bestiary for the Credulous* (W118), and the overture to *The Women of Trachis* (W115).

NOTES

I. BIOGRAPHY

1. Youth and Education, 1922-43

1.   This work has not been located among Sapp's papers and is presumed to be lost.

2.   Allen Sapp, interview with the author, 5 January 1991. Hereafter, the reader should assume that all interviews were conducted by the author unless otherwise specified. Tapes for all interviews are located in the Oral History Collection, Music Library, SUNY at Buffalo.

3.   Howard Pollack, *Walter Piston* (Ann Arbor, Mich.: UMI Research Press, 1981), 45. In 1936, the Columbia Broadcasting System commissioned Piston's *Concertino* as well as Copland's *A Saga for the Prairie*, Gruenberg's *Green Mansions*, Hanson's *Third Symphony*, Harris' *Time Suite*, and Still's *Lenox Avenue* for broadcast premieres. The 20 June 1937 broadcast of Piston's *Concertino* was conducted by Howard Barlow, with Jesús María Sanromá as soloist.

4.   Piston's *Concertino* remained an influential work for Sapp for many years: Sapp and his wife, Norma Bertolami Sapp, performed the work in a two-piano version several times in Cambridge in the late 1940s and 1950s.

5.   Money continued to be an issue for the Sapp family throughout the early 1940s. The composer remembered receiving at least one eviction warning from Harvard due to his university housing bill not having been paid; his parents were responsible for this portion of his college expenses. It took several years for the family to pull out of the financial difficulties, which began in 1940. Sapp also remembers taking Robert Middleton to his large childhood home for spring vacation in 1940 and sensing that all was not well; a few weeks later, he received a letter from his parents explaining that they had moved into an apartment. All the large furniture was in storage for the summer, including the piano, which made that summer particularly difficult both personally and musically for the young composer.

6.   Sapp interview, 5 January 1991.

7.   Ibid.

8.   Nadia Boulanger, "Concerts Colonne," *Le Monde musical* (November 1919), 350; quoted as translated in Teresa Walters, "Nadia Boulanger, Musician and Teacher: Her Life, Concepts, and Influences" (D.M.A. diss., Peabody Institute of Music, Johns Hopkins University, 1981), 88.

9.   Sapp interview, 12 January 1991.

10.   Ibid.

11.   Sapp interview, 5 January 1991.

12.   Sapp interview, 5 January 1991: "I took orchestration with [William] Denny, who had been brought in to replace Hill on a three-year appointment of some kind. Bill Denny was a bright fellow, a good, solid musician. He had had the experience in Europe of the German training, and was interested in the music of Berg and Schoenberg. He was also interested in Scriabin. All the kind of music that was not acceptable around Harvard."

13.   These included epigrams by Thomas Bancroft, John Donne, Sir John Harrington, Robert Hayman, and John Weever in *Seven Epigrams (Both Sweet and Sour)* (W86), John Donne's "Epithalamion" in *A Song of Marriage* (W98), and poems of Robert Herrick in *The Lady and The Lute* (W87).

14.   A letter of 6 May 1940 to his parents (personal papers, home of Allen Sapp, Cincinnati, Ohio; hereafter, "Sapp papers") tells of working very long hours on the production of *The Ascent of F-6*. "Starting last Sunday I have rehearsed from 2-5:30 and 7-1:30 every day. This is not the slightest exaggeration. We all slaved as much as we could to make the play a success.   I have done practically no work [for college courses] for weeks—barely getting by."

15.   Sapp's supplemental music appears to have been only in sketch form; if the sketches still exist, they have not been located among the composer's papers, the Harvard University Archives, or the Harvard Theatre Collection.

16.   His incidental music for *The Family Reunion* (W134) was primarily improvised, save the overtures. The scores to the overtures have yet to be located among the composer's papers; they were not in the collection of the Harvard University Archives or the Harvard Theatre Collection as of January 1994.

17.   See WB134a-c.

18.   One such broadcast took place on 4 March 1941 from 8:30 to 9:00 p.m., where he performed "original compositions" (*Harvard Crimson*, 4 March 1941). Sapp continued his association with the radio staff the following year. In a letter to his parents (25 October 1941, also discussed in his interview of 12 January 1991), Sapp tells of a comedy skit he performed in during the previous week in which he was interviewed as "the student with the hardest class at Harvard."

19.   The exact date of the première broadcast performance is unknown. The composer remembers that it was performed shortly after he finished composing the work; the manuscript score is dated April 1940.

20.   Sapp interview, 16 January 1991.

21.   This was actually his second sonata for violoncello, the first having been written in Philadelphia, dedicated and given to one of his Haverford School teachers, a certain Mr. Jamison. The composer apparently did not retain a copy of this work, and Jamison's copy has not been located as yet.

22.   Letter of 4 May 1941 to the composer's parents, Sapp papers. Fine also advised Sapp on the composition of this work in their tutorial sessions, and made some revisions in the passage work (Sapp interview, 12 January 1991). The most notable of these is a section paper clipped onto the manuscript in Irving Fine's hand, replacing measures 168-85 of the second movement.

23.   Sapp interview, 12 January 1991.

24.   Sapp interview, 5 January 1991. Sapp did institutionalize the tutorial concept in the system of colleges he helped to design at the State University of New York at Buffalo in the late 1960s and early 1970s. At the University of Cincinnati College-Conservatory of Music, he personally took on many additional students, including non-composers, in private tutorial sessions over and above his assigned academic load.

25.   Sapp interview, 5 January 1991.

26.   This was probably his manuscript to the *Andante for Orchestra* (W110), which Sapp submitted for the Young Composers' Contest of the New York Philharmonic in which he would win second prize.

27.   Letter from the composer to his parents, 30 November 1941, Sapp papers.

28.   Letter from the composer to his parents, 4 May 1941, Sapp papers.

29.   First prize went to Andre Mathieu, third to Dika Newlin. "Composer, Aged 12, Wins First Prize," *New York Times*, 3 February 1942.

30.   Telegram, Edilh Sawsin to Sapp, 5 February 1942, Sapp papers.

31.   Sapp interview, 5 January 1991.

32.   The following sections of the holograph orchestral score of *Andante for Orchestra* are newly composed music, or revisions of the analogous passage from the *Piano Sonata I* (W1): 1) Two measures before letter E until letter I (34 measures); 2) Third measure of letter J (one measure only); 3) Second measure of letter L until sixth measure of letter L (four measures); seventh measure of letter N until letter P (nine measures); and the final cadential passage extended for four measures. Sapp remarked that he had private sessions with Piston to work on the orchestration of this work, so perhaps some of these alterations were at the suggestion of Piston (Sapp interview, 12 January 1991).

33.   Robert Lawrence, "Philharmonic Ends Series for Young People," *New York Herald Tribune*, 19 April 1942.

34.   Stravinsky's Norton Lectures were first published in the original French version, *Poétique musicale sous forme de six leçons* (Cambridge: Harvard University Press, 1942), and later in an English translation, *Poetics of Music in the Form of Six Lessons* (Cambridge: Harvard University Press, 1947).

35.   Although Sapp was not enrolled in Piston's *Seminar in Composition* (Music 109) in his freshman year, he was invited by Piston to attend these sessions (Sapp interview, 5 January 1991).

36.   Sapp interview, 5 January 1991. "I had a few private short sessions with Stravinsky in which he looked at my music and said some rather vague things about it, you know. He was very kind, and of course he was very inspirational."

37.   Allen Sapp, "An Introduction to Orchestral Analysis as Applied to Seven Works of Igor Stravinsky," (A. B. honors thesis, Harvard University, 1942). Donald Grout was his advisor for the thesis, and was apparently "extremely complementary" of Sapp's work (Sapp interview, 5 January 1991). "Nobody else was doing any work like that at that time . . . and I had no reference points at all." (Ibid.) The seven works studied were *Suite from "Pulcinella"* (1922), *Apollon musagète* (1928), *Four Etudes for Orchestra* (1928), *Violin Concerto* (1931), *Jeu de cartes* (1936), *"Dumbarton Oaks" Concerto* (1938), and *Symphony in C* (1940).

Robert Commanday, music reviewer for the *San Francisco Chronicle* and former college friend of Sapp's, recalls that Sapp had initially wanted to write his thesis on the music of Charles Ives. "In 1941, Charles Ives was not generally known. Very few of his major works had come out. But Allen discovered him and was all caught up with him. He proposed to the Harvard Music Department that he write his dissertation on Charles Ives. They turned him down flat. It was a very conservative department. People like Tillman Merritt and Walter Piston and the other faculty, I guess they must have just rejected Ives out of hand as an eccentric and not worth his time and certainly not worth the dissertation at Harvard. It's too bad, because Allen would have done pioneering work and probably [would have] come out with a seminal study at the very beginning of the Charles Ives revival. And it might have made an enormous difference in his career. But that's the way Harvard was. It was a very conservative place." (Robert Commanday interview, 6 February 1993).

38.   Sapp interview, 5 January 1991.

39.   Sapp believes he is the only student to have had extensive private lessons with Copland (Sapp interview, 5 January 1991), but Copland's biographer Vivian Perlis could neither confirm nor deny this fact (Vivian Perlis to the author, 25 January 1993).

40.   Sapp interview, 12 January 1991. Boulanger fled Paris for southern France in the spring of 1940 when the Germans invaded Belgium. She eventually made her way to Lisbon, where she sailed to New York in December 1940. She began teaching at the Longy School of Music (Cambridge, Mass.) in 1941, and accepted a second concurrent position at the Peabody Conservatory of Music in spring 1942. Jérôme Spycket, *Nadia Boulanger* (Stuyvesant, N.Y.: Pendragon Press, 1992), 106, 111.

41.   Sapp is listed as class of 1943 in most Harvard documents, including his official transcript, which reads "Received the degree of A. B., Magna cum Laude (Music) at Commencement, 1942 as of the Class of 1943."

42.   Archibald T. Davison to Captain McClung, Chief of Naval Operations, 11 December 1942, Sapp papers.   Walter Piston and A. Tillman Merritt also wrote letters of recommendation for Sapp's application for a Navy commission.

43.   Sapp interview, 12 January 1991.

44.   Aaron Copland and Vivian Perlis, *Copland, 1900 through 1942* (New York: St. Martin's, 1984), 364. Sapp remembers that John Cowell was also a member of the Copland group of students, but he is listed as a student of Martinů in the above source.

45.   *Lincoln Portrait* had just been premiered by Andre Kostelanetz and the Cincinnati Symphony on 14 May 1942, and the work received its first radio broadcast on 16 August 1942. The first Boston Symphony Orchestra performance took place on 3 April 1943, Serge Koussevitzky conducting.   Aaron Copland and Vivian Perlis, *Copland, 1900 through 1942* (New York: St. Martin's, 1984), 343-46.

46.   Sapp interview, 12 January 1991.

47.   Aaron Copland and Vivian Perlis, *Copland: 1900 through 1942* (New York: St. Martin's, 1984), 365.

48.   Sapp interview, 12 January 1991.   Also from this interview session, Sapp comments on the personal significance to Copland and himself of this careful study of Shostakovich: "The work that we mostly concentrated on . . . in those seminars was the Shostakovich *Piano Quintet*, which, as you know, is a marvelous piece.   It sort of shows Shostakovich developing the whole piece out of his fondness for Bach, but also [being] very popular, very realistic, very appealing.   It was clearly part of Copland's getting into the second style of his, you see. Rationalizing in terms of a music which would reach a large population.   Obviously a well-formulated doctrine.   That's the first time I had really ever come across that.   Shostakovich was not a name that I really knew and I didn't know that piece.   It made a very powerful impression then and it remained.

"It has led me to an increasing [awareness] over the years . . . [of] the influence of Shostakovich [on my music].   It is very strong.   I think as I get to know the late quartets, from about the eighth on, I realize that there is a very close relationship of compositional attitudes and methods.   These diatonic planes of reference, and the polymodality and the affected use of multitonal sectors.   Much of that which I thought was my own way of writing, of thinking.   I realize now [that] it is parallel with Shostakovich."

49.   From Sapp interview, 12 January 1991: "He talked about style.   We were a pretty heterogeneous group and that's the way he liked it.   I remember one other thing that he said that was very impressive to me which was that he was much less interested in technique, in the technical skill of composers than he was in originality and personality.   I guess that was rather striking, because I had built a lot of my own sense of security as a composer on the basis that I had a fluency and a technical underpinning that was pretty solid.   So I think he was essentially giving me a back-handed complement, because I had . . . a sufficiency of technique and fluency with handling problems.   But he was saying in effect that there was personality somehow that he detected as well.   But he said originality was what he looked for when he talked with young composers or heard music.   Some voice which was different out of the crowd.   He made quite a bit of that.   Technique is all very well and good, but it only gets you so far."

50.   Sapp interview, 12 January 1991.   In this latter point, Copland apparently discussed how university support of composers was becoming more important as the level of private financial resources for the arts was on the decline.   It is interesting to note that Sapp, together with Lukas Foss, would in 1964 establish one of the most ambitious efforts to support young contemporary composers within the university, the Center of the Creative and Performing Arts at the State University of New York at Buffalo.

51.   "Three Commissions," *New York Times*, 7 June 1942.   Norman Dello Joio of the Juilliard School and William Bergsma of the Eastman School of Music were also

commissioned, and their works were to be performed on the same concert (17 February 1943, by the Saidenberg Little Symphony, conducted by Daniel Saidenberg at Town Hall). The composers "were selected by their respective schools as the outstanding students, whose work in composition was felt deserving of recognition by performance before the city's music public and critics." Unfortunately, this performance of Sapp's *Concertino* (W111) was canceled. Since Sapp had been inducted into war service several months earlier, his parents arranged for the parts to be copied by a local university student; these parts turned out to be rather faulty, causing Saidenberg to remove the piece from the program. Sapp would have to wait until after the war to hear his *Concertino*.

52.   Sapp's manuscript for this setting for the Piston *Seminar in Fugue* has not been located as yet among the papers of the composer.

53.   Sapp interview, 12 January 1991. No program or newspaper account of this concert could be located among the composer's papers or in the Boston Symphony Archives, so the exact date of the concert is not known. It probably was not performed on the last day of concerts, 14 August 1942, since it did not appear on the programs for both the student orchestras as reported in the following article: "Tanglewood Nets More Than $12,000 at Benefit Concert," *Springfield News* (Springfield, Mass.), 15 August 1942.

The free-standing fair copy manuscript score of *Passacaglia on a Theme by Piston* is almost certainly the version performed at Tanglewood, and its title page is dated "1942 - July"; the colophon of the *Concertino*, which contains the extensively revised "Passacaglia on a Theme by Piston" as its second movement, is dated "Bryn Mawr, August, 1942." Since the first concerts at Tanglewood did not take place until July 14 that year, it is probably safe to assume that the performance of the first version of the *Passacaglia* took place some time between 14 July and 13 August 1942. Both manuscripts are in the possession of the composer.

54.   Sapp interview, 12 January 1991.

55.   Sapp's lessons were mostly held at Copland's loft on Sixty-third Street, but were also occasionally at his room at the Hotel Empire (Electronic mail, Allen Sapp to the author, 10 May 1994). In the autumn of 1942 Copland also rented a country retreat, Dellbrook Farm, near Oakland, N.J. (Copland and Perlis, *Aaron Copland, 1900 through 1942*, p. 366), but Sapp did not have any lessons with him at this residence.

56.   Sapp interview, 12 January 1991; incidentally, Aaron Copland was also beginning the composition of his *Sonata for Violin and Piano* (1942-43) at this time. Sapp's *Violin Sonata I* (W52) was awarded the 1943 George Arthur Knight Prize in Composition at Harvard.

57.   Sapp interview, 5 January 1991.

58.   Sapp interview, 12 January 1991.

59.   Ibid.

60.   Paul Vidal, *Manuel pratique d'harmonie* (Paris: Enoch & cie, n.d.).

61.   Electronic mail from Allen Sapp to the author, 10 May 1994.

62.   Sapp interview, 12 January 1991.

63.   The première took place on 21 January 1945, Viviane Bertolami, violin, Norma Bertolami Sapp, pianoforte, at City Center Chamber Music Hall, New York, N.Y., at a League of Composers concert. Copland was also apparently in attendance at this concert, as Sapp also received a congratulatory letter from him while in the Army in Europe (Sapp interview, 12 January 1991).

64.   Telegram from Sapp to his mother, 21 February 1943, 9:21 P.M. from St. Louis (Sapp papers): "AM IN STLOUIS, MISSOURI TRAVELLING FOR UNKNOWN DESTINATION STOP KEEP YOUR COURAGE UP I AM TRYING TO CALL UP BUT CIRCUITS ARE BUSY WILL WRITE OR WIRE AT FINAL DESTINATION ALLEN.

2. Service in World War II, 1943-47

1.   Vint Hill Farms Station was an "estate which had been turned over to the army for the war" (Sapp interview, 12 January 1991). It is not listed in the 1942 edition of Charles J. Sullivan's *Army Posts and Towns: The Baedeker of the Army* (Los Angeles: Haynes, 1942); Camp Crowder is listed in this source on p. 45. Vint Hill Farms Station is still listed as an active station in the pamphlet "United States Army Installations and Major Activities" (Department of the Army Pamphlet 210-1), [Washington, D.C.]: Headquarters, Department of the Army, 1977, p. 8. Camp Crowder does not appear in this pamphlet.

2.   Sapp interview, 12 January 1991.

3.   Nadia Boulanger returned to Paris in mid-January 1946 (her ship arrived at La Pallice on 17 January), after having fled to the United States in 1940. Jérôme Spycket, *Nadia Boulanger* (Stuyvesant, N.Y.: Pendragon Press, 1992), 116.

4.   Lucienne Barbier's nickname was "Dédé," to whom Sapp's *Sonatina I* (W12) is dedicated. Allen Sapp to the author, 25 April 1990.

5.   Sapp interview, 12 January 1991. Sapp learned of this performance in the letter which accompanied the package containing the fair copy of the *Sonata* in Lucienne's hand; see also endnote 8.

6.   It was perhaps at Verviers that Sapp composed another work for piano, *Novelette* (W11), dated "Feb. 21, 1945" at the colophon; however no location was recorded there.

7.   This work is dated "July 1945" on the title page, and at the colophon "Pullach b[ei] München, Sept. 1, 1945."

8.   Sapp had left his manuscript behind with the Barbier family when he left Namur since they had expressed an interest in performing the première. This holograph is no longer in the possession of the composer (perhaps retained by the Barbier family), but Lucienne's fair copy is. Her manuscript reverses the order of the two movements from Sapp's intended order. The work was probably performed in this inverted state at its première.

9.   This listening session probably took place at the sound recording archives of Radiodiffusion Française in Paris. This recording eventually made its way into the Archives de la phonothèque de l'Institut national de l'audiovisuel, Maison de Radio-France (Maic Chomel to Alan Green, 4 December 1995). The original recording was made on 19 April 1945 on an instantaneous acetate disc, and later transferred to analog tape.

10.   Allen Sapp to the author, 24 November 1993. The theory that Nadia Boulanger made the arrangements to have Sapp's *Concertino* performed is entirely possible. She was certainly very familiar with the work from Sapp's lessons with her in 1942-43. She might have known that the composer's parents had access to his scores and may have arranged for the *Concertino* to be shipped to someone in Paris for proper editing of the faulty orchestral parts (see Chapter 1, endnote 51). As noted earlier, Boulanger herself did not return to Paris until January 1946.

11.   Lt. Col. Clarence S. Howe to Allen D. Sapp, 29 October 1947, Sapp papers.

12.   Because of the large number of U.S. troops in Europe after the war, a priority system had to be established for returning home for discharge. Infantrymen generally had higher priority than most signal intelligence personnel since they had accumulated "battle points" in greater numbers; thus Sapp would have been very low on the priority list for normal discharge.

13.   Lt. Col. Clarence S. Howe to Allen D. Sapp, 29 October 1947, Sapp papers.

14.   Sapp interview, 12 January 1991.

3. A Return to Harvard

1.   Sapp interview, 12 January 1991. Sapp served unofficially in this capacity since it was too late to be offered a fellowship for the year.

2.   A. Tillman Merritt to Allen Sapp, 21 May 1948, Sapp papers; and Sapp interview, 12 January 1991. His appointments at Harvard are also partially documented in Elliot Forbes, *A History of Music at Harvard to 1972* (Cambridge: Department of Music, Harvard University, 1988), 97, 121-124, and 134-135. They are as follows: Teaching Fellow, 1948-50; Instructor, 1950-53; Assistant Professor, 1953-58.   See Appendix A for a complete list of Sapp's academic appointments.

3.   Forbes' *A History of Music at Harvard to 1972* provides a listing of "Courses of Instruction" in the index (p. 215-221).   Prior to 1972 there apparently was never offered a graduate or undergraduate course on the music of any composers associated with the Second Viennese School; however, there were courses offered on other twentieth century composers like Bartok, D'Indy, Hindemith, and Stravinsky. The names of Berg and Webern do not appear at all in the index to Forbes' book. Schoenberg is mentioned, primarily in connection with his being commissioned to write his *String Trio* (op. 45) for Harvard's "Symposium on Music Criticism" on 1 May 1947 (p. 104).   This is the only mention in Forbes' book of Schoenberg being performed at Harvard until a 1971 performance of his *Ode to Napoleon Bonaparte* (p. 177).   Perhaps most indicative of the reception of serial music at Harvard during this era was Sapp's remembrance of a Webern performance in the early 1950s, "in which Merritt and Piston were just laughing.   The Webern Symphony, laughing!   I mean openly laughing! I was so ashamed" (Sapp interview, 16 January 1991).

4.   After joining the Harvard faculty as Instructor in 1950, Sapp worked with several students on projects concerning serial technique.   One of these was Peter Westergaard, who in his 1953 senior honors thesis on the Schoenberg string quartets acknowledged his debt to his tutor: "Without [Sapp's] exhaustive knowledge of the music treated here, this essay could never have been written." Peter Westergaard, "Harmony in the Four String Quartets of Arnold Schönberg," (B.A. honors thesis, Harvard University, 1953), i.

5.   Dr. Davison was apparently very impressed with Sapp's presentation in the graduate-level Seminar in Music History *(Music 203)*, so much so that he asked Sapp to write a lecture on serial music for his undergraduate *Survey of Music History* (Music 1) course to replace his own. "His lecture on serial music . . . had been very traditional and disdainful and essentially 'What a monstrous aberration it was,' and 'Thank God we have Stravinsky and other sensible composers!' [Laughter] But he realized that he had just not kept up. So I wrote the lecture for Music 1. . . . [I took] some pleasure that I somehow was able to rectify what was so clearly a wrong view of this music and to . . . [present] lots of evidence and lots of material in support of it" (Sapp interview, 12 January 1991).

6.   Howard Pollack, *Harvard Composers: Walter Piston and His Students from Elliott Carter to Frederic Rzewski* (Metuchen, N.J.: Scarecrow Press, 1992), 225-26.

7.   Ibid., p. 226.

8.   One exception to this is *Anoia* (W93, 1988) in which the composer was purposely mocking the minimalist style.

9.   Of course Sapp was by no means the first composer to write serial music with strong references to tonality.   Perhaps the most famous of such works is Alban Berg's *Violin Concerto* (1935), which also employed a tone row with several embedded triads: G - B♭ - D - F♯ - A - C - E - G♯ - B - C♯ - D♯ - F.

10.   Sapp interview, 7 December 1991.

11.   A. Tillman Merritt to Allen Sapp, 23 January 1950, Sapp papers.

12.   Allen Sapp to A. Tillman Merritt, 28 January 1950, Sapp papers.

13.   Phelps would engage Sapp frequently with extra teaching for the University Extension courses, even after he left Harvard for Wellesley in the late 1950s.

14.   Howard Pollack, *Walter Piston* (Ann Arbor, Mich.: UMI Research Press, 1981): 187-93. Only one vocal work is listed in Pollack's catalog of works by Piston in these pages, his *Carnival Song for Men's Chorus and Brass Instruments* (1938).

15.   *Harvard University Catalogue*, June 1951, p. 348; and A. Tillman Merritt to Allen Sapp, 23 January 1950, Sapp papers.

16.   The exact date of the final concert is not known, but it most likely occurred in the spring of 1956. This is inferred by the date of a letter from Wallingford Riegger to Allen Sapp, 28 May 1956 (Sapp papers). Sapp had obviously had the unpleasant task of telling Riegger that the Creative Concerts Guild could not honor its promise of a commission for the following season. Riegger responded with very sympathetic words: "Through lack of any government support of the arts, such as is found in most countries the world over, it is hardly surprising that the CCG is having hard sledding, so don't feel too badly about the commission. I hadn't really started on it anyway."

17.   Sapp interview, 16 January 1991. Sapp immediately preceded William Pierce, who began substituting for Sapp in 1953 when he became too busy with his Harvard faculty duties to maintain his parallel career as a radio announcer. Pierce remained the radio voice of the BSO for the next 38 years, until retiring in the spring of 1991. Pierce gradually took over the broadcasts from Sapp: "In 1953 I substituted for a colleague at a Pops broadcast, and then I took over the Friday afternoon concerts, and then the rest of them." Richard Dyer, "And Now William Pierce is Bowing Out," *Boston Globe*, 14 April 1991.

18.   Both of these series were also rebroadcast in the early 1950s on WMEX-AM in Boston under the series title "The Music's the Thing."

19.   A fuller description of this two day conference (10-11 August 1953) appears in Forbes, *A History of Music at Harvard to 1972*, p. 129.

20.   McGeorge Bundy later served as National Security Advisor to President John F. Kennedy.

21.   Sapp interview, 16 January 1991.

22.   The Walgreen Lectures, funded by the drugstore tycoon Charles Walgreen, were on topics dealing with the history of American institutions. Craven was himself a past Walgreen lecturer and published his speeches, *Democracy in American Life: A Historical View*, with the University of Chicago Press in 1941. Other preceding lecturers in this distinguished series included Daniel J. Boorstin, John H. Hallowell, and Jacques Maritain.

23.   Randall Thompson to Allen Sapp, 1 August 1953, Sapp papers; also, Forbes, *A History of Music at Harvard to 1972*, 123.

24.   Sapp interview, 16 January 1991; also Dr. Sanford Gifford to Allen Sapp, 8 April 1955, Sapp papers.

25.   McGeorge Bundy to Allen Sapp, 6 May 1955, Sapp papers. Although this letter came nearly a month after Sapp began his leave, Bundy made clear that this was just a written confirmation of permission granted earlier by telephone.

Sapp's courses were taken over by several of his colleagues: Thompson continued Sapp's Elementary Harmony (Music 51); Bach scholar Karl Geiringer of Boston University took over Sapp's The Art of Bach (Music 126); and Merritt assumed the Bartok seminar begun by Gombosi (Music 203). Forbes, *A History of Music at Harvard to 1972*, 123.

26.   Sapp's two sons, Christopher and Anthony, were born in 1952 and 1954, respectively.

27.   McGeorge Bundy to Allen Sapp, 29 March 1956, Sapp papers.

28.   Sapp interview, 16 January 1991.

29.   Sapp interview, 14 December 1991.

30.   Ibid.

31.   Sapp interview, 14 December 1991. In a concert at Harvard on 17 May 1956, Sapp performed a nebulous form of his *Piano Sonata II* (W16) with only the first two movements completed; as a third movement he performed the piano score of the *adagietto* movement of the *Second Suite for Orchestra* (113), and partially improvised the fourth movement, which was largely still in sketch form at that time (telephone conversation, Allen Sapp to the author, 22 March 1994).

32.   Sapp interview, 14 December 1991.
33.   This was certainly not an uncommon occurrence for Harvard's Music Department, since they had not granted tenure to a junior faculty member since G. Wallace Woodworth in 1940 (Forbes, *A History of Music at Harvard to 1972*, 195). Among the other junior faculty who were not granted tenure at Harvard in mid-century were such well known figures as Grosvenor W. Cooper, Donald J. Grout, Irving Fine, Robert Moevs, and Billy Jim Layton. (Sapp interview, 16 January 1991; see also Pollack, *Harvard Composers*, 229, 325).
34.   Randall Thompson to Allen Sapp, 12 December 1956, Sapp papers.
35.   Among the institutions who solicited Sapp in 1958 were Swarthmore College (Peter G. Swing to Allen Sapp, 3 March 1958, Sapp papers) and the University of California at Berkeley (David D. Boyden to Allen Sapp, 2 May 1958, Sapp papers). Prior to that year he was also solicited by Cornell University (Donald J. Grout to Allen Sapp, 5 April 1955, Sapp papers) and the University of Chicago (Sapp interview, 14 December 1991).
36.   Sapp especially remained active with the Harvard Extension Courses after joining the Wellesley faculty. He also continued occasional radio work, substituting for G. Wallace Woodworth as the host of WGBH-FM's "Tomorrow's Symphony" program periodically throughout the late 1950s. Sapp also wrote and delivered on-air program notes for at least six programs of the Boston Pops in 1960 (Arthur Fiedler to Allen Sapp, 13 December 1960, personal papers of the composer.)
37.   Sapp interview, 16 January 1991.

4. Wellesley College

1.   Sapp believes this offer came about through the intercession of noted Boston organist Melville Smith, head of the Longy Conservatory, where Sapp's wife Norma was active as a piano instructor (Sapp interview, 16 January 1991). Smith had heard that Sapp was leaving the Harvard faculty, and suggested to Hubert Lamb that Sapp be appointed at Wellesley, in the twilight of the tradition of closed-door college appointments.
2.   Sapp interview, 16 January 1991.
3.   Hubert Lamb to Margaret Clapp, 10 March 1958, Faculty Record Files ("Sapp, Allen"), Wellesley College Archives, Wellesley, Mass.
4.   Sapp interview, 16 January 1991.
5.   Sapp's incidental music for Barbara McCarthy's 1960 production of *The Trojan Women* (W136) was revived for the 1966 Wellesley College production. Martha Craven to Allen Sapp, 15 October 1965, Sapp papers.
6.   Due to an illness, Barbara McCarthy apparently had to withdraw as director of this production to be replaced by Paul R. Barstow. The new director apparently did not care for Sapp's taped percussion incidental music and asked him instead to perform excerpts of his orchestral overture to *The Women of Trachis* (W115); the composer reluctantly complied (Sapp interview, 16 January 1991).
7.   The Commission on Extension Courses was established in 1910 by A. Lawrence Lowell, then President of Harvard University. It offered extension courses through the following Boston area institutions: Harvard University, Tufts University, Boston University, Massachusetts Institute of Technology, Boston College, Simmons College, Wellesley College, Museum of Fine Arts, Lowell Institute, Massachusetts Department of Education, and the School Committee of the City of Boston. Reginald Phelps served as Chairman of the Commission, and Director of University Extension of Harvard University.
8.   This most likely occurred well before 20 February 1961, the date for the Music Department faculty meeting where Sapp's name is first mentioned in the minutes (University Archives, State University of New York at Buffalo). He is spoken of as if he has already accepted the position: "The Slee Committee report will be shelved until Mr. Sapp has been here one semester. Mr. Sapp is to give lectures and programs in the first semester and have

a hand in selecting the Slee Professor for 2nd semester." However, the search process was apparently not finalized until much later, since a letter of thanks from Dean Albrecht to Dr. Irving Cheyette for serving as a departmental representative on the search committee was dated more than a full month later, 26 March 1961 (University Archives, State University of New York at Buffalo).

9. Sapp interview, 16 January 1991.

10. Frank A. D'Accone to the author, 10 February 1994.

5. From Composer to Administrator: Buffalo, 1961-68

1. See Appendix A for a complete list of academic positions held and a partial list of appointments to artistic institutions and foundations.

2. Sapp even discussed this issue with the *Buffalo Courier-Express* in a story published 30 April 1967, "Sapp's Busy Program Inhibits Composing."

3. John Dwyer, "Magic is Essential Power of Composer, Says Slee Professor," *Buffalo Evening News*, 20 October 1961.

4. Sapp delivered his Slee Lectures on 19 October 1961, 30 November 1961, and 5 February 1962. Unfortunately, the Recording Archives at the State University of New York at Buffalo Music Department do not have recordings of Sapp's lecture-recitals, although they do hold recordings of many other Slee Lectures including those by Copland, Rochberg, and Pousseur.

5. Allen Sapp to Josef Krips, 8 March 1962, University Archives, State University of New York at Buffalo. This document is an example of a detailed letter giving recommendations to Krips on program lengths, character, and individual works for the next season. Among other comments, Sapp recommends formalizing the arrangement of performing a work by the composer named to the rotating Slee Professorship at the University.

6. Sapp added Foss' name to the list of conductors to be considered by the Music Advisory Committee, of which he was Chairman. Foss had been a member of the UCLA faculty since 1953 and occasional guest conductor with the Los Angeles Philharmonic, was not actively seeking the Buffalo position. Sapp heard that Foss had recently suffered the loss of his home in the Bel Air fire of 1962, resulting in the loss of many of his manuscripts and his wife's art works; this tragic event greatly influenced Foss' decision to accept the Buffalo position (Foss interview, 21 March 1994). Sapp, in a letter of 11 December 1962 to David Laub, President of the Buffalo Philharmonic (University Archives, SUNY at Buffalo), recommended Foss, along with Eugen Jochum, Paul Kletzki, and Rafael Kubelik, but singled out Foss as the committee's endorsed candidate, describing him as an example of a "conductor-performer-composer" in the manner of Leonard Bernstein who had "successfully led the Buffalo Philharmonic as a guest conductor . . . [and] would carry on the same devotion to music and loyalty to the orchestra characterized by Mr. Krips."

7. Seymour H. Knox to Allen Sapp, 26 November 1962, University Archives, State University of New York at Buffalo, Buffalo, N.Y.

8. For a fuller account of the early years of music at the University of Buffalo, see Sharon G. Almquist, "Music at the University of Buffalo—The Baird Years," *American Music* 10 (Spring 1992): 53-79. This article is a reworking of portions of her 1986 M.A. thesis from SUNY at Buffalo, "A History of the State University of New York at Buffalo Music Department to 1968."

9. Almquist, "A History," p. 59. In 1926, Cameron Baird "graduated from Williams College with a Bachelor of Arts degree. He also attended the Harvard University School of Business Administration from 1926-27."

10. Ibid., p. 60.

11. Ibid., p. 124.

12.   Ibid., p. 69.

13.   "The Last Will and Testament of Frederick C. Slee and Alice Slee," 24 October 1952, University Archives, State University of New York at Buffalo.

14.   The complete cycle of the seventeen Beethoven String Quartets is performed in six concerts each year in the exact order set by Frederick Caldecott Slee; the order is reprinted in Nat Brandt, *Con Brio: Four Russians Called the Budapest String Quartet* (New York: Oxford University Press, 1993), p. 237 (endnote 13).

15.   Nat Brandt, *Con Brio: Four Russians Called the Budapest String Quartet* (New York: Oxford University Press, 1993), 161. The first Slee Beethoven Cycle began in September 1955, according to the obituary of Alice Slee, "Mrs. Frederick C. Slee Dead; Served Red Cross in 2 Wars," *Buffalo Evening News*, 21 May 1956.

16.   Almquist, *A History*, p. 120, provides a list of degree programs offered by the SUNY at Buffalo Music Department through 1968: her list indicates that the M.Ed. in Education offered since 1954 was discontinued in 1961, and does not list a Ph.D. in Education. However, in a letter from Sapp to Dean Milton C. Albrecht dated 19 July 1962 (University Archives, State University of New York at Buffalo), Sapp states "Our real role, I think, in Music Education is going to be the establishment of a firm graduate area to take care of the M.E. and Ph.D. in education programs which have just been established." (Author's emphasis.)

17.   Sapp interview, 25 March 1991.

18.   A memo of 9 October 1962 from Sapp to Dean Milton C. Albrecht indicates that the payroll forms for the quartet were being processed by this date.

19.   Brandt, *Con Brio*, p. 173, states information from an interview with Spivacke's administrative assistant Frances Gewehr, indicating that the quartet's patroness at the Library of Congress, Mrs. Whittall, was upset over the increasingly poor reviews of the concerts and decided to discontinue the relationship with the quartet following the 1961-62 season.

20.   Brandt, in *Con Brio*, makes a serious error in his statement on page 174: "The Quartet's leaving the Library sparked an idea in the mind of their good friend in Buffalo, Cameron Baird, head of the music department at the University of Buffalo. . . . Would they like to be the quartet-in-residence at the university?" Cameron Baird died on 6 May 1960; the quartet would play another two concert seasons at the Library of Congress following his death (ibid., p. 173). It is clear that the "friend" in Buffalo who proposed this arrangement was really the current chairman, Allen Sapp.

21.   Sapp interview, 14 December 1991.

22.   Among the several recordings of solo recitals by Budapest Quartet members held in the tape archives of the SUNY at Buffalo Music Department are two by Boris Kroyt on which he performed the Sapp *Viola Sonata* (W55): 19 April 1965 (with Norma Bertolami Sapp, piano) and 29 March 1967 (with Murray Perahia, piano). Kroyt had apparently planned to record this work for Columbia Records, but became ill and passed away before this could take place. "Boris liked my sonata very much and had actually agreed to do it with Murray Perahia . . . and had the Columbia Records people all committed." (Sapp interview, 14 December 1991).

23.   Allen Sapp, "Music at the State University at Buffalo: A Report for the Provost of State University, October 1965," University Archives, State University of New York at Buffalo, p. 10. Also a mail advertisement produced by the SUNY at Buffalo Music Department, "String Player's Institute Conducted by the Budapest String Quartet, March 30 to April 2, 1964," personal papers, home of Allen Dwight Sapp.

24.   "Schneider Inspires Players in First Harpsichord Event," *Buffalo Evening News*, 7 November 1963. Also quoted in Almquist, "A History," p. 103, endnote 20.

25.   Allen Sapp to Milton C. Albrecht, 3 October 1962, University Archives, State University of New York at Buffalo.

26.   Allen Sapp to Milton C. Albrecht, 11 April 1962, University Archives, State University of New York at Buffalo.

27.   William B. Ernst to Otto Kinkeldey, 13 April 1964, University Archives, State University of New York at Buffalo. The university purchased the materials from Kinkeldey's library for $3,000; it was personally packed and delivered by truck by Prof. Herbert Kellman.

28.   In a letter to the author (10 February 1994), Professor D'Accone described the recruitment of Professors Kellman and Fuller. "Even before I was awarded a Fulbright for 1963-64, we realized that we would need someone to replace me should I receive one and also that we needed to have another musicologist if we were to have the kind of curriculum we felt the department should have. . . . We had decided to seek a single replacement. But when we got [to the American Musicological Society convention] and heard Herbert Kellman give one of the best papers ever, and when he learned that David Fuller, whom we both knew and very much admired, was looking for a job, we agreed that we should try to get both of them. Which Allen then did."

It is remarkable that so many bright young musicologists could be attracted to a university which did not yet have a reasonable music library. Commenting on this, D'Accone added that "when I left on my Fulbright in September 1963, I had been teaching at Buffalo for three years as an assistant professor. Two offers had come my way during that time, but the idea of working with Allen and being part of the exciting things that were happening at Buffalo kept me from ever considering them seriously. While I was away, I was informed that I had been promoted to associate professor with tenure. To my mind this is also indicative of how Allen, and perhaps [Dean] Milton [Albrecht], were thinking in terms of musicology and the department's future."

29.   Sapp interview, 25 March 1991.

30.   Myles Slatin to Allen Sapp, 26 June 1964, University Archives, State University of New York at Buffalo.

31.   Dual scholar-librarian appointments were still uncommon in the 1960s, but such positions were to be found at that time at institutions with strong musicology programs. Indeed, it was hardly a new idea. Otto Kinkeldey was appointed in 1930 as the first Professor of Musicology in the United States, and also served Cornell University as University Librarian (Carol June Bradley, *American Music Librarianship: A Biographical and Historical Survey* (Westport, Conn.: Greenwood Press, 1990), 14). George Sherman Dickinson, who was appointed Assistant Professor of both music theory and history at Vassar College in 1916, was appointed Music Librarian at the same institution in 1927, and later also served concurrently as Chairman of the department (ibid., p. 84).

32.   Sapp interview, 25 March 1991.

33.   Allen Sapp to Milton C. Albrecht, October 3, 1962, University Archives, State University of New York at Buffalo.

34.   The Buffalo Philharmonic was one of several major U.S. orchestras to receive generous grants from the Rockefeller Foundation to spend "extra time on university campuses performing works primarily by young, lesser-known American composers." In fact, The Buffalo Philharmonic received the third largest grant ($30,000) in 1965, behind only the Chicago Symphony ($60,000) and the Detroit Symphony ($40,000). *The Rockefeller Foundation Annual Report for 1965* (New York: The Foundation, 1965), 112.

35.   For a complete listing of concerts both in and outside of Buffalo in the "Evenings for New Music" series, see *Evenings for New Music: A Catalogue, 1964-77* (Buffalo: Music Department, State University of New York at Buffalo, 1978), and its supplement, *Evenings for New Music: A Catalogue, 1977-80* (Buffalo: Music Department, State University of New York at Buffalo, 1981).

36.   Allen Sapp, "Music at the State University at Buffalo: A Report for the Provost of State University, October 1965," 13-14. University Archives, State University of New York at Buffalo.

37.   Lukas Foss, "Preface, laying the groundwork of the project." In "A Proposal for the Establishment of a Center of the Performing and Creative Arts with Emphasis on New Music, for Consideration by the Rockefeller Foundation, October 1963," by Lukas Foss and Allen Sapp.

38.   "Talk of the Town: Foss," *The New Yorker* (30 January 1965): 23.
39.   Sapp interview, 25 March 1991.
40.   "A Proposal for the Establishment of a Center," section II; also Sapp interview, 14 December 1991.
41.   The Rockefeller Foundation, *The President's Review from the Annual Report 1966* (New York: The Foundation, 1966), 85.
42.   Allen Sapp to Gerald Freund (Associate Director for Humanities, Rockefeller Foundation), 1 February, 1965, University Archives, State University of New York at Buffalo, Buffalo, N.Y.
43.   Renee Levine to Albert Cohen, 10 September 1971, University Archives, State University of New York at Buffalo, Buffalo, N.Y.
44.   Jan Williams interview, 17 February 1993. It is interesting to also note the comments of Lukas Foss concerning the recruitment of musicians for the Center: "I didn't do most of the recruiting; I think that actually I probably did less than Allen in terms of recruiting." Lukas Foss interview, 21 March 1994.
45.   Renee Levine interview, 23 March 1994.
46.   A letter from Foss to Sapp dated 24 June 1965 (University Archives, State University of New York at Buffalo) is very indicative of this relationship. Foss was returning from a recruiting trip to Europe in which he attended concerts in Berlin, Zagreb, and other centers. He asked Sapp for help in deciding between selecting Frederic Rzewski or Carlos Alsina as a pianist for the next season. (Rzewski was chosen for the position (spring 1966), but Alsina came for the next two seasons (1966-68); David Tudor also served as a pianist during the 1965-66 season.) He also discussed several other musicians and programming decisions.

Additional illustration of the relationship between Foss and Sapp is contained in the latter's annual report memo to Dean Milton C. Albrecht, (24 June 1965, University Archives, State University of New York at Buffalo). Sapp reports that the Creative Associates were "carefully and laboriously chosen by Lukas and myself." Yet he noted that there were some difficulties with co-direction, particularly in programming decisions. Sapp would defer to Foss' judgement since he felt that "two cooks here would certainly spoil the broth," but he noted that "my interest in music is rather catholic, [while Foss'] is, at the moment, extremely focused on one segment of music."

47.   Renee Levine interview, 23 March 1994.
48.   Almquist, in "A History," p. 108, mistakenly reports the initial grant award as two million dollars.
49.   Charles Balkin (Assistant Treasurer, SUNY at Buffalo) to John H. Greenfieldt (Assistant Comptroller, Rockefeller Foundation), 3 September 1964, University Archives, State University of New York at Buffalo, Buffalo, N.Y.
50.   The Rockefeller Foundation, *Annual Report for 1964* (New York: The Foundation, 1964), 128-30.
51.   Allen Sapp to Clifford C. Furnas, 18 February 1965, University Archives, State University of New York at Buffalo, Buffalo, N.Y. Also The Rockefeller Foundation *Annual Report for 1965* (New York: The Foundation, 1965), 111.
52.   Allen Sapp to Martin Meyerson, 30 September 1966, University Archives, State University of New York at Buffalo, Buffalo, N.Y. Also The Rockefeller Foundation *Annual Report for 1966* (New York: The Foundation, 1966), 158.
53.   Renee Levine to Albert Cohen, 10 September 1971, University Archives, State University of New York at Buffalo, Buffalo, N.Y.
54.   Minutes of the Music Department Faculty Meeting, 13 February 1968, Music Department, State University of New York at Buffalo, Buffalo, N.Y.
55.   Sapp interview, 3 April 1994. "We needed about $150,000 a year to run the [Center], which seems like a pittance in retrospect for all of the glamour and excitement that it brought to the city. Seymour Knox gave some money, and I gave quite a lot of money too—I gave a good bit of my inheritance money to keep the Center going during one or two years. But you know, that's just while we maneuvered to try to get some other source."

A detailed account of the number and funding source of Creative Associates positions is contained in a memo from Renee Levine to Albert Cohen, 10 September 1971, University Archives, State University of New York at Buffalo.

56.   Sapp interview, 3 April 1994; Foss interview, 21 March 1994.

57.   Susan K. Tepas, "Buffalo's Revolution in the Arts: January 1963 through June 1965," unpublished paper, University Archives, State University of New York at Buffalo, 95. Sapp also recalled the meeting of the steering committee of the 1965 festival. "The question was 'How much did the whole thing cost? Who was going to pay for it?' And I remember so vividly Seymour Knox saying 'Oh, let's not waste any more time with all these details, just tell me how much to write a check for.' And that was pretty staggering! He sat down and wrote a check for, I don't know, four hundred and twenty one thousand dollars and eighteen cents or something like that." (Sapp interview, 3 April 1994).

58.   "2nd Buffalo Festival of the Arts Today, Mar. 2-17, 1968" [festival program], Sapp papers.

59.   "Visitors Stand in Line to Enter Art Gallery," *Buffalo Courier-Express*, 8 March 1965.

60.   *Bedlam Galore for Two or More, Foursome, L'Impromptu*, and *The Leader*.

61.   "Avant-garde: Did You Ever, Ever, Ever," *Time* 85 (19 March 1965): 55.

62.   Rosalind Constable, "Can This Be Buffalo?," *Life* 58, no. 16 (23 April 1965): 68.

63.   Howard Taubman, "Festival: Buffalo Offers Arts of Today," *New York Times*, 8 March 1965.

64.   "Avant-garde: Did You Ever, Ever, Ever," *Time* 85 (19 March 1965): 55; Rosalind Constable, "Can This Be Buffalo?" *Life* 58, no. 16 (23 April 1965): 63-71; "Talk of the Town: Foss," *New Yorker* (30 January 1965): 22-24; Howard Taubman, "Festival: Buffalo Offers Arts of Today," *New York Times* (8 March 1965): 34; segment on the festival in television program "Sunday," NBC television network, 7 March 1965; segment on Foss in television program "The Way Out Men," ABC television network, 13 February 1965.

65.   This is illustrated by the continued national media attention paid to Buffalo arts organizations following the festival. For instance, the CBS Evening News featured a report on the Center of the Creative and Performing Arts and their upcoming performances of works by Maryanne Amacher and Cornelius Cardew, with interviews of both Foss and Sapp by correspondent George Herman in December 1966 (J. Don Schlaerth, "CBS to Televise New Music at UB," *Buffalo Evening News*, 14 December 1966. As further evidence, *Saturday Review* sent reviewer Henry Hewes to cover the opening of the new Studio-Arena Theater production of Eugene O'Neill's *A Moon for the Misbegotten* (*Saturday Review* 48 (23 October

66.   "Avant-garde: Did You Ever, Ever, Ever," *Time* 85 (19 March 1965): 55.

67.   Rosalind Constable, "Can This Be Buffalo?" *Life* 58, no. 16 (23 April 1965): 63.

68.   *Rain Forest* (1968), music by David Tudor (performed along with Gordon Mumma), choreographed by Merce Cunningham, with decor by Andy Warhol; dancers were Merce Cunningham, Carolyn Brown, Barbara Lloyd, Sandra Neels, Albert Reid, and Gus Solomons, Jr. "Program, Saturday, March 9, 1968," Sapp papers.

69.   Robert Creeley interview, 12 October 1989.

70.   *Evenings for New Music: A Catalogue, 1964-1977,* (Buffalo: Music Department, State University of New York at Buffalo, 1978), 18-21.

71.   Roger Sessions was to be Slee Professor in autumn 1965, but had to cancel because of illness; Sapp himself gave the first Slee Lecture of that semester, entitled "Music and Language" (see B23). (11 October 1965, tape recording in the sound archives of the Music Department, State University of New York at Buffalo.)

72.   *Canticum Novum Pro Pace* (1962; W107), *Variations on "A Solis Ortus Cardine"* (1962; W63), and *Colloquies I* (1963; W117).

73.   Sapp interview, 7 December 1991.

74.   For a partial list of his major consultancies and non-academic appointments, see Appendix A.

75.   James B. Hartgering to Allen Sapp, 7 January 1963, University Archives, State University of New York at Buffalo. Eric Salzman, "Teachers under Fire," *New York Times*

(7 July 1963), provides a brief summary of the conference. A complete conference report, partially written by Sapp, was published in 1964 (see B21).

76.   Allen Sapp, "Matrices and Lattices: Federal Help for Music in the Last Quarter of the 20th Century," National Endowment for the Arts Library, Washington, D.C.; Sapp interview, 8 December 1991.

77.   Allen Sapp, "Monthly Report for June 1965, Department of Music," University Archives, State University of New York at Buffalo, Buffalo, N.Y.; Sapp interview, 25 March 1991.

78.   Interview, Myles Slatin, 17 January 1994. In fact, Sapp was a leading member of the Committee to Reorganize the College of Arts and Sciences, and assisted the committee's chairman, Oscar Silverman, in the writing of the final report. Allen Sapp to Oscar Silverman, 18 March 1965, University Archives, State University of New York at Buffalo.

79.   Minutes of the Music Department Faculty Meeting, 26 September 1967, University Archives, State University of New York at Buffalo. Larrabee thanked Sapp "for substituting for him during the summer months."

80.   Sapp interview, 25 March 1991.

81.   Sapp's 1966 appointment book lists this visit as 7-9 January 1966 (Sapp papers).

82.   Allen Sapp to Martin Meyerson, 7 August 1967, University Archives, State University of New York at Buffalo; C. C. Furnas to Allen Sapp, 18 June 1966, University Archives, State University of New York at Buffalo; Sapp interview, 25 March 1991; Sapp interview, 3 April 1994.

83.   [University at Buffalo] *Gazette*, 30 August 1968. Meyerson decided "that there would be collegiate system, like the Yale, Harvard, Oxford, Cambridge system. Meyerson was a great Anglophile. He wanted to transfer a lot of the best in the British educational system. So he asked me to be the head of the college system." (Sapp interview, 25 March 1991).

84.   A supposed quote of Meyerson assistant Saul Tauster during the recruitment of Warren Bennis from M.I.T. Warren Bennis, *The Leaning Ivory Tower* (San Francisco: Jossey-Bass, 1973), 112.

85.   Interview, Robert Creeley, 12 October 1989, paraphrasing a conversation with Saul Tauster, an assistant to President Meyerson.

86.   Myles Slatin interview, 17 January 1994. This "embarrassment of riches" period is illustrated by a letter from President Meyerson to Dr. Slatin, Acting Dean of the College of Arts and Sciences (14 October 1966): "I am very anxious that the University pursue its efforts at recruitment of faculty as expeditiously as possible at all instructional levels. . . . I am allocating forty-one new FTE instructional positions for 1967-68 for immediate recruitment. These new positions are in addition to those vacant positions in your current budget. . . . Circumstances now indicate that you might possibly be able to have an additional thirty-five positions." University Archives, State University of New York at Buffalo.

87.   Warren Bennis, *The Leaning Ivory Tower*, 137.

88.   Ibid, p. 136-7.

89.   Ibid, p. 137.

90.   Sapp interview, 26 March 1991.

91.   Allen Sapp to Eric Larrabee, 15 August 1967, University Archives, State University of New York at Buffalo. Sapp may have inherited (or at least shared) this preference for administrative rotation from President Meyerson, who held "a conviction that administrators should be scholars and that a five-year period was about the optimum number of years one should stay in an administrative capacity before returning to one's scholarship." Warren Bennis, *The Leaning Ivory Tower*, 119.

92.   Minutes of the Music Department Faculty Meeting, 23 May 1968, Music Department, State University of New York at Buffalo, Buffalo, N.Y. Most notable of Sapp's commitments was the policy "blueprint" commissioned by Roger Stevens, Director of the National Endowment for the Arts. Stevens was also recruiting Sapp to consider heading the new Kennedy Center for the Arts in Washington D.C., a position Sapp resisted since he saw "the whole thing [as being] so involved with politics and complicated and [with] badly set up

administrative arrangements." Allen Sapp to Martin Meyerson, 7 August 1967, University Archives, State University of New York at Buffalo.

6.   University and National Arts Leadership: Buffalo, 1968-75

1.   Robert Ketter, "Martin Meyerson Advisory Committee Report," University Archives, State University of New York at Buffalo.

2.   Karen Brady, "UB to Start Six Colleges on Amherst Site in Fall," *Buffalo Evening News*, 19 June 1968. Sapp apparently served as Chair of the Council of College Masters until April 1970, at which point the Faculty Senate created a successor, the Collegiate Assembly; Sapp was elected Chairman Pro Tem at its first meeting on 29 April 1970, and was succeeded by Konrad von Moltke in August 1970.

3.   Allen Sapp, "Matrices and Lattices: Federal Help for Music in the Last Quarter of the 20th Century," Archives, National Endowment for the Arts, Washington, D.C.; Sapp interview, 8 December 1991.

4.   Sapp interview, 25 March 1991.

5.   Information Services Press Release, State University of New York at Buffalo, 24 March 1971, Allen Sapp Biographical File, University Archives, State University of New York at Buffalo.

6.   Wayland P. Smith to Robert L. Ketter, 14 May 1973, University Archives, State University of New York at Buffalo.

7.   [Allen Sapp, course listings for College B], "The Colleges: Catalogue, Spring 1971, University Archives, State University of New York at Buffalo.

8.   Warren Bennis, *The Leaning Ivory Tower* (San Francisco: Jossey-Bass, 1973), 16.

9.   Ibid., 126.

10.   Arthur Levine, *Why Innovation Fails* (Albany: State University of New York Press, 1980), 58. The departing "superstar" faculty cited by Levine included John Barth, James Dannieli, Edgar Friedenberg, Gabriel Kolko, and C. H. Waddington; on page 47 he also states that two of the original six college masters, John Huddleston and Mac Hammond, also resigned during this period.

11.   Allen Sapp, quoted in "UB Professor Takes Arts Post," *Buffalo Evening News*, 26 February 1971.

12.   Allen Sapp, quoted in James R. De Santis, [press release], Information Services, State University of New York at Buffalo, 26 February 1971.

13.   "UB Educator Sapp Elected Council for Arts Director," *Buffalo Evening News*, 26 June 1972.

14.   Ted Foote, "The Arts Organize," *School Arts* (October 1972): 10.

15.   Paul Gardner, "Conference to Study Urban Arts Centers as Links to Schools," *New York Times*, 19 June 1972.

16.   Allen Sapp, quoted in "UB Professor Takes Arts Post," *Buffalo Evening News*, 26 February 1971.

17.   Sapp interview, 8 December 1991.

18.   Ibid.   For a more complete listing of Sapp's leadership positions in artistic organizations, see Appendix A.

19.   Sapp interview, 25 March 1991. Sapp was in charge of a project conducting educational programs for the museum in the community, an extension of his work with Arts/Worth.

20.   Allen Sapp to The Fellows and Staff of College B, 13 January 1974, University Archives, State University of New York at Buffalo.

21.   Ibid.

22.   "Sapp Resigns College B Post, Stays in Music Department," Buffalo Evening News, 17 January 1974.

23.   Sapp interview, 25 March 1991.

24.   Kenneth P. Service, [press release], Information Services, State University of New York at Buffalo, 9 September 1975. Biographical File, Allen D. Sapp, University Archives, State University of New York at Buffalo.

25.   Sapp interview, 25 March 1991.

26.   Ibid.

27.   "Prof. Sapp to Leave UB for Fla. State U. Post," *Buffalo Courier-Express*, 11 September 1975.

28.   Sapp's address, "New Buildings: New Obligations" (see B44) was delivered at ceremonies in Slee Hall on 22 November 1981.

29.   The first *Festspiel* for Sapp took place on his sixtieth birthday, 10 December 1982; the concert in honor of his seventieth birthday was delayed due to planning problems, and took place on two evenings, 16-17 February 1993.

7. A Disappointing Detour: Florida State University, 1976-78

1.   Sapp interview, 25 March 1991.

2.   Ibid.

3.   Sapp interview, 26 March 1991. Even more incredibly, this situation persisted for an entire three months before his office was properly furnished and decorated.

4.   Pat Harbolt, "Marshall Resigning from Florida State," *Tallahassee Democrat*, 8 March 1976. Marshall announced his resignation on 8 March 1976.

5.   Creston Nelson, "Marshall Calls It Quits," *Florida State Flambeau*, 9 March 1976.

6.   [Press release, no author], "Mr. Allen Sapp, Special Assistant to the Vice President for Academic Affairs and Director of Cultural Affairs," Office of Information Services, Florida State University, 10/21/77. Biographical file, Allen D. Sapp, University Archives, State University of New York at Buffalo.

7.   Sapp interview, 25 March 1991.

8.   One of the Florida Secretary of State's "primary responsibilities [is] serving as state cultural ambassador." "Secretary of State," *United Press International* (dateline: Tallahassee, Fla.), 1 March 1982, in: Lexis/Nexis "News: ARCNWS" (database file). Sapp even apparently wrote some speeches for Smathers, who eventually ran as the Democratic candidate for Governor of Florida in 1978 (Sapp interview, 25 March 1991).

9.   Allen Sapp to John McCall, 18 June 1978, personal papers.

10.   Sapp interview, 26 March 1991.

8. The Muse Returns: Cincinnati, 1978 to Present

1.   Marian Jo Souder, "The College-Conservatory of Music of Cincinnati, 1955-1962: A History," master's thesis, University of Cincinnati, 1970.

2.   Kevin Grace (Archives and Rare Books, University of Cincinnati) to the author, 3 June 1994. In autumn quarter 1978, CCM had 300 graduate and 725 undergraduates enrolled, for a total student population of 1025.

3.   College Music Society, *Directory of Music Faculties in Colleges and Universities, U.S. and Canada, 1976-78*, 6th ed. (Binghamton, N.Y.: College Music Society, 1976). Larger music faculties existed at the following institutions: Manhattan School of Music (171); Indiana University (136); and New England Conservatory of Music (135).

4.   College Music Society, *Directory of Music Faculties in Colleges and Universities, U.S. and Canada, 1978-80*, 7th ed. (Boulder, Colo.: College Music Society, 1979). Larger music faculties existed at the following institutions: Manhattan School of Music (152); New England Conservatory of Music (150); Indiana University (137); New York University (118) and University of Southern California (118).

5.   Later named Percussion Group Cincinnati.

6.   Sapp interview, 26 March 1991.

7.   The Friends of CCM was established by Sapp's predecessor as dean, Eugene Bonelli, in the mid-1970s. In the beginning, it was "a small group, raising a few thousand dollars. Now it is an extremely active group" (Assistant Dean W. Harold Laster, interview, 22 March 1994).

8.   Sapp interview, 26 March 1991.

9.   Ibid.

10.   College Music Society, *Directory* (1976-78): 187-88. Contains final CCM listing for Professors John Q. Bass, Raymond Dudley, and Assistant Professor Ilona Voorm.

College Music Society, *Directory* (1978-80): 194. Contains final CCM listing for Professor Jeanne Kirstein and Associate Professor John L. Meretta.

11.   W. Harold Laster interview, 22 March 1994.

12.   Sapp interview, 26 March 1991.

13.   W. Harold Laster interview, 22 March 1994.

14.   From Sapp interview, 26 March 1991: "The financial [support staff member for CCM] . . . went to pieces during this time . . . because her husband was dying of cancer. . . . She was just not herself for six to eight months. In other words, the things weren't done right. She was working only about one-quarter of her energy. . . . That meant that I didn't get proper reports from her."

Assistant Dean Harold Laster (who held the same position during Sapp's tenure as dean), in an interview on 22 March 1994, further explained that the financial support staff person for CCM was "from sort of the old school kind of approach. We had just gone [to] state [funding], and there were many, many, many more reports that were mandated out of the state beginning in '77 than probably anybody ever dreamed there would be. We were not computerized in this college at that time, so everything was done by hand entering and by typewriters. So I'm sure that some of the needs that were felt by Allen—he didn't have the support staff to carry through those kinds of things. Now whether or not that was because of [the staff member's] family illness with her husband and subsequent death, whether or not it was because of going state and people being used to doing things the old way in the old College and the old Conservatory, and then the merger with the University and then the state system, lack of equipment, lack of staff support . . . who knows whether or not you can put one thing on it."

15.   Sapp interview, 26 March 1991.

16.   Felicia Lee, "CCM Dean Resigns after Budget Disclosures," *Cincinnati Enquirer*, 10 November 1980.

17.   Ibid.

18.   James Chute, "Music Dean Resigns, May Stay as Teacher," *Cincinnati Post*, 7 November 1980. Further illustrating this point, Harold Laster (interview, 22 March 1994) stated that "the thing that Allen needs to get credit for is his vision. And looking at wanting to bring in the top people to attract students and to attract an international visibility for CCM. And he probably got caught not being able to support what he wanted the school to be. Now who is at fault for that? Is it the Provost at fault? Is it the President at fault? Is the internal workings at fault? I don't know. . . . Allen is just one of those dear, you know almost like a 'Renaissance man' of the twentieth century. A dear humanist, a very caring person, who always wants the right thing to happen for the people, for the students and the faculty and the staff. . . . And whether he got in over his head, or whether or not he thought things would happen support-wise and they didn't happen, I can't tell you. I just don't know."

19.   Sapp interview, 26 March 1991.

20.   John McCall to Allen Sapp, 24 November 1980, personnel folder of Allen D. Sapp, Office of the Dean, University of Cincinnati College-Conservatory of Music (permission granted by Dean Robert J. Werner, 23 October 1990; letter of permission held by the author). In 1985, Sapp's title was changed from Professor of Composition to Professor of

Music, since in addition to teaching students in composition he also led courses in music theory and history topics and held private tutorial sessions with performance majors.

21.   Sapp interview, 26 March 1991.

22.   Ibid.

23.   Ibid.

24.   Ibid.

25.   There is also evidence that he had sketched many other small works which might have been composed during this period.   Sapp had apparently given several of his manuscripts as gifts to CCM patrons in the spring of 1979.   Letters of thanks from some of these patrons are located in Sapp's personnel folder, Office of the Dean, University of Cincinnati College-Conservatory of Music (access by permission of Allen Sapp and Dean Robert Werner; letters of permission in the possession of the author).   These letters give the identity of some of these manuscripts of works and sketches which are believed to be unica and have never been publicly performed: Sketch for *Trio II*, to John J. Strader (letter of 2 June 1979); *Double Dirge*, to Samuel F. Pogue (letter of 4 June 1979); unidentified "fragment of music," to Mary Bergstein (letter of 1 June 1979); and apparently several unidentified scores to Melissa Lanier (letter of 5 June 1979): "We just couldn't get over these lovely scores.   When you said 'musical fragment' I expected a bar perhaps, but nothing like what you sent!   We shall treasure our scores especially because we are so fond of you."

26.   Judging from colophon dates, *Piano Sonata V* (26 August 1980) appears to be the first major work Sapp completed at the beginning of his latest series of consecutive productive years.   Interestingly, this work sprouted from a Buffalo era sketch: "The first three or four pages from the *Fifth Sonata*, that terribly disjunct toccata-like figure, I had written that in Buffalo in about 1968. . . . But then some administrative crisis came and I did not [finish the work]" (Sapp interview, 7 December 1991).   It is particularly interesting that he recalls the sketch as dating from 1968, the year he saw many of his plans for SUNY at Buffalo begin to wane, largely due to the student body political demonstrations; as it would turn out, and perhaps as he already realized by late summer, 1980 would also be a very difficult year personally.

27.   Allen Sapp to Robert E. Middleton, 16 January 1982, personal papers, home of Robert E. Middleton.

28.   Robert E. Middleton to Jorge L. Carro (Chairperson, Rieveschl Award Committee), 7 April 1986, personal papers, home of Allen D. Sapp.

29.   Jan Williams to Donald B. Parker (Rieveschl Award Committee member), 1 April 1986, personal papers, home of Allen D. Sapp.

30.   Jonathan D. Kramer to Donald Parker, 27 March 1985, personal papers, home of Allen D. Sapp.

31.   Howard Pollack, *Harvard Composers*, 229.

32.   Among the instrumental works prior to 1981 there are only a handful of evocative titles, most coming toward the end of his earlier productive period, e.g., *The Double Image* (W114, orch., 1957), *The Heptagon* (W127, unfinished, orch., 1957), and *Fantasy I: The Pursuers* (W21, piano, 1960).   Prior to *Imaginary Creatures*, Sapp had also subtitled his *Piano Sonata VII: "Conversations with Friends"* (W25).

33.   It is interesting to note that Sapp had apparently planned to order bells identical to those at Lowell House for the Amherst Campus.   Robert B. Po-Chedley (I. T. Verdun Bell Company) to Allen Sapp, 20 February 1967, University Archives, State University of New York at Buffalo.

34.   Typescript for program notes of *Taylor's Nine*, dated 9 October 1981, Sapp papers.

35.   Sapp interview, 26 March 1991.

36.   Jonathan D. Kramer to Donald Parker, 27 March 1985.

37.   Howard Pollack, "Favored Sons: Robert Middleton and Allen Sapp." In *Harvard Composers: Walter Piston and His Students from Elliott Carter to Frederic Rzewski* (Metuchen, N.J.: Scarecrow Press, 1992): 208-30.

38.   The first movement of the *Concerto* is the first movement of *Piano Sonata III* (W19); the second movement of the *Concerto* is the third movement of *Piano Sonata IV* (W20); the third movement of the *Concerto* is the first movement of *Piano Sonata II* (W16); the fourth movement of the *Concerto* is the fifth movement of *Polyhedra* (W83).

39.   Gerhard Samuel instead performed Sapp's *Suite for Orchestra, no. 2* (see P113c).

II. WORKS AND PERFORMANCES

1.   The composer remarks in a letter to his parents dated 4 May 1941 that this work was premiered on a recent "beautiful spring evening," which most likely places the date of the première between 21 March and 3 May.

2.   Allen Sapp, telephone interview with the author, 22 March 1994.

3.   Also referring to Sapp's *Piano Sonatas III* and *IV*.

4.   The composer has reordered the movements in the following sequence: V - IV - I - III - II (Allen Sapp to the author, 10 April 1990).

5.   Allen Sapp to the author, 10 April 1990. These assignments pertain to the original 1980 ordering of movements, not the 1990 reordering.

6.   10 December 1992; the concert was delayed for two months due to scheduling problems.

7.   Allen Sapp to the author, telephone conversation, 22 March 1994.

8.   Actually, the entire work is performed at the same tempo, Eighth note = 128. To the listener, it might sound as if the tempo gradually increases as the work progresses, but what actually occurs is a gradual increase in the number of notes performed per measure, i.e., the use of smaller rhythmic values.

9.   This title appears on several concert performance programs, including the première.

10.   This title, which matches the poem title from Schevill's collection *The American Fantasies* (Agana, Guam: Bern Porter, 1951), was given in a list of works in a resumé of the composer dating from ca. 1953.

11.   This title appears on the title page of the piano-vocal score published by the American Composers Alliance (New York, N.Y., 1952).

12.   *Harvard University Gazette*, 10 November 1954, p. 53.

13.   Allen Sapp, telephone interview with the author, 1 October 1995. The score for Sapp's *Four Motets* (W143) is missing.

14.   Maic Chomel to the author, 4 December 1995.

15.   Sapp interview, 12 January 1991. No program or newspaper account for this concert could be located among the composer's papers or in the Boston Symphony Archives, so the exact date of the concert is not known. It probably was not performed on the last day of concerts, 14 August 1942, since it did not appear on the programs for both the student orchestras as reported in the following article: "Tanglewood Nets More Than $12,000 at Benefit Concert," *Springfield News* (Springfield, Mass.), 15 August 1942.

The free-standing fair copy manuscript score of *Passacaglia on a Theme by Piston* is almost certainly the version performed at Tanglewood, and its title page is dated "1942 - July"; the colophon of the *Concertino*, which contains the extensively revised "Passacaglia on a Theme by Piston" as its second movement, is dated "Bryn Mawr, August, 1942." Since the first concerts at Tanglewood did not take place until July 14 that year, it is probably safe to assume that the performance of the first version of the *Passacaglia* took place some time between 14 July and 13 August 1942. Both manuscripts are in the possession of the composer.

16.   This is a reference to a preservation project carried out by the author (at the suggestion of James B. Coover and Carol June Bradley) between 1990 and 1993, making photocopies of the holographs of Sapp's compositions on acid-free paper. Six copies of each

holograph were made. Two sets of holographs were organized in volumes by genre and bound, one for the composer, and one for the author. Another two sets were requested by the music libraries at the State University of New York at Buffalo, and the University of Cincinnati College-Conservatory of Music; these libraries have bound and cataloged each work separately. The remaining two copies remain unbound, and at the time of this writing are located at the Ohio State University Music & Dance Library.

17.   Britten's unpublished score (British Library Additional MS No. 60622), composed in February 1937, calls for female voice, 2 male voices, chorus (SATB), percussion, ukelele, and two pianos. John Evans, Philip Reed, and Paul Wilson, *A Britten Sourcebook* (Aldeburgh, Suffolk: Published for the Britten-Pears Library, Aldeburgh by the Britten Estate, 1987), 146-47.

18.   The holograph of Sapp's supplementary incidental music to *The Ascent of F-6* was not found in the Harvard Theatre Collection, Harvard University Archives, or the home of the composer as of this writing.

19.   The holograph of Sapp's incidental music to *The Family Reunion* was not found in the Harvard Theatre Collection, Harvard University Archives, or the home of the composer as of this writing.

20.   Sapp interview, 5 January 1991.

21.   The holograph of Sapp and Fine's incidental music to *Alice in Wonderland* was not found in the Harvard Theatre Collection, Harvard University Archives, or the home of the composer as of this writing.

22.   The medium of performance is ascertained from an undated letter from Miss Martha Craven to the composer, ca. 20 October 1965 (date of the composer's response): "I have listened to the tape recording made of the 1960 production, and cannot tell you how much I admire the music you wrote for it. It seems to capture beautifully the mood of the play, besides being lovely in itself. Of course we want to use it again [in a new student production at Wellesley College], but Mrs. Lefkowitz can find copies only of the three choral odes, with their flute accompaniment. We do not have any of the parts for harp, the background orchestration for flute and harp (since it will be outside we cannot use a harpsichord), and the duet between Hecuba and Andromache."

This information is confirmed by an interview with the composer on 16 January 1991, when he recalled that for "*The Trojan Women* . . . I wrote a "Hecuba's Lament" and I wrote some other incidental march music. Some of it for harp and so on. And I think those are in scraps. . . . I remember giving the harpist a part to play and I remember somebody sang "Hecuba's Lament." I think there was a sort of incidental music at the time. Some choral excerpts. In fact a fairly large number of choral excerpts are there."

23.   The holographs of Sapp's incidental music to *The Trojan Women* were not found in the Wellesley College Archives, or the home of the composer as of this writing.

24.   The holograph of Sapp's incidental music to *The Way of the World* was not found in the Wellesley College Archives, or the home of the composer as of this writing.

25.   Allen Sapp, telephone interview with the author, 1 October 1995.

III. DISCOGRAPHY/WEBOGRAPHY

1.   Bibliographic record for this item, CATNYP (New York Public Library Research Libraries on-line catalog).

APPENDIX A: ACADEMIC AND NON-ACADEMIC POSITIONS

I. University Positions

Harvard University
    Teaching Fellow, 1948-50
    Instructor, 1950-53
    Assistant Professor, 1953-58
    Tutor in Music, Kirkland House, 1949-55
    Acting Chairman for Summer School, summers of 1953 and 1954
    Secretary, Committee on Educational Policy, 1953-55

Wellesley College
    Lecturer, 1958-61

University of Buffalo (later, State University of New York at Buffalo)
    Frederic Slee Visiting Professor of Composition, autumn 1961.
    Professor, 1961-75
    Chairman, Department of Music, 1961-68
    Co-Director, Center of the Creative and Performing Arts, 1964-68
    Head, Division of Languages, Literature and the Arts, 1965-67
    Director of Cultural Affairs, 1966-71
    Chairman, Council of College Masters, 1968-70
    Master of College B, 1968-74

Florida State University
    Provost, Division of Communication and the Arts, 1976-77
    Professor of Music, 1976-78
    Director of Cultural Affairs, 1977-78
    Special Assistant to the Vice President for Academic Affairs, 1977-78

University of Cincinnati College-Conservatory of Music
    Dean, and Thomas James Kelly Professor of Music, 1978-80
    Associate Dean for Special Projects, and Professor of Composition, 1980-85
    Professor of Music, 1985-93; Emeritus Professor of Music, 1993-

II. Other Academic and Scholarly Appointments

The Salzburg Seminar in American Studies, Lecturer, summer 1954
University of Chicago, Charles F. Walgreen Visiting Lecturer in American Studies,
October 1955
Brandeis University, Summer Institute of Music, Lecturer, summer 1959
Senior Rockefeller Fellow in Education, Metropolitan Museum of Art, 1973-74
Florida State University, Visiting Lecturer, School of Music, October 1974

III. Selected Consultation and Advisory Positions

New York State Council on the Arts, 1962-63
Yale Seminar on Music Education, 1963
University of California, San Diego, Advisor on Music, 1965
University of Minnesota, Twin Cities, Advisor on Music, 1965
Danforth Foundation of St. Louis, Advisory Council on Teacher Training Grants,
1965-68
Consultant to: Bard College, Duke University, New England Conservatory of Music,
Ohio University, Rutgers University, Yale University.

IV. Selected Leadership Positions in Cultural Organizations

Creative Concerts Guild (Boston), Vice-President, 1952-54; President, 1954-56
Nova Concerts (Boston), Director, 1959-60
Buffalo Fine Arts Academy, Trustee and Music Advisor to the Chairman of the
Board, 1961-75
Buffalo Philharmonic Orchestra, Director, 1961-75
Studio Arena Theater (Buffalo), Director and Vice President, 1962-74
Composers Recordings, Inc. (CRI), Director, 1964-65.
Buffalo Ballet Company, Trustee and Vice President, 1969-75
Project ARTS/WORTH (American Council for the Arts in Education), Executive
Director, 1971-74
American Council for the Arts in Education (ACAE), Executive Director, 1972-74
Great Lakes Association for the Dance, Director, 1972-? [parent organization for
Festival Ballet of New York, primarily serving cities in Western New York]
Dance Notation Bureau, Trustee, 1972-75
New York State Council on the Arts, Review Committee, Chairman, 1972-75
New York Foundation for the Arts, Director and Chairman, 1972-79
Creative Artist Public Service Program (New York City), Director and Chairman,
1972-84
Arts Development Services, Director, 1973-75
Museums Collaborative (New York City), Director and Chairman, 1972-76
Charles MacArthur Center for American Theater, Director, 1976-79
State Theater of Florida, Trustee, 1976-78
Arts Council of Tallahassee, Director, 1976-78

Cincinnati Arts Commission, Trustee, 1978-81
Cincinnati Ballet Company, Trustee, 1978-81
Cincinnati Opera Company, Trustee, 1978-81
Cincinnati Symphony Orchestra, Trustee, 1978-81
Cincinnati Chamber Orchestra, Trustee, 1978-
National Guild of Community Schools of the Arts, President, 1979-80
American Music Scholarship Association, Trustee and Chairman, 1980-84

APPENDIX B: CHRONOLOGICAL INDEX OF COMPOSITIONS

Viola Sonata (W55) .... September 1948
In Grato Jubilo (W99) 1949
Suite for Orchestra, no. 1 (W112) 1949
Suite for Piano (W14) 1949
Piano Trio (W56) .... April 1949
Five Landscapes (W100) 1950
Intermezzo for Orchestra (W126) 1950
String Quartet I (W57) 1951
The Bridal Song (W84) 1951-52
American Fantasies (W101) .... ca. 1952
Nursery Rhymes (W85) .... ca. 1952
Seven Epigrams (Both Sweet and Sour) (W86) 1952
Four Motets (W143) .... ca. 1953
The Little Boy Lost (W102) .... 1 July 1953
Chaconne for Violin and Organ (W58) .... 1 August 1953
A Birthday Piece for A. T. D. (W103) .... September 1953
A Prayer for Commencement (W104) .... May 1954
Four Dialogues for Two Pianos (W43) 1953-55
Suite for Orchestra, no. 2 (W113) 1952-56
Seven Bagatelles for Piano (W15) .... October 1956
Six Ricercare for Viols (W59) .... October 1956
The Lady and the Lute (W87) .... 1952; revised 1957
Piano Sonata II (W16) .... 1954-56; revised 1957
Four Impromptus for Piano (W17) .... February 1957
String Trio (W60) .... February 1957
Piano Sonatina II (W18) .... 3 March 1957
Piano Sonata III (W19) .... 15 March 1957
The Double Image (W114) .... April 1957
Piano Sonata IV (W20) .... August 1957
The Heptagon (W127) .... Begun 29 June 1957; continued in 1959
A Maiden's Complaint in Springtime (W105) .... summer 1959-60
The Trojan Women (W136) .... ca. winter 1960
Six Variations on the
        Hymn-Tune "Durant" (W61) ..... [Between 1 January and 17 April] 1960
The Way of the World (W137) .... ca. spring 1960
Fantasy I: "The Pursuers" (W21) .... 6 July 1960
How True Love is Likened to Summer (W106) .... September-October 1960
Overture, "The Women of Trachis" (W115) .... November 1960
Violin Sonata III (W62) .... November 1960
The Frogs (W138) .... ca. winter 1961
The Women of Trachis [incidental music] (W139) .... ca. spring 1961
June (W116) .... 8 June 1961
Canticum Novum Pro Pace (W107) .... December 1962
Variations on "A solis ortus cardine" (W63) .... December 1962
Colloquies I (W117) .... June-September 1963
Prayer (W108) .... 4 January 1964
Untitled [four preludes for piano] (W22) .... ca. 1972 or 1973
Irregular Polygon (W64) .... 12 November 1973
Nocturne for Solo Violoncello (W65) .... March 1978
Piano Sonata V (W23) .... 26 August 1980

Dix chansons sphériques (W95) .... February-March 1989
Piano Sonata IX (W34) .... 12 April 1989
Piano Sonata X (W35) .... spring 1989
Rose Petals Falling (W36) .... October 1989
A Bestiary: 25 Preludes for Piano (W37) .... 30 October 1989
Four Lyrics of Absence and Loss (W96) .... June-July 1983, and June 1990
The Farewell (W38) .... 1 June 1990
Fantasy II: "A Piece of the Rach" (W39) .... spring-8 July 1990
Five Impromptus (W40) .... 24 April 1990-23 April 1991
Inscriptions and Commentaries (W82) .... spring-8 August 1991
Fantasy III: "Homage to Mendelssohn" (W41) ...... summer-21 September 1992
Polyhedra (W83) .... July-24 November 1992
A Concerto for Chamber Orchestra,
      "The Four Reasons" (W122) .... February-December 1993

APPENDIX C: ALPHABETICAL INDEX OF COMPOSITIONS

Colloquy V: "The Cage of All Bright Knocks"
    SEE: Colloquies V: "The Cage of All Bright Knocks" (W79)
Concertino for Piano and Chamber Orchestra (W111)
Concertino no. 1
    SEE: Concertino for Piano and Chamber Orchestra (W111)
A Concerto for Chamber Orchestra, "The Four Reasons" (W122)
Concerto for Piano and Orchestra (W123)
Concerto for Piano in One Movement (W124)
Conversations with Friends
    SEE: Piano Sonata VII: "Conversations with Friends" (W25)
Crennelations (W119)
Dix chansons sphériques (W95)
The Double Image (W114)
Easter Day (W97)
Eaux-Fortes (W47)
Eight Songs to Texts of Robert Herrick
    SEE: The Lady and the Lute (W87)
Epithalamium (W32)
Er, der Herrlichste von Allen
    SEE: Motet, "Er, der Herrlichste von Allen..." (W109)
The Family Reunion (W134)
Fanfare for WGUC (W129)
Fantasia for Violin and Piano (W78)
Fantasy I: "The Pursuers" (W21)
Fantasy II: "A Piece of the Rach" (W39)
Fantasy III: "Homage to Mendelssohn" (W41)
Fantasy for Piano, "The Pursuers"
    SEE: Fantasy I: "The Pursuers" (W21)
The Farewell (W38)
First Viola Sonata
    SEE: Viola Sonata (W55)
First Violin Sonata
    SEE: Violin Sonata I (W52)
Five Impromptus (W40)
Five Inventions for Piano (W29)
Five Landscapes (W100)
Five Pieces for Solo Violin in the Language of Flowers (W72)
Five Pieces to Texts of T.S. Eliot
    SEE: Five Landscapes (W100)
Five Toccatas for Solo Harpsichord (W26)
For Debbie (W27)
For Vicky (W28)
Four Dialogues for Two Pianos (W43)
Four Hand Piano Sonata I (W42)
Four Hand Piano Sonata II (W44)
Four Hand Piano Sonata III (W45)
Four Hand Sonata
    SEE: Four Hand Piano Sonata I (W42)
Four Impromptus for Piano (W17)
Four Lyrics of Absence and Loss (W96)

Piano Trio (W56)
A Piece of the Rach
    SEE: Fantasy II: "A Piece of the Rach" (W39)
Pigeons (W7)
Polyhedra (W83)
Prayer (W108)
A Prayer for Commencement (W104)
Prelude and Finale (W8)
The Pursuers
    SEE: Fantasy I: "The Pursuers" (W21)
Rhapsodie pour les courageux (W141)
Romance for Solo Violin (W77)
Rose Petals Falling (W36)
Second Suite for Orchestra
    SEE: Suite for Orchestra, no. 2 (W113)
Second Violin Sonata
    SEE: Violin Sonata II (W54)
The Septagon
    SEE: The Heptagon (W127)
Serenade for Flute and Strings after Lyrics of Simonides at Ceos (W120)
A Set of 12 Canons (W92)
Seven Bagatelles for Piano (W15)
Seven Epigrams (Both Sweet and Sour) (W86)
Seven Songs of Carew (W88)
Seven Songs to Texts of Thomas Carew
    SEE: Seven Songs of Carew (W88)
Sirius :: Stella Canis; The Companion of Sirius :: The Serious Companion (W73)
Six Ricercare for Viols (W59)
Sixth Sonata for Piano
    SEE: Piano Sonata VI (W24)
Six Variations on the Hymn-Tune "Durant" (W61)
Socrates and Phaedrus Speak of Love by the Banks of the Illisus
    SEE: Colloquies VI: "Socrates and Phaedrus Speak of Love by the Banks of
          the Illisus" (W81)
Sonata III for Violin and Piano
    SEE: Violin Sonata III (W62)
Sonata IV for Violin and Piano
    SEE: Violin Sonata IV (W68)
Sonata for Piano
    SEE: Piano Sonata I (W1)
Sonata for Piano and Cello
    SEE: Cello Sonata (W51)
Sonata Movement for String Trio (W50)
Sonatina II
    SEE: Piano Sonatina II (W18)
Sonatina for Piano
    SEE: Piano Sonatina I (W12)
A Song of Marriage (W98)
String Quartet I (W57)
String Quartet II (W66)

INDEX

About the Author

ALAN GREEN is Music Reference Librarian, Cataloger, and Instructor at Ohio State University, Columbus. In addition to writing on music and librarianship, he is also active as a composer.

Recent Titles in
Bio-Bibliographies in Music

Peter Sculthorpe: A Bio-Bibliography
Deborah Hayes

Germaine Tailleferre: A Bio-Bibliography
Robert Shapiro

Charles Wuorinen: A Bio-Bibliography
Richard D. Burbank

Elliott Carter: A Bio-Bibliography
William T. Doering

Leslie Bassett: A Bio-Bibliography
Ellen S. Johnson

Ulysses Kay: A Bio-Bibliography
Constance Tibbs Hobson and Deborra A. Richardson, compilers

John Alden Carpenter: A Bio-Bibliography
Joan O'Connor, compiler

Paul Creston: A Bio-Bibliography
Monica J. Slomski, compiler

William Thomas McKinley: A Bio-Bibliography
Jeffrey S. Sposato

William Mathias: A Bio-Bibliography
Stewart R. Craggs

Carl Ruggles: A Bio-Bibliography
Jonathan D. Green

Gardner Read: A Bio-Bibliography
Mary Ann Dodd and Jayson Rod Engquist